No Sanctuary

NO SAN

CTUARY

**Teachers and the School Reform
That Brought Gay Rights to
the Masses**

STEPHEN LANE

ForeEdge

ForeEdge
An imprint of University Press of New England
www.upne.com
© 2019 Stephen Lane
All rights reserved
Manufactured in the United States of America
Designed by Lindsay Starr
Typeset in Dante by Monotype

Library of Congress Cataloging-in-Publication Data
Names: Lane, Stephen, author.
Title: No sanctuary : teachers and the school reform that
    brought gay rights to the masses / Stephen Lane.
Description: Lebanon, NH : ForeEdge, [2018] | Includes
    bibliographical references and index.
Identifiers: LCCN 2018017534 (print) | LCCN 2018018871 (ebook) |
    ISBN 9781512603156 (epub, pdf, & mobi) | ISBN 9781512603149
    (pbk. : alk. paper)
Subjects: LCSH: Gay students—United States—History. |
    Gay teachers—United States—History. | Homophobia in
    high schools—United States—History. | Gay and lesbian
    studies—United States—History. | Gay rights—United
    States—History.
Classification: LCC LC2575 (ebook) | LCC LC2575 .L36 2018 (print) |
    DDC 370.86/64—dc23
LC record available at https://lccn.loc.gov/2018017534

5 4 3 2 1

To teachers everywhere. Keep fighting the good fight.

Contents

Acknowledgments

HISTORY TEACHERS constantly enjoin their students to understand the writer in order to understand the writings—that uncovering the author's unstated biases is the first step in analyzing the work itself. My own biases are fairly transparent, and were largely shaped by my fellow teachers. I am especially indebted to Tom Hart, who first encouraged me to get back into teaching after a long hiatus, and to Denis Cleary, Robert Furey, Kevin Harding, Andrei Joseph, Mary O'Connor, and Joe Zellner—the old guard when I first started, all of whom worked thirty or more years in the same building. They instilled in me the belief that the teaching faculty has a far greater influence on educational outcomes than do administrators, school committees, or even state politicians—who, by comparison, are only a transient presence in the system. Rightly or wrongly, my colleagues are the ones who first pointed me toward studying the impact of teachers on education reform.

My research began in the master's program at Simmons College in Boston, and I could not have asked for a more supportive, committed faculty to guide me. In particular, I must thank Dr. Laura Prieto. She gave me enough confidence in my abilities as a researcher and writer to believe I had something worthwhile to contribute. Without her encouragement and positive feedback, I never would have had the conviction to pursue writing this book.

WRITING IS A SOLITARY PURSUIT; publishing a book is a group effort. It was stupid of me not to realize just how significant a difference this is. The dedicated efforts of an entire team are responsible for turning what I wrote into a polished, professional, and publishable final product. Their impact on the book itself is hard to overstate, but more important to me has been the simple comfort of knowing I'm not doing this alone.

First among those on the team is my agent, Amaryah Orenstein. Her initial belief in the value of this story and her unflagging work on its behalf are primarily responsible for shepherding it to completion. Her relentless positivity and enthusiasm provided much comfort to me during the long slog of finishing the book, and her advice on both editorial and business matters has proved invaluable.

My editor at UPNE, Richard Pult, provided great insight into how to turn my research and ideas into a much better story. He has helped make the book less an academic treatise, and more a narrative. To the extent that the book is an entertaining read, most of the credit belongs to him. The copy editor Richard chose, Glenn Novak, did a wonderful job smoothing out my prose, helping create a more consistent voice throughout, and generally cleaning up the fairly haphazard style of my drafts. And Amanda Dupuis's efforts in shepherding this work through all stages of production were invaluable.

THE GREATEST INSPIRATION for this book is the incredibly brave work of the teachers and students who founded the movement to support LGBT youth in schools, and who continue this important work today. Their work should be held up as the ideal of the true meaning of education. I am grateful to them not only for the example they provide, but for their time and patience in sharing not only their work, but in many cases their own personal struggles to survive in a hostile world. Since some of them have chosen to remain anonymous, I think it is best not to thank by name any of the dozens of students and teachers who were willing to share stories and documents with me. But to all of you, thank you.

In addition, I would be remiss if I didn't also thank the administrators who shared their perspective on the movement with me. In many cases, this meant admitting to their own shortcomings on this issue—never an easy thing to do.

FINALLY, I WANT TO THANK my family. To my lovely wife Jess: Your patience and support got me through this project. You are the rock on whom I rely constantly. And to our new addition, Elliot: Thank you for giving me the ultimate deadline, as I desperately tried to finish the final draft before your due date. I barely succeeded. You are far too young to read or understand this book, but I do hope at some point (even if you never read it), you will appreciate that there are brave and inspirational people in the world, trying to make it a better place, and that I was lucky enough to write about some of them.

No Sanctuary

The Path to Reform

No one should have to go through
the loneliness that I and the tens of
millions like me had to endure. I write
this letter because I am finally able to
say . . . those words I longed to hear
when I was their age. You are not
alone.

   —High school teacher Peter Atlas, coming
     out in an open letter in his school's
     newspaper, 1993

O**N WHAT HAD BEEN** an unremarkable school day in 1990, the
principal at a suburban Boston high school was suddenly
confronted with an issue he felt could easily erupt into a
full-blown crisis. He rushed into one of the faculty offices and asked
for a private word with one of his teachers. "Some of your students
just asked me if you're gay! What should I tell them?"

"The truth, I suppose," replied the teacher. The teacher in question,
well liked by students and remarkable primarily for his near-inhuman
calm, had given an admittedly flippant answer, one that expressed
little concern with his boss's worries. The principal was an understanding and progressive man; he had known the teacher was gay,
and had consistently been supportive. But like many in his position,
the principal shied away from controversy, and the students' question
promised not just controversy, but potential fallout of unpredictable
levels. The students' simple question required more than a simple
answer—it required a plan of action. How would students react to

the truth? What about parents? Other faculty? The school committee? If the principal's tone reflected some degree of fear, these unknowns were its source.

The teacher was no more certain than his boss about what came next, and had much more at stake. His job, at least in theory, was not: in 1989, the state of Massachusetts had amended its nondiscrimination laws to include sexual orientation. He couldn't be fired for coming out, but his relationships in the community, with the faculty, and with his students were certainly at risk. Tension and hostility could create an environment in which doing his job effectively was no longer possible. Suburban Boston was, relative to the rest of the country, a progressive enclave—no doubt many in the community would rally to his side. But just as certainly, there would be some backlash. The nature of his job was going to change, and there was no way to know how. Still, he was significantly better prepared than the principal. He had a supportive network of colleagues, and had seen teachers at other schools go through the same process. Moreover, he had decided it was time; he would be happier living and working openly. More important, he wanted his school to make a statement of unambiguous support for gay students who faced a society that was at best indifferent to them and at worst openly hostile.

The first step, he felt, was to make administrators see the problem. This in turn required the school community, from leadership to the student body, to recognize that gay and lesbian students and teachers did indeed roam the halls of their school—that homosexuals were not some exotic species found only in the wilds of Greenwich Village and San Francisco. And further, that they were, in a sense that an affluent suburban population in Massachusetts could understand, just normal people. For most Americans in the early 1990s, the term homosexuality still conjured any number of negative associations: psychosis, predation, disease, deviance, lewdness, promiscuity, immorality. The American imagination envisioned a whole menagerie of butch women, effeminate boys, and sinister older men cruising bars, clubs, and bathhouses—all engaged in activities beyond the moral pale. Homosexuality was to be mocked, feared, and avoided, lest one be somehow tainted or infected. Even for many inclined to be more open-minded on the subject, it was a thing apart, existing elsewhere, outside regular society. To humanize and normalize homosexuality in his own school, the teacher decided to make an example of himself.

He was not the first public school teacher to come out, nor was he the first to seek to improve school climate for gay and lesbian students. His story is not unique or particularly dramatic (at least, not to hear him tell it); however, it is illustrative of how change came to schools. He came of age as the gay rights movement grew increasingly vocal and political, part of a generation insistent on living as equal members of society. His was also the first generation afforded some measure of antidiscrimination protection—by the late 1980s, two states (Wisconsin and Massachusetts) and a handful of municipalities offered statutory protection, and there were allies in the legal community (the American Civil Liberties Union among them) ready and willing to fight dismissals in court. But even as the social and political landscape began to shift, schools were still generally hidebound by antiquated stereotypes of gay men as predators and remained steeped in a culture that targeted for bullying those students marked as different. A small number of teachers at a handful of schools sought to change this environment, to make others aware of the particular hardships that LGBT youth faced.

For LGBT youth, school was (and, in many cases, still is) a special sort of nightmare. They were easy marks—often targets of violent harassment, rarely objects of much sympathy. They faced (and still face) higher dropout rates, higher teen homelessness and substance abuse rates, and a suicide rate perhaps three times that of their straight peers.[2] Statewide hearings conducted in Massachusetts in 1992 shed some light on their experience: "We were picked on. We were called 'queer' and 'faggot,'" testified high schooler Chris Murther. "We were . . . used as punching bags by our classmates, just for being different."[3] At those same hearings, many students reflected on their own suicide attempts, or on those who succeeded in taking their own lives out of a desperate feeling that life held nothing for them but abuse and desolation.[4]

Fear, isolation, and violence were recurring themes for those growing up gay, yet their plight went generally unnoticed—or at least unremarked on—by teachers, counselors, or administrators. It was this dynamic that teachers hoped to change. In the beginning, they did not attempt formal, programmatic reforms in their schools, but sought only to change perception in the wider community, and to offer hope for those who most needed it. In 1993, Peter Atlas, a teacher at Concord-Carlisle High School in Massachusetts, came out publicly in an open letter published in his school's newspaper. He noted the higher rate of suicide among LGBT youth and the bullying they faced, but also stated, "Despite the recent spate of political messages to the contrary, it is entirely possible, in fact common place [sic], to be happy, secure, well-adjusted, honest, loving, respectable, even religious, and, at the same time, be openly gay, lesbian, or bisexual." He ended by saying, "No one should have to go through the loneliness that I and the tens of millions like me had to endure. I write this letter because I am finally able to say . . . those words I longed to hear when I was their age. You are not alone."[5]

IN MASSACHUSETTS, the work of gay teachers and students, along with their allies, led to a remarkable set of statewide education reforms known as the Massachusetts Safe Schools Program. In 1992, Republican governor William Weld convened the Governor's Commission on Gay and Lesbian Youth, which held the aforementioned hearings on the crisis facing LGBT youth. The commission delivered its report, *Breaking the Silence: Making Schools Safe for Gay and Lesbian Youth*, in February 1993. Among its recommendations: policies to protect students from bullying, anti-harassment training for teachers and staff, information in school libraries for gay and lesbian adolescents, and the creation of school-based support groups. Perhaps more important, the state provided extensive funding to establish such support groups—dubbed Gay-Straight Alliances (GSAs)—AND train faculty to lead them. The work of the Governor's Commission and subsequent implementation efforts by the state board of education marked a watershed change in the relationship between schools and their LGBT students. However, the work started much earlier, well before the 1990s, and has had an impact well beyond the schoolhouse doors. Values taught in schools can spill out into the larger community, and it is perhaps not coincidental that reform in schools preceded fundamental shifts in American views on gay marriage or gays in the military.

Reform began almost invisibly. The first efforts to support LGBT youth were little more than covert, tentative steps by teachers unsure of how to proceed or even of their final goal. Then, in the 1970s, teachers began to push more openly for antidiscrimination language that included protection for homosexual teachers. Even before they had statutory protection, a few brave teachers came out publicly—in 1980, Arthur Lipkin, a high school teacher at Cambridge Rindge and Latin, was perhaps the first to do so in Massachusetts. In the mid-1980s, the small steps got bigger. In 1984 in Los Angeles, a science teacher, Dr. Virginia Uribe, created the first school-based intervention program for gay and lesbian students, which she called Project 10. In 1987, Lipkin and fellow teacher Al Ferreira spearheaded faculty assemblies to promote tolerance, after which Ferreira started an extracurricular club to support LGBT students and their allies. His students chose the name Project 10 East for their group. In 1988, also in Massachusetts, Kevin Jennings and one of his students created the first Gay-Straight Alliance at Concord Academy, a small, exclusive boarding school outside Boston. That same year, at Phillips Andover, another suburban Boston prep school, a group led by student Sharon Tentarelli and counselor Cilla Bonney-Smith launched a similar project. And in 1990, Bob Parlin began the process of creating the first Gay-Straight Alliance in a public school—Newton South High School, also just outside Boston.

MUCH OF THE TEACHERS' EARLY WORK began informally, and spread by word of mouth as much as anything else. In some ways, this is problematic for the telling of the story; often, the narrative hinges on conversations only half remembered, or on dates, places, or people almost entirely forgotten. Any portrayal of these teachers' work—especially in its early stages—is necessarily impressionistic, an attempt to fill in a picture around the few dots that can be reliably placed on the canvas. Although the historical trail is still fairly warm, very little organized documentation exists. It consists of scattered notes from early meetings, a few teaching materials, the very rare memoir—in Jennings's words, "Who has time to archive?"[6]

The telling of this story also involves the interesting question of how ideas are spread and adopted in education. At the embryonic stage, ideas often spread through informal networks—which can retard progress if educators are siloed in their schools, or even in their own particular classrooms. Even in public schools, which (at least in theory) have the institutional mechanism—state departments of education—to develop and spread new educational practices, the lag between the creation of useful ideas and their formalization as educational policy can be extensive. And the implementation of new policy initiatives is neither automatic nor immediate. The creation of supports for LGBT youth is not merely the story of a handful of teachers being willing to go out on a limb to help students at risk. It is also the story of how their ideas were adopted and implemented on a larger scale—never a sure thing in the educational world.

Further, although this book is about the creation and spread of in-school supports for LGBT youth, it would be a mistake to turn the few teachers highlighted in this story into singular heroes working to save LGBT students. Nor is it constructive to focus too much on the question of "firsts," of which program actually preceded all others, which one truly originated the idea of the Gay-Straight Alliance as it exists in schools now. As we shall see, none of the programs highlighted above may actually claim to be first—a short-lived GSA appears to have sprung up at a school in Washington Heights, New York, in the early 1970s. This book should not be read as a story of firsts, nor of individual teachers. The characters highlighted herein may certainly be heroic in their work, but it is best to consider them exemplars of the type of work that was likely happening throughout the American educational system.

It is also important to note that this book is not meant to be a complete history of the many ways in which schools began to support LGBT youth. This is only one story, but one that illustrates the almost unfathomable success of the movement to change schools' relationship with the LGBT students under their care. Teachers had begun their work essentially underground, their efforts not even coordinated enough to be called a grassroots campaign. Gradually, their work became more visible and their goals more coherent. They built networks, cultivated political allies, and developed strategies for advancing their cause. What began with a few teachers working in isolation transmogrified into a state-led reform program and a national model. It is a story of the many ways individuals took risks, threw out lifelines, and made significant differences for countless young people in their care.

The health risks facing LGBT youth have not disappeared, nor have schools uniformly become bastions of tolerance and understanding. Still, this reform effort has had a remarkable impact. GSAs have extended their reach across the nation and throughout the world. According to research by the Gay, Lesbian, and Straight Education Network (GLSEN), schools with GSAs offer a safer environment for LGBT youth: students are less likely to hear homophobic remarks, less likely to experience harassment, less likely to miss school because they feel unsafe, and more likely to feel connected to faculty members and the school community.[7]

Further, by bringing homosexuality into the open and making it part of the dialogue within school communities, these reforms influenced perceptions of homosexuality in American society. Schools have forced large swaths of the population to come to terms with the gulf between their deeply held fears of homosexuality and the affable, intelligent, understanding, and gay teacher at the front of the room (or, for that matter, the ill-humored, aloof, and intimidating gay teacher at the front of the room). While it would be intemperate to overstate the impact of school climate on broader nationwide cultural trends, the existence of openly gay teachers and students, and of Gay-Straight Alliances, has helped generations of students and parents get used to the idea that homosexuality is a normal part of mainstream society. Schools have helped condition individuals and communities to a new reality.

This book has two purposes. First, and foremost, it is a work of history. The story is a remarkable one, partly because the reform effort has worked (an all-too-infrequent outcome in the history of education), but mostly because the Safe Schools program has had a profound impact on the health, safety, and dignity of a population that has often been marginalized and degraded. Further, changes in schools have influenced the larger conversation regarding the LGBT community and American society. Schools will continue to have an important role in shaping this dialogue. It is important to understand the story so far, and the many ways in which school reform and the LGBT rights movement have influenced each other.

The almost organic nature of the development of the Safe Schools program brings us to the second purpose of this book. It demonstrates a process of education reform that is different from what is typically described by the policy makers, historians, and academic researchers who make up the expert class of the American educational system. In the traditional model, education reform is driven by the ideas of these elites. It is understood to be a top-down dynamic, in which teachers— characterized as fearful of change and wedded to outdated ideas and practices—resist those who would seek to modernize the American educational system. According to this traditional model of education reform, the manner and intensity of this resistance can vary—from unions engaging in direct and large-scale action, to a single teacher in a single classroom simply ignoring the dictates of a far-off educational bureaucracy. However, the Safe Schools program offers a counterexample. It began with the ideas and initiative of those at the bottom of the educational hierarchy, and their efforts were often resisted by administrators and politicians who feared change and sought instead to preserve the status quo. This story inverts the traditional understanding of education reform, and it is highly unlikely that it is unique in this regard. Despite the persistence of the traditional top-down narrative in policy and academic circles, other examples of bottom-up reform surely exist.

This hole in the historical record does necessarily represent a willful, elitist disregard for the efforts of students and teachers; historians can describe only what the available evidence allows. All too often, teachers and students do not leave the same type of paper trail as administrators and policy makers. Further, the cause-and-effect narrative that turns a collection of facts into memorable history is often difficult to uncover where teachers are concerned: classroom teaching often occurs in what has been described by education researcher Larry Cuban as a "black box,"[8] and the connection between the work of individual teachers and the development of education policy is often obscure. However, in this instance, the chain of events is quite clear: the state department of education implemented reforms that were based entirely on models developed by teachers working at their individual schools. It is a process that began with teachers seeking to address the problem directly in front of them, and ended with a statewide program to support LGBT youth, key elements of which have been copied by many other states.

Differing views on the process of reform matter, because the traditional model profoundly colors popular perceptions of school reform efforts. As a result, conventional wisdom has developed and hardened in policy circles: successful implementation of education reform is seen to hinge on the degree to which teachers can be made to abandon their instinct to cling to past practice and "buy in." This narrative is not entirely wrong, but merely incomplete. Top-down reform is well documented, and has had significant impact on American education; what remains is to work toward a better understanding of the dynamics and impact of reform that is initiated by those at the bottom of the hierarchy. If nothing else, doing so may raise some interesting questions about broad-based reform efforts with other marginalized groups in schools. Perhaps we can use the specific story of how teachers sought to change school climates for LGBT youth to look more generally at how the work of educators shapes societal views on any number of issues.

Perhaps more important, a better understanding of the myriad origins of reform efforts may well open the door to new ideas for how to bring meaningful change to schools. What happens if teachers—typically seen as those upon whom reforms are imposed—are seen as leaders of reform efforts? How do processes and strategies for reform change if school administrators—at school, district, or state levels—are the ones who need to be induced to buy in to reform efforts? Can schools benefit from nurturing an environment in which teachers take a more entrepreneurial role in directing change? This book is certainly not intended to be the last word on school reform, merely to raise some questions about how we view the process.

Nor is this book meant to be an exhaustive history of the gay rights movement in education; it is an attempt to trace efforts to improve the experience of LGBT students in the school system—a significant part of the story to be sure, but only one strand of the larger history. It begins with a look at how schools have sought to teach values—with a particular focus on the effort to instill traditional gender and sexual norms in their young charges. It then offers a brief survey of the early gay rights movement—its beginnings in the 1950s, and efforts to combat the tremendous antigay hysteria in postwar America. These two threads—the larger gay rights movement and efforts to teach values in schools—connect in the work of the early school reformers who faced tremendous obstacles in addressing LGBT issues in schools. Finally, the book shows how this work snowballed into a statewide reform movement, and how this movement became the basis for statewide policy, which in turn became the model nationwide, and indeed internationally. And above all, it seeks to bring much-deserved recognition to a remarkable group of students and teachers, whose work began a series of changes that have rippled through American society in the twenty-first century.

Out of the Shadows and into Parades

CHAPTER 1

The Drama Club!

—Director of the Massachusetts Safe
Schools program Jeff Perrotti's partially
tongue-in-cheek response when asked
where LGBT youth could have found a
safe place in schools in the early 1980s

The Drama Club!

—Massachusetts high school teacher Peter
Atlas's response to the same question

I know of no sanctuary.

—Massachusetts high school teacher
Arthur Lipkin's response

O N A CLEAR AND COOL SATURDAY in June 1993, downtown
Boston prepared for the annual onslaught of color, costumes, and unbound flamboyance that is the Boston pride
parade. Although a staid affair compared to the parades in San Francisco or New York—more in keeping with the reserved New England
character—the event still boasted its share of glam, camp, and provocation. Marching bands and flag-snapping drill teams, the backbone
of any all-American parade, were present, but dressed in Speedos and
little else. Carnival drag queens coquetted down the parade route in
all their finery, led by Miss Boston Pride, who presided with queenly
extravagance. Leathermen gyrated suggestively on floats. Dozens of
masked figures clad in fairy wings danced joyously down the street.
Black-booted Dykes on Bikes revved their motorcycles. And out of this
riotous rainbow swirl marched perhaps the most shocking group of
all: a gaggle of conservatively dressed, visibly nervous and excited high
school students, and their faculty adviser, history teacher Bob Parlin.

The sight of the "Newton South High School Gay-Straight Alliance" banner caused a greater stir than many of the more provocative floats and costumes—the rest, outrageous as they may have been, had all been seen before. But high schoolers, gay and straight alike, marching together? With a teacher? This was new. Onlookers cheered and clapped and rushed into the street to greet the small contingent, as if they weren't quite convinced of its reality. Tears were shed. Parlin was enveloped by complete strangers. Pictures were taken. That LGBT youth could find acceptance and support in their schools, that they could march publicly and proudly—on what amounted to a school field trip, no less—strained even the wildest imaginings of the most optimistic dreamers in the crowd.

The students were pleased and proud, if slightly taken aback by their newfound celebrity status. On one level, they understood why their presence generated such an outpouring. For members of the Gay-Straight Alliance at a place like Newton South, school, while certainly not idyllic, was not quite the nightmare it had been for the adults clamoring around them. For generations of LGBT men and women before them, talk of surviving high school was not mere hyperbole. Gay youth, frequent targets of abuse, often found no safe haven; for many, the teenage years were a constant struggle to suppress whatever "signs" they might give off. Being outed at school turned classmates into bullies. School leaders had ignored their plight, or made it worse. Faculty were not immune to the biases of the time, and jokes and epithets might just as easily come from the teacher at the front of the class as from the students in the halls. Being outed at home could be worse. Many gay youth were kicked out of their homes and disowned by their parents. Some never reconciled with their families—they became orphans in their teenage years, and remained so.

Doubtless many among the parade goers had contemplated suicide at one time or another. A disproportionate number had attempted it, and many knew at least one friend who had succeeded. Fear, isolation, a double life, a desperate need for secrecy, and the longing for acceptance—this is how many of the parade goers reminisced about high school. And then, to see this group of kids marching, with straight allies and teachers—here, in front of them, was a new possibility: that high school reminiscence could recall something better than the anger and hopelessness that clouded many of their own memories. It was the essence of the pride parade—a victory march.

THROUGHOUT THE TWENTIETH CENTURY, Americans' reflexive response to homosexuality was revulsion. They equated it with deviance, and assumed (wishfully, in most cases) that the "sickness" of homosexuality did not taint their own communities. It wasn't until after World War II that organized activism for gay rights began in the United States, and in those early days police harassment, a right to privacy, and protection from violence were seen as more pressing issues. The individuals and groups that made up this nascent movement fought many small battles against many forms of discrimination, sought support for the larger fights, and, to be frank, lost nearly as often as they won. And they avoided addressing the issues facing gay youth. Advocacy in schools was never at the top of the movement's priority list, and often was consciously avoided—the stereotype of the gay predator as seducer of children was pernicious enough to keep homosexual adults from working to help school-age children. Until the 1990s, progress in schools lagged behind that of the larger gay rights struggle.

Further, school leadership, perhaps more than leaders of other public institutions, consistently endeavored to maintain the fiction that homosexuality existed only elsewhere, and often actively purged gay and lesbian teachers from their ranks. Only a few years before the Newton South GSA joined the parade, a teacher's open participation in a pride march would have been unthinkable—most teachers feared attending gay pride rallies even anonymously, lest they be discovered and outed, and their jobs forfeit. A handful of teachers marched with bags over their heads. Those who sought to support LGBT students in schools could do so only covertly, while support networks for youth outside the school system were tentative and sporadic. Schools in the 1980s did not appear markedly more tolerant than those of generations before—for the most part gay students were either invisible or attacked.

Even if the larger gay rights movement shied away from addressing the problems of gay youth, there is a clear (if circuitous) line connecting the work of these activists with the GSA movement. Work in the 1950s helped create a new consciousness, a willingness to fight openly against the often violent contempt with which straight society viewed gay men and women. The increasingly activist mentality within the gay community eventually gave rise to teachers and students working from the inside to change their schools' culture and the values those schools taught. The nascent movement of the 1950s, one mostly concerned with preventing police harassment and keeping its members safe from harm, laid the foundation for teachers like Parlin to forge a fundamentally different relationship between gay and straight members of their school communities. On the one hand, the Newton South GSA's participation in the 1993 Pride Parade appeared to be a watershed moment in the history of gay rights, a sudden and unexpected display of support for LGBT youth. On the other, it was merely another incremental step, part of a largely unseen progression of work by students and teachers to make schools safer and more supportive for all.

THE GAY RIGHTS MOVEMENT exploded into the popular consciousness with the Stonewall riots of 1969, a violent protest against police harassment, named for the gay bar at its epicenter in New York City's Greenwich Village. Stonewall was a public flashpoint, but the movement itself began many years earlier, in much more prosaic fashion—the result of hundreds of different conversations in hundreds of living rooms, bedrooms, bars, and at parties. Chuck Rowland, who in the 1950s helped found what was perhaps the first gay rights group, the Mattachine Society, recalled that talk about organizing a rights movement long preceded any actual organization: "I don't think there was any thinking person who hadn't, at some time back in the 1920s or 1930s, said at a bar one night, 'You know, we should get together and have a gay organization.' And usually you would be laughed out of the place."[1] Shirley Willer, an early activist in Chicago (and later one of the first members of the Daughters of Bilitis—a groundbreaking lesbian rights group founded in 1955), asked a lawyer how she could go about starting an advocacy group, to which the lawyer replied, "You don't. It's too dangerous."[2]

Perhaps her lawyer referred her to the case of another Chicago activist, Henry Gerber. In 1924, Gerber, a U.S. Army veteran, founded the Society for Human Rights, an ill-fated gay rights discussion group. He could attract only three others to join, but he did manage to publish—briefly—an advocacy journal entitled *Friendship and Freedom*. Gerber's organization fell apart only a few months after its inception, when the wife of one member outed the group to an acquaintance who in turn reported them to the police. Gerber was arrested just after he arrived home, alone, from a walk. The others were similarly detained. A headline blared, "Strange Sex Cult Exposed." The case against Gerber and the others was dismissed, as there was no actual evidence of homosexual activity, but Gerber was fired from his job with the Postal Service. He drifted to New York, and in 1927 he re-upped with the army. Gerber served through the end of World War II and retired with an honorable discharge and a pension.[3]

The very idea that homosexuals should have rights was radical at the time. Homosexuality was believed—even by many homosexuals—to be a problem of "moral weakness, criminality, or pathology."[4] Every possible source—church, school, doctors, police, media—sent the same message. "Everything I read said that we were deviants," recalled one early activist. "So that's what I thought about myself."[5] Coming to terms with one's homosexuality often involved doing clandestine research in abnormal psychology texts, receiving diagnoses from doctors or clergymen, with prescriptions ranging from marriage to shock therapy. In most states, even serving drinks to homosexuals was illegal—a reaction to the proliferation of gay bars that sprang up with the end of Prohibition. Antisodomy laws were in place, with penalties as serious as lengthy prison sentences with solitary confinement. Stories of forced sterilization and even castration at the hands of authorities were whispered throughout the gay community.[6] Fears—often well-founded—of isolation, harassment, and ostracism from friends and family drove many either to deny their own identity or to hide it as deeply as possible.

Enter Harry Hay, Communist organizer, lifetime radical, the man who largely built the foundation for the gay rights movement, and who first articulated an identity for homosexuals as members of a minority group that suffered from discrimination at the hands of the straight majority. Despite his marriage to Anna Platky, Hay, a veteran of the violent labor battles along the West Coast waterfront in the 1930s, carried on a long-running affair with actor Will Geer—later known to mainstream America as Grandpa Zeb from *The Waltons*. When Hay first broached the idea of a homosexual discussion group in 1948, Geer was dismissive: "But honey, what would we talk about?"[7] Nevertheless, Hay was persistent, and in 1950, he and four other activists—Rudi Gernreich, Dale Jennings, Bob Hull, and Chuck Rowland—founded what became known as the Mattachine Society to advocate for gay rights, a term and an idea that did not exist at the time. Their original prospectus outlines material goals that appear relatively modest to twenty-first-century eyes: legal reform to counter police brutality, funds for legal support and bail money for those arrested, and political advocacy for right-to-privacy laws. Still, the extent to which they were breaking new ground is apparent in the founders' calls for study groups and forums "to understand ourselves." As Hay himself often noted in later years, in 1950 there was no "us," no gay community or identity. There was not even a name—any of the words of the time, even "homosexual," carried such negative freight that they were deemed unusable. Hay started with "Bachelors Anonymous" and referred to his constituency as "the Androgynous Minority" in his first prospectus.[8]

Hay's legacy within the movement is complicated. His identification of homosexuals as culturally distinct in society meant separating gay culture from the dominant straight culture, and celebrating the differences—even the most extreme libertine excesses. For Hay, to be gay was to be free from the constraints of all mainstream norms. He embraced all aspects of what he saw as gay culture—including the North American Man-Boy Love Association (NAMBLA), which most considered morally indefensible as well as politically suicidal. Others in the early movement wanted instead to identify as nothing more than completely normal members of mainstream society—who just happened to be homosexual. The fractious history of the Mattachine Society, from which Hay departed (or was ousted, depending on whose telling one believes) in 1954,[9] reflects some of this separatist vs. assimilationist divide. In the twenty-first century, Hay is often left on the periphery of the history of the gay rights movement. His celebration of the most radical fringe of gay culture, and his association with groups as reprehensible as NAMBLA, leave many in the movement uncomfortable with lionizing him. But his most important contribution to the movement is simple and undeniable: Hay was the first organizer. He created, for gay Americans, an "us."

The Mattachine Society and the Daughters of Bilitis both took many small steps to support the larger gay community, as did other activists working on their own. They published newsletters and attempted to build a social community where previously there was little. They intervened with the police when possible, offered advice on what to do if arrested, and protested instances of particularly egregious or violent harassment. They attempted to forge connections to religious leaders and build a coalition of supportive church communities. But they could not yet coordinate a broader attack on the vast array of barriers to mainstream acceptance of homosexuality. In many cases, members of the groups disagreed about both goals and methods. ("Get two gays together, you have three opinions," joked one early activist.)[10] Still, the movement, such as it was, chipped away at a variety of problems—even if this early work often passed unnoticed by the mainstream—and helped create a community and identity.

This chipping away gave rise to a generation of men and women who desired to live openly and proudly, who were unwilling to accept the place in society to which they had been consigned. The goal of right-to-privacy morphed into a demand for public acceptance. Beginning in the late 1950s, activists pushed the medical community to reconsider the clinical definition of homosexuality as an illness, and in 1973 the American Psychiatric Association voted to remove homosexuality from the list of mental disorders. The Stonewall riots of 1969—the "we're not gonna take it anymore" moment of its generation—was both emblematic of a changing mentality within the gay community and a catalyst for greater activism. In 1971, Boston held its first pride parade. LGBT leaders organized the first National March on Washington for Lesbian and Gay Rights in 1979 (after an aborted attempt in 1973). Where many in the gay community had grown up believing their desires were the problem, they now saw straight society as the problem. And they became louder and more public in their demands for equal treatment.

Then AIDS happened. There could be no bigger issue for the gay rights movement, and nothing with as significant an impact on popular perceptions of the gay community, both for better and worse. It reinforced popular conceptions of homosexual promiscuity. It ushered Rock Hudson, among many others, out of the closet. The AIDS crisis completely unhinged society from its previous values and beliefs about homosexuality. It brought increased awareness and sympathy, but also notoriety, fear, revulsion, and suspicion. Activism surged, as did condemnation. Above all, AIDS made it impossible to ignore questions of homosexuality and American society. It brought new opportunities to discuss the issue, but also erected one more barrier in the minds of many: if gay people were perceived as a threat before, AIDS made them a lethal one. And if coming out was political before, AIDS only magnified the stakes.

The activism of the 1960s and '70s, coupled with the social upheaval wrought by AIDS, had done little to make the job of supporting LGBT youth any easier. Certainly activists well understood the nature of the risks gay teenagers faced. Many could look to their own past experiences, and by the 1970s a few in the medical community began to publish clinical data on those risks—the high incidence of substance abuse, the increased dropout rates, the bullying, and the exceptionally high number of suicides.[11] More compelling than the statistics were the heartbreaking stories that young gay men and women could tell the few social workers and activists trying to help: the parents who erected a gravestone and ran a newspaper obituary rather than acknowledge their very much living and breathing lesbian daughter;[12] a fifteen-year-old boy kicked out of a group home after being gang-raped and beaten, because he was gay;[13] numerous runaways, throwaways, and young addicts driven to petty crime or forced into sex work. Gay health professionals recognized the crisis, but in many cases could do very little. Early homophile organizations feared that reaching out to the neediest youth—the homeless, the runaways, the suicidal—could lead to criminal charges. After all, if state liquor boards prohibited serving gays, and if dancing with a same-sex partner led to arrests for lewd behavior, then even speaking to younger boys or girls represented a whole new level of danger. Beginning in the 1950s and '60s, the Daughters of Bilitis counseled youth via telephone and mail, and individuals offered some limited support, but working directly with youth was simply too risky.

Young people themselves didn't need others to point out they had been neglected. In 1972, a short-lived group in Boston, High School Gays United, gave voice to the frustration of their generation:

> A separate segment of the gay movement is being formed because, although there are several people in the gay community who can be contacted by phone or mail, many of these do not want to become involved in any way with people under 18 for fear of being charged with "contributing to the delinquency of a minor." The mere fact that they cannot give us the help we seek is contributing to our delinquency and possible self-destruction by leading us into reinforced depression and lonliness [sic], hostility for the society that forces us to hide, and in some instances excessive drinking, drug abuse—and maybe even suicide for some.
>
> Being gay and in high school presents many problems, the worst of which, in my opinion, is having to hide our sexual identity. We cannot reveal ourselves without running the risk of harassment and rejection by peers and teachers, the first of which hurts more deeply. We cannot walk arm in arm with our lovers as heterosexuals do without being ostracized. A generally quite [sic], non-joining type of person's loneliness is augmented because of the "front" he or she has to build. The outgoing class officer or member of the Student Council is forced into a "role"—a code of behavior dictated

and reinforced by the heterosexual student body. Many popular students who do not want their homosexuality discovered may "go steady" with members of the opposite sex who are in the same limelight simply to limit suspicion and maintain a "straight" reputation; and they are miserable because they must hide their natural preference and portray a different person. Many become ashamed of their homosexuality and think it is a sickness; but, on the other hand, there are many who are proud and want it to be recognized as a lifestyle—a way of expressing love for a person.[14]

If this manifesto is taken at face value, its authors may be considered fortunate in one respect—they were, at least, still in school and not among the dropouts trying to make it on the streets. Homelessness has always been a particularly acute problem for gay youth, although it was not always recognized as such. More recently, studies have shown that between 20 and 40 percent of the homeless youth population identify as homosexual or bisexual. Data of this nature is difficult to come by for earlier periods, as agencies working with homeless youth rarely broached the topic. Traditionally, serial runaway youth were diagnosed as deviant and were hospitalized or entered into the juvenile criminal system in great numbers.[15]

In the mid-1970s, adult-led activist groups, working independently from the schools, began to work more directly with youth in crisis. In Boston, Project Lambda formed in 1975 to support gay teens and to "plead the causes of youth . . . wherever necessary: court, probation officer, doctor, etc."[16] For a brief, shining moment, the project received public funding through a Boston city program with the descriptive title "Treatment Alternative to Street Crimes—Juvenile." Although public funding dried up in 1976—it was about the lowest possible funding priority in the city budget—the group reformed in 1977 as the Committee for Gay Youth, "a watchdog for the needs of often neglected Boston Gay Youth."[17] Among other initiatives, CGY sought to provide places for homosexual boys and girls to meet (as the social centers of the gay community were often bars). However, this group was riven by disputes over leadership, and a splinter group known as the Boston Alliance of Gay and Lesbian Youth—led by students and focused specifically on the needs of high school youth in the Boston area—formed. In 1981, BAGLY hosted its first (and likely the nation's first) prom "by and for GLBT youth," which was proudly attended by over one hundred students and their dates.[18]

In New York, a professional couple—psychiatrist Emery Hetrick and New York University professor Damien Martin—undertook a notable series of efforts to address the youth crisis in 1979. The Hetrick-Martin Institute began as the Institute for the Protection of Lesbian and Gay Youth (IPLGY) after its two founders heard the story of a fifteen-year-old who had been severely beaten while staying at a homeless shelter. The boy had subsequently been kicked out of the shelter, as his homosexuality was considered to be the cause of the disturbance.[19] Hetrick and Martin brought together a group of acquaintances to discuss how they might help in such cases. If this work with the young seemed risky, even for (or especially for) a dowdy middle-aged couple, it likely was, as the gay-men-as-seducers-of-youth trope appeared to be a concern of all who learned of Hetrick and Martin's work. Representatives from NAMBLA had to be disinvited from early IPLGY meetings.

Still, the two persisted, and slowly, the IPLGY took shape—beginning without a staff or even a plan for how to go about helping gay youth. In 1983, at last in possession of an office, the institute began doing contract work for the city of New York, running intervention programs for gay youth living on the streets. In 1984, it launched an AIDS and HIV prevention education program for adolescents, a project no other group dared touch.[20] In 1985, after two years of discussion with the New York City Board of Education, IPLGY and the board opened the Harvey Milk School, aimed at providing a safe space to educate homosexual students who had dropped out of traditional public schools. The *New York Times* ran a front-page article (which included the subhead "No recruitment") about the opening of the Milk School. The article noted Damien Martin's insistences that "the organization has no outreach or recruitment plan of its own, and that students . . . come to the institute on their own initiative." The school's only teacher, Fred Goldhaber, also sought to put suspicious minds at ease:

"Neither in the school nor here at the Institute do we convince the kids to be one way or another." The article did mention, however, that "one of the aims of the program is to teach the teen-agers . . . to be comfortable with their own homosexuality." Program director Steve Ashkinazy noted "nervousness" and "stalling" on the part of the board of education, despite backing from staffers in the mayor's office and the office of the Manhattan borough president. The article also took pains to mention—on four separate occasions—that the city government provided funding for the school and the institute.[21]

The school, such as it was in the beginning, first operated out of a church basement in Greenwich Village. Goldhaber taught all five subjects to a student body of twenty. While the board of education was concerned about the inevitable controversy that would follow, then-mayor Ed Koch appeared to support the idea, and his office nudged the board along. However, it appears that members of the New York City Board of Education never explicitly approved the program: the BOE's spokesman stated that the board's "professional staff" approved of the program, so the board did not need to vote expressly to ratify it. In press coverage at the opening of the school, it is notable that the then-chancellor of public schools, Anthony Alvarado, was not available for comment, and that those who did speak to the press emphasized repeatedly the "no recruitment" angle.

Ashkinazy also emphasized what became the foundation of teachers' push for changing school cultures: a safe environment for all. "When I started working here . . . we were dealing with lots of gay kids 15 or 16 years old who had been out of school for a year or more . . . The reason they gave us was that when it became known in their schools that they were gay, they were harassed verbally or . . . beaten up." Both the school board and institute members rejected the idea of trying to work within the traditional school setting—concerned that "immature teen-agers" would lead to continued harassment of gay students. Goldhaber concurred: "For the most part, the males are overtly effeminate, some are transvestites, and the girls are all tough . . . All of them would be targets for abuse in regular schools." In the end, the Harvey Milk School worked like a hospital emergency room: it provided immediate and lifesaving care, and addressed the acute problem. Its mission was not to create a healthier system. As a member of the board's professional staff explained, "If these kids don't want to go to school anywhere but this one place, what are you supposed to do? The important thing is to get them back into a school, address their problem, and get them on the diploma track."[22]

THESE EARLY, out-of-system efforts were important, but limited in their impact. Although they attempted to build coalitions with local governments, they received little and only sporadic funding, and often reluctant or tepid support. Further, they aimed only to help the most acute cases—those who had already left school and were on the streets. Such a choice may perhaps have been dictated by the necessities of triage, but from an educational perspective, it was nonetheless an exercise in deploying lifeboats well after the ship had sunk: Even now, only a minority of students who drop out of high school ever return to graduate. More importantly, providing supports in alternative settings, separate from the mainstream student population, could only serve to widen the gulf between straight society and the homosexual teenagers it cast out. Such measures sought to alleviate the effects of the antigay culture in schools without addressing the cause. Schools, better positioned to intervene before troubled or bullied students became youth in crisis, missed a chance to become more involved. While government institutions demonstrated some willingness to reach out a sympathetic hand, sympathy extended only so far.

There existed at least one tantalizing example of this missed opportunity for schools to extend support to gay youth on a system-wide basis. George Washington High School in Manhattan's Washington Heights can lay claim to perhaps the first Gay-Straight Alliance in a high school in the nation. In 1972, a group of students launched the Gay International Youth Society (GIYS)—a club composed of gay, bisexual, and straight students, both male and female, and, as the name suggests, students of ethnically diverse backgrounds as well. In the years prior to 1972, George Washington was riven by conflict and violence, a school on fire—often literally, as students used arson to protest

inadequate school funding, heavy-handed treatment by school officials, and substandard educational resources. By 1972, a new principal,
Samuel Kostman, had restored order—not by instituting harsh disci-
plinary measures but by fostering a sense of community and responsibility among all stakeholders. His message of inclusiveness included
the LGBT community, and he was open to the idea of a student-run LGBT
group.

The GIYS appears to have struck a fairly strident tone—perhaps in
keeping with the time and the mentality within the school community. It organized weekly meetings, held dances (although, fearful of
possible harassment by others in the school, the group held these at
off-campus venues), and pushed its members to come out and be politically active. GIYS quite perceptively noted that it might be easier for
the students to come out than for teachers, and its work actually preceded the creation of the first gay teachers organization in New York,
the Gay Teachers Association, which formed in 1974. "Gay teachers,"
one member wrote, "are still not ready to come out and support such
student groups . . . Gay teachers fear coming out for many reasons, but
a main one is the fear that it would impair their functional ability as
teachers . . . It is up to these students to create an atmosphere that will
help them too."[23] The students further sought to spread their model
for student-run activist groups to other schools, but had limited success. At George Washington, the group itself slowly lost momentum
and membership, and this early, proto-GSA movement died out by the
late 1970s. What could have been the beginning of the movement to
change schools in the early 1970s withered, and the idea disappeared
from public schools until the late 1980s.

Still, by fits and starts, the gay rights movement was on the
march—on occasion literally. Born in the 1950s, the movement could
point to some small victories and a few signature moments over the
ensuing decades: reduced harassment, the removal of homosexuality from the list of mental disorders, the Stonewall uprising, the first
pride parades, the first march on Washington. But work in schools
would have to wait. Americans expected their schools to beget a certain type of graduate, into whom had been insinuated a particular

vision of the American character—one that certainly did not include homosexuality. Schools—where it was assumed that bedrock values could be impressed upon malleable youth—were trapped in an odd place. They could not be seen to be harboring deviants, so school leaders were often tempted to purge even a hint of homosexual behavior. However, moving to root out the problem was an admission they had allowed it to fester in the first place, and—in the minds of their constituents—put children at risk of exposure. In the words of lawyer and scholar Karen Harbeck, schools had trapped themselves behind "a wall of silence."[24] So school officials often preferred to ignore the issue altogether. Teachers—no matter their personal views on the wisdom of ignoring kids in crisis—were expected to play their part, and gay teachers were expected to stay in the closet or, when threatened with exposure, to resign and move on.

For most of the twentieth century, it was a successful strategy—if success is defined as turning a blind eye to the problem. But an increasingly activist mentality bred a generation of teachers (and students) less inclined to surrender quietly or remain in the closet. It began slowly, and almost invisibly; before these teachers could support LGBT students openly, they would first need to make Americans see LGBT students and teachers as not so different, to move associations away from notions of deviance and danger and toward the idea that homosexuality was normal, healthy, and respectable. And they would have to emphasize a different set of values as definitional of the American character. This battle over values—what schools should attempt to instill, and how teachers should model them—is central to many stories of reform, and this one is no different. In this particular case, the conflict over values and character has its roots in the early years of the century, and in the fear that the very essence of American manhood was in decline.

Fears of a Petticoat Regime

CHARACTER AND EDUCATION
IN THE UNITED STATES

CHAPTER 2

It takes a man to raise a man.
—Arthur Evans, quoted in "Men Teachers in the United States," a doctoral dissertation by Joseph Alva Baer, 1928

[They] don't learn to take initiative that men need to do. A group of women sit like bumps on a log in a business meeting.
—Anonymous survey response cited in Baer's dissertation

Woman does not grasp what is meant by "sense of honor."
—C. W. Bardeen, quoted in Baer's dissertation

I N 526 CE, Queen Amalasuntha of the Ostrogoths, youngest daughter of Theodoric the Great and regent to the child king Athalaric, and perhaps the most cosmopolitan woman in sixth-century Europe, took on what turned out to be an insurmountable challenge: continuing her father's legacy. Theodoric, the greatest and wisest of the Gothic kings, overran the barbarian chieftains governing the tatters of the Western Roman Empire and established an Ostrogothic empire that extended from Southern France in the west to Serbia in the east. As king, Theodoric sought to resurrect the ghosts of the Rome around him, to create an oasis of civilization among the bellicose and unlettered chiefdoms of Europe. He died in 526, and having no sons, he left the kingdom to his ten-year-old grandson Athalaric—which in practical terms meant putting his daughter, Amalasuntha, on the throne.

Amalasuntha was truly her father's daughter. As regent, she insisted Athalaric be educated by Roman scholars and learn classical poetry, history, and philosophy. Like Theodoric, she fervently wished to civilize her subjects. The Gothic nobility, however, saw little use for education beyond that needed to make war, and chafed under the rule of a woman—a Romanized woman at that. They were singularly unmoved by Athalaric's argument (or Amalasuntha's, as she was its likely source) that while "other nations have arms, the lords of the Romans alone have eloquence." After all, hadn't they conquered the Romans? Roman learning, the nobles were convinced, instilled no useful character traits, and promoted nothing but "effeminacy and cowardice." The Gothic chiefs took a similarly dim view of their young ruler—a frail mama's boy who clearly lacked the temperament and strength of a warrior king. Unfortunately, Athalaric lived down to their expectations: he dissipated what strength he had in pursuit of all manner of vices, and died in his teenage years. Shortly thereafter, Amalasuntha, still trying to drag the Goths toward her Roman ideal, was murdered—strangled in her bath at the behest of nobles with more traditional views of what constituted a proper Gothic way of life.

Save for the violent end, the story of Amalasuntha and her chieftains has much in common with more recent battles over American schooling. Conflicts about values and character and education are as old as education itself. What should be taught? Who is suited to do the teaching? And who decides? An educational program represents an ideal vision for the future of society and an effort to instill in the next generation the morals, values, skills, and knowledge needed to secure it; failure to instill the right characteristics, to produce the right kind of person, is seen to have calamitous consequences. Leaving aside the question of whether youth are simply blank slates ready and willing to be programmed by their elders, conflicts over education often take on both aspirational and apocalyptic tones, and the character of the teacher often becomes part of the battleground. History, both recent and ancient, demonstrates a consistent belief that educators should both teach proper values in the classroom and model them in their daily lives. In this context, the conflict over whether homosexuals are fit to teach, and how schools should address homosexuality, is but one battle (admittedly a major one) in the long history of conflicts over values in education.

If the character of the teacher is seen as instrumental either in molding an ideal future society, or hastening the downfall of civilization, it is not surprising that teachers have often been held to higher standards of morality and comportment than the rest of society. In the United States in the early twentieth century, administrators imposed codes of behavior on teachers—female teachers especially—that included bans on smoking, marriage, and dancing in public.[1] In New York, Rose Friestater was denied a teaching license in 1935 for being, in the words of the New York City Board of Examiners, "thirty pounds more than the maximum allowed for her height."[2] Their justification: "Teachers should [be] . . . acceptable hygienic models for their pupils in the manner of weight."[3] As one prominent author of education texts cautioned the young female teacher, "Her health and vitality will be a large element in her success in teaching . . . for without health she cannot have enthusiasm or buoyancy or attractive ways."[4]

One of the most extreme examples of this type of effort to ensure educators conformed to an idealized type comes from a teaching contract ascribed to a "certain southern community" in the 1920s:

I promise to take a vital interest in all phases of Sunday-school work, donating of my time, service, and money without stint for the uplift and benefit of the community.

I promise to abstain from all dancing, immodest dressing, and any other conduct unbecoming a teacher and a lady.

I promise not to go out with any young men except in so far as it may be necessary to stimulate Sunday-school work.

I promise not to fall in love, to become engaged or secretly married.

I promise not to encourage or tolerate the least familiarity on the part of any of my boy pupils.

I promise to sleep at least eight hours a night, to eat carefully, and to take every precaution to keep in the best of health and spirits, in order that I may be better able to render efficient service to my pupils.

I promise to remember that I owe a duty to the townspeople who are paying me my wages, that I owe respect to the school board and superintendent that hired me, and that I shall consider myself at all times the willing servant of the school board and townspeople.[5]

It is a contract for a cipher, naïve in its longings, shaped by the most fervent hopes and ideals for what a proper young lady should be. And while its demands are surely excessive, administrators have often attempted to impose upon their subordinates such visions of propriety. Nor are such attempts merely relics of a distant past. In the social media age, examples abound of teachers being punished for violating some unwritten code of morality while off-duty. In 2009, a Wisconsin teacher was placed on leave after posting a picture of herself aiming a rifle (for which she was licensed). That same year, a Georgia teacher was forced to resign for what her superiors called "promoting alcohol use"—to wit, posting a picture of herself holding a drink while vacationing in Europe. In 2010, a teacher in Pennsylvania was fired after someone else posted a picture of her at a bridal shower with a male stripper. In that case, a school board member stated, "Everybody has a right to do what they want on their own time, but once kids and parents see it on the Internet, it becomes the school district's problem."[6]

While reasonable people may disagree on acceptable standards of behavior and social media activity for teachers, the above examples highlight an important dynamic of the teaching profession: when the behavior, comportment, or personal characteristics of the teaching class diverge from the vision of school leadership (or of educational policy makers, politicians, or even popular media), conflict is inevitable. If the divergence is particularly great, the conflict takes on a special urgency. In the early decades of the twentieth century, administrators and educational experts in the United States espied such a crisis—a problem that, in the words of one newspaper editorial, "[filled] one's heart with grave concern for the future."[7] The crisis? Too few men in the teaching profession.

It was feared that young boys were so under the spell of their female teachers that the nation risked losing its industry, its dynamism, even its honor. A generation educated by women portended a nation soon to be rendered emasculate. "Boys too effeminate, say principals, when they haven't had male instructors," declared the *New York Times*. Administrators described the dearth of male teachers as a "distinct discrimination" against boys in their early years, many of whom, they feared, left school early, without ever having had the benefit of instruction by men.[8] "The vast majority of boys are the victims of petticoats," lamented one newspaper columnist in 1925. "They are raised by their mothers, go to school to women clear up to the time they enter college and even their religious education is given over largely to women . . . our boys are under a petticoat regime in the school, the church, and even in the home."[9]

It is certainly no coincidence that rising concern over "the petticoat regime" came just on the heels of the women's suffrage movement. In many ways, this so-called crisis foreshadowed future conflicts over gay teachers and support for gay students. At the heart of both are questions about what it means to be a man or a woman in American society. That schools would be central to answering these questions is unsurprising; certainly in the early twentieth century, traditionalists hoped that more male teachers would help restore "proper" notions about gender roles, return women to their rightful sphere of influence in the home, and leave men firmly in charge of the political and economic realms. In 1914, education writer E. F. Chadwick predicted dire consequences if this "Woman Peril" was not addressed. For, he stated, "despite all the claims of the feminist movement," it was not the girls, but the future men who would "do the main work of the world: build and handle steamships and railways, command armies and fleets, fight our battles, tunnel our mountains and make our steel." That these young men, "in whom force of character is a first essential," should be taught by women "is of all things the most unreasonable and illogical." The end result, according to Chadwick, would be "a feminized manhood, emotional, illogical, non-combative against public evils . . .

I lay down the broad statement that no woman, whatever her ability, is able to bring up a man child."[10]

THIS LATEST CRISIS had its roots in a problem that has bedeviled educational systems throughout history. While society's aspirations for its future generations are often bound up in its idealistic vision of what a teacher should be, the hard reality of public finance has often compromised that vision. In colonial America, qualifications for teaching were virtually nonexistent: "If a man was in need of support, could read a chapter in the Testament, teach the Shorter Catechism, and whip the boys, he was sufficiently qualified as a teacher."[11] One writer reminisced about growing up in Georgia in the mid-1700s, during which time most instructors "were either indentured servants or felons."[12] Or, if communities did wish to hold their teachers to some standard of competence, they often found suitable candidates lacking. William Bradford of the Plymouth Colony wrote in 1624, "We have no common school for want of a fit person or hitherto means to maintain one."[13] To be fair, pastors or recent male college graduates would often take on teaching duties as a way to make some small living before embarking on more remunerative professional careers. But few men could support a family on a teacher's wage (in colonial times a teacher might get paid in commodities rather than cash), so few men of quality could be attracted to the profession.

Over the course of the nineteenth century, more and more women entered the field of education. By the 1870s, still 40 percent of all elementary and high school teachers were men, but by 1920, that number had dropped to 14 percent.[14] Young single women were cheaper to hire and thought to be more malleable, and for a time, in the eyes of school administrators, they became nearly ideal employees—until those same school administrators began to fear the petticoat regime. Men abandoned the profession for a host of reasons, not least of which was this increased competition and downward pressure on salary—although male teachers still made between 15 and 20 percent more than their female peers.[15] Other men left because they felt they were held in particularly low esteem. Salmon Chase, who taught secondary school while at Dartmouth and later founded a prestigious school in Washington, D.C., before embarking on a political career that included service in President Lincoln's cabinet and as chief justice of the Supreme Court, once commented that even a "drunken, miserable dog who could thre'd the mazes of the Alphabet" might become a teacher, and that the whole profession was held in "utter contempt."[16] In addition, many men were driven out by the inability to take real initiative in the classroom, being "systematized to death," or being at the mercy of the vicissitudes of local politics or small-minded administration.[17] The job was low-paying, low-prestige, involved caring for children, and was viewed as unmanly. "Looked upon as being a member of 'the third sex,'"[18] complained one teacher—a reference to education writer G. Stanley Hall's 1904 characterization of single women as an entirely new "other," a "third sex."[19]

According to a 1928 survey of superintendents and principals—part of a study that aimed to address this "woman peril"—school leadership shared the popular concern. Both male and (the very few) female school principals and superintendents saw the dearth of male teachers as a problem: of 541 male high school principals who responded to the survey, 512 agreed that there was need for more male teachers. Of 17 female principals who responded, 15 saw the same need.[20] However, not just any man would do. "If it were possible," one superintendent wrote, "I should like to see one teacher in every three or . . . four above the fifth or sixth grade, a man. I am afraid it would be very difficult, though, to secure enough men of the kind needed to carry out such a plan." "I believe every boy eleven or twelve years of age, or older, should come under the influence of a live, wide-awake man," wrote another. "For such teachers, however, I should want strong, vigorous, 'manly' men. To fill such positions with men of effeminate tendencies would be decidedly unfortunate." Regarding the goal of hiring more male teachers, another cautioned, "I wish to say that we think this is highly desirable, if we can improve the quality of men going in for teaching." And another wrote most succinctly, "Good strong men are OK, a weakling is dangerous."[21]

CONCERN OVER THE LACK OF "proper" men in teaching was not solely about gender. In the late nineteenth and early twentieth century, another bogeyman arose to disquiet the sleep of American parents, pressmen, and school leaders: a newly taxonomied deviant branch of humanity, the homosexual. While homosexuality has existed throughout human history, something important changed in the late nineteenth century: homosexuality went from being understood as a behavior—stigmatized and punished to varying degrees depending on place and time—to being considered a pathologized identity. It changed from something one does to something one is. Doctors of all stripes raced to identify its particular morphological markers or psychological origins. One British amateur scholar proposed a geographic cause, citing the locus of homosexuality specifically between latitudes 30 and 43 degrees north; others—noting that Germany seemed to be the origin of much scholarly investigation into same-sex attraction—wondered whether something in the Teutonic character or racial makeup inclined one toward homosexuality.[22]

As scholars and doctors diagnosed same-sex attraction as pathological rather than behavioral, homosexuality became the subject of greater attention, and aroused greater suspicion. Certainly religious authorities had consistently and explicitly disapproved of homosexual acts, but what had been condemnation of a sin now became an outspoken denunciation of the sinner. Intellectual and social movements of the time also expressed increased public antipathy toward homosexuals. The late nineteenth century saw a widespread fear of degeneracy—the general decline of civilization. While this decline might manifest itself in many ways, of particular concern were "moral stigmata," or signs of moral decay—defined by one writer as "any evil thought, feeling, or action . . . which is a permanent element or tendency in the character of a person."[23] In other words, homosexuality, once just an immoral act, could now bring about the fall of Western civilization. At the same time, theories of social Darwinism percolating throughout Europe and the United States provided a pseudoscientific rationale for antigay attitudes: homosexuals could not reproduce, and could only seduce others into their fold and further weaken the race. And finally, homosexual identity represented yet another crack in the foundation of a traditional society marked by well-defined gender roles. The essential character of men and women was at least partly understood in terms sexual and familial relations: men were providers and protectors, women were nurturers and caregivers, and together, they made a family—what, then, were homosexuals?

The "discovery" of homosexuals presented a clear challenge to society, and became, by the turn of the twentieth century, a "national problem."[24] In particular, homosexuality threatened the vital character of American manliness—more so even than the petticoat regime. Perhaps inevitably, schools were both blamed for incubating homosexuality and charged with solving the problem, whatever that problem actually was. Compared to their twentieth-century counterparts, nineteenth-century same-sex schools offered what may have been a relatively safe environment for same-sex attraction. Girls professed mad crushes on older students. Boys cultivated deeply intimate friendships with one another, often between a younger and older student. Schools sought to channel rather than discourage these overt displays of affection; older students were supposed to direct their youthful protégés toward salubrious and public-minded purpose. No doubt, in most cases these relationships were nothing more than teenage hormonal excess enabled by fashionable encouragement of lighthearted youthful enthusiasm. At the same time, though, a school culture tolerant of such friendships also provided an environment in which same-sex attraction could find fuller expression. But as fear of homosexuality increased in the early twentieth century, this tolerance disappeared. Writers warned of pervasive homosexual activity at all-girls schools, and urged parents to watch out for signs of sexual deviancy. Among boys, one writer warned, homosexual practices were "nowhere quite so general" as in the United States, and, he further claimed, universities the world over were bastions of same-sex relations "between fine-natured young collegemen."[25] Male-only schools clamped down on any signs of intimacy between students, and looked to cultivate in their pupils the proper art of manliness—namely, emotional restraint, vigorous physical activity, and self-control in all areas of life.

The early twentieth century similarly witnessed increased worries over teachers' deleterious influence on the character of their students. If women at the head of the classroom feminized boys, officials feared the degenerating effect of homosexual teachers would be significantly worse. Administrators and academics began to rethink schools' reliance on unmarried teachers, particularly women—who now were guilty of unmanning the boys, luring girls into same-sex deviancy, or just generally representing a lifestyle that broke with traditional family norms. Spinsters (as they were known in the popular lexicon) went from being a model of female virtue to being sexually suspect. A 1934 study purported to show that the "measured mental growth" of students taught by married women was greater than that of students taught by single women.[26] Although change came gradually, the percentage of single women in education dropped from 86 percent in 1920, to 29 percent by 1960.[27]

At the same time, single male teachers also found themselves suddenly under a cloud of suspicion. In the 1930s, leading educational scholar Willard Waller argued that "nothing seems more certain than that homosexuality is contagious."[28] He further claimed that, in his experience studying the profession and observing teachers, "the homosexual teacher develops an indelicate soppiness in relations with his favorites, and often displays not a little bitterness toward the others. He develops ridiculous crushes, and makes minor tragedies of little incidents when the recipient of his attentions shows himself indifferent."[29] Waller went on to outline a colleague's process for identifying homosexuals in the hiring process:

"Do you like boys?" he would ask. Often the answer betrayed the applicant. An over-enthusiastic answer was taken as probably betraying a homosexual, latent or active . . . It is also possible for such a question, suddenly injected into the conversation, to precipitate a conflict, and to obtain a confused, emotional, delayed or unduly hurried answer that is very diagnostic. In using such a device, it is necessary to have in mind an answer that is neither too thick nor too thin and to have a sharp eye for all kinds of self-betrayal. A more sophisticated technique would probably depend somewhat more upon such personality traits as carriage, mannerisms, voice, speech, etc.[30]

In cases where it was too late, where a school had already hired a homosexual teacher, Waller argued that psychiatry may be needed to prevent undue harm to the students: "Perhaps the strongest argument in favor of psychiatric work with teachers is that unadjusted teachers pass on their personality problems to their students . . . The teacher whose attitude toward sex is not wholesome engenders a similar maladjustment in her students."[31]

Self-control and propriety became the new watchwords. Waller declared that "if the schools ever decide to take their task of character education seriously, they will need to set it up as one of their major objectives to produce individuals normally heterosexual."[32] But how to teach it? Waller argued that schools must aggressively instill heterosexual norms, going so far as to state that "dramatic productions in which boys play the roles of girls or girls take the part of men are very undesirable . . . because of their possible influence in fostering homosexual attitudes."[33] Teachers were called on to model these new norms at all times, and to police any activity that was even remotely suggestive of same-sex attraction. Waller related a case study in which a "virile man teacher," who witnessed a group of boys displaying unfortunate tendencies, "was able by means of a downright speech to define clearly what expressions of affection were and what were not proper in a group of boys."[34] A report by the American Federation for Sex Hygiene (whose honorary president at the time was Charles W. Eliot, president emeritus of Harvard University) offered further tips. Aiming to promote sexual rectitude among youth, the federation exhorted schools to educate any physical intimacy out of their charges, to prepare students for a life of abstinence and self-control until marriage—at which time it was a couple's duty to produce healthy and fit children to propagate the race.[35] The purpose of sex education, the report argued, was "to impart such knowledge of sex . . . as may be necessary to preserve health, develop right thinking, and control conduct."[36] Further, sex education "must not seek to create interest and awaken curiosity," and that "the less children and youth think of sex, and the later they mature sexually, the better both physiologically and ethically."[37]

AMERICANS IN THE EARLY TWENTIETH CENTURY awoke to a two-pronged pink menace: the deteriorating quality of manliness and the viral spread of homosexuality. Could American values survive this nascent generation of mollycoddles and butch women? A nation feeling its oats after years of territorial expansion and industrial growth, one just beginning to flex its muscle on the global stage, could scarcely tolerate such creeping fey gentility among its men, nor any hint of mannish independent-mindedness among its women. Schools became the first line of defense. The traditional virtues that fortified the backbone of American character had to be reclaimed. Students found their behavior more rigidly constrained, their conduct more closely regulated. Teachers were expected to be models of decorum—the more conventional in their dress and behavior, the better. Administrators became less likely to view single women as ideal teachers, and single men, too, raised suspicion—for what red-blooded American male would be attracted to such a feminine (not to mention low-paying) profession? Certainly, traditional American society always viewed homosexual activity as abnormal; however, while schools in the nineteenth century never openly encouraged or accepted it, neither had they sought to eliminate even the slightest tint of what they now called deviant behavior. But by the early twentieth century, sexual deviance seemed sure to weaken the national character, and schools were called upon to root it out.

Postwar Hysteria

THE RED MENACE AND LAVENDER LADS

You can't hardly separate
homosexuals from subversives.

> —Senator Kenneth Wherry, on security risks
> working in the U.S. government, 1950

They were homosexuals.

> —John Peurifoy, testifying before Congress
> as to why ninety-one employees of the
> State Department were fired, 1950

I F HOMOSEXUALS aroused increasing concern in the early twentieth century, after World War II they became something like the monsters under the bed of the American psyche. In the fevered imaginations of the citizenry, they not only multiplied in number, but grew ever more threatening and depraved. In fact, they became an object of terror: in the postwar era, the vision of the gay man as a dangerous predator became ingrained in the American consciousness. Further, gay men and women were prime suspects in the obsessive hunt for Communist spies; as the World War ended and the Cold War with the Soviets took shape, fears of homosexuality became intertwined with—and often indistinguishable from—the fear of communism.

The war years were a boon to the development of active gay communities—men and women from all over the country were thrown together in single-sex environments, and finding others who desired same-sex love became significantly easier.[1] As the military demobilized, communities of gay men and women sprang up in urban centers across the nation. But Cold War America was an unfriendly place for such deviance. The containment policy abroad birthed what historian Elaine Tyler May has called a domestic containment, one that constrained Americans to increasingly rigid behavioral norms. At the same time, fears of sallow middle-aged degenerates preying on unwitting American boys gripped the nation. Once again, schools found themselves on the front lines. Suspect teachers were hunted and removed, and schools (if they addressed the issue of homosexuality at all) were expected to prevent the virus from catching, if not cure it outright.

More importantly, the American mind came to conflate homosexuality and communism, and the pink menace of the early twentieth century took on darker red undertones after the war. They became the twin perils on the domestic front, spurred by a near-manic hysteria that sought to purge the country of anything that might undermine American character and values. In fact, the frenzied panics—first over Communists, then homosexuals—often masked a deeper concern about what exactly those values were. The 1947 blacklisting of alleged Communist sympathizers in the film industry—perhaps a strike at libertine Hollywood culture as much as a defense against enemy infiltration—was a sign of things to come; events soon turned what might have been a run-of-the-mill culture war into an intensely charged fight against an existential threat.

First, Alger Hiss, convicted in 1948 of spying for the Soviets during the war (or more accurately, convicted of perjury for lying about it), gave a face to the spectral menace of Soviet infiltration. Then, in 1949, Mao and the Chinese Red Army rolled over the American-backed Guomindang, and in short order America had "lost" the most populous country in the world to the Communists. Finally, on September 23, 1949, President Truman announced that, in August, the Soviets had completed their first test of a nuclear weapon—an event intelligence analysts had predicted was still years away. In a few short years, communism went from abstract threat to insidious global force, bent on world domination, capable of spreading its tentacles into the heart of the country, and possessed of the means to wipe America off the face of the earth.

Almost immediately, many Americans—and not a few of President Truman's political opponents—sought a scapegoat. The day after Truman's announcement, Republican representative Harold Velde of Illinois and Democratic senator Herbert O'Conor of Maryland declared, in a heartening display of bipartisanship, that an appalling lack of vigilance "from the White House on down" left the United States "wide open to Communist infiltration," which could be remedied only by much stricter immigration controls on suspect nationalities.[2] Others were a little slower to capitalize on the crisis: it took the House Un-American Activities Committee (HUAC) a full week to out a mild-mannered professor, Joseph Weinberg, as "Scientist X"—a shadowy figure they claimed passed atomic secrets on to the Soviets. Meanwhile, perennial Republican presidential candidate Harold Stassen waited two full weeks (he was on a ship returning from England when the news broke) before declaiming, "The Russians gained through espionage and the reason is a loose administration." Two months later, in December, HUAC called on General Leslie Groves to answer charges that members of President Roosevelt's inner circle pressured him to release bomb-related material and information to the Soviets. On a near-daily basis, newspapers fanned American fears of the Red menace, and political opponents tarred the Truman administration as lax, or worse, as sympathetic to communism. All the while, President Truman and his secretary of state, Dean Acheson, sought to calm the nation and demonstrate that they took the Soviet threat seriously.

Then, of course, came Senator Joseph McCarthy. Born in 1908, senator at thirty-eight, dead of liver ailments at forty-eight, he lived as though he knew he was running out of time. His first bout of schooling (his was a one-room schoolhouse) ended at age fourteen when he dropped out to work the family farm. He raised chickens, and began trucking them from Grand Chute, Wisconsin, to the Chicago poultry markets at age fifteen. He did not enter high school until age twenty, but soared through in nine months, finished college and law school in five years (working odd jobs to pay his way the entire time), became a judge at thirty, and left the bench in 1942 for the marines.

Primarily a desk-bound intelligence officer without much to do, he may have given himself the nickname "Tail-Gunner Joe" and embellished both his combat record and the circumstances surrounding his war wounds. He did fly combat missions (fourteen, seventeen, or thirty-two, depending on when he was asked)—primarily as a recon photographer—and did indeed suffer an injury aboard a ship engaged in the Pacific theater. But it was a drunken hazing incident, not combat, that left him with three broken bones in his foot and an ugly burn scar, though the injury did earn him a commendation from his squadron leader, Everett E. Munn, for continuing to perform his desk duties ably while on crutches. He resigned his commission in early 1945 and launched his campaign for an open Senate seat in 1946.[3] Small-town farmer, judge, war hero, tireless campaigner, and energetic speaker, McCarthy was an irresistible candidate and won election easily. But in Washington he was adrift—wrong-footed by the collegial Senate atmosphere and languid pace of legislating. Finally, in 1950, he found his issue and the means to vault himself to national prominence.

McCarthy's speech on Lincoln Day in Wheeling, West Virginia, captured the public's imagination—and tapped into its deepest fears. His list of 205 (or 57, or 81, depending on when he was asked) Communists in government made an indistinct threat real. Enemies were everywhere—if 205 (or 57, or 81) traitors had wormed their way into the State Department, surely there were more? A paranoid, fantastical mentality gripped much of the nation. Years later, historian Richard Hofstadter tried to make sense of the McCarthyist phenomenon in his seminal analysis, "The Paranoid Style in Politics." This mentality, he argued, might be a constant undercurrent in American history, "a persistent psychic phenomenon . . . affecting a modest minority of the population." But, at times, it might explode into more: "Certain historical catastrophes or frustrations may be conducive to the release of such psychic energies, and to situations in which they can more readily be built into mass movements or political parties."[4] What was the rising Communist threat if not such a catastrophe? Had Americans sacrificed so greatly during the war, only to face an existential crisis so soon after?[5] Why had they fought, if not to defend the values and freedoms that now seemed threatened?

McCarthy framed the issue as something much larger than great powers competing on the world stage. "The great difference between our western Christian world and the atheistic Communist world is not political . . . it is moral," he declared. The "religion of immoralism," he argued, would "more deeply wound and damage mankind than any conceivable economic or political system." And who had allowed evangelists for this religion to creep into American government? "It has not been the less fortunate, or members of minority groups who have been traitorous to this Nation—but rather those who have had all the benefits that the wealthiest Nation on earth has had to offer— the finest homes, the finest college education and the finest jobs in government we can give."[6] Their Svengali, according to McCarthy, was Secretary of State Acheson, a "pompous diplomat in striped pants, with a phony British accent." (McCarthy's choice epithets rubbed off on another young anticommunist crusader in Congress, Richard Nixon, who later fulminated about the "striped-pants faggots" at State.)[7] To McCarthy, beating the Soviets was a character issue. The silver spooned, the striped of pants, the Eastern educated elite did not represent the American character; McCarthy—a war hero, raised on a farm, educated in a one-room schoolhouse—did.

AND WHO ELSE LIVED IN THE SHADOWS, hiding their true selves? Who else undermined bedrock American values? Preyed on unsuspecting innocents? Lacked the strength of character to resist blackmail when Communist agents came calling? The anticommunist terror spun off other whorls of paranoid mania, and the leap from targeting and purging suspected Communists to doing the same to suspected homosexuals was, perhaps, not much of a leap at all. The two were easily (and perhaps intentionally) conflated: was it not obvious that homosexuals, lacking the will to resist their degenerate urges, posed a clear threat to national security? That homosexuals were unmanly and lacked the fortitude required for the coming fight? McCarthy forged a connection between communism and homosexuality, describing Communists as deviant in a way that Americans often thought of homosexuals: "Practically every active communist is twisted mentally or physically in some way," he declared in a speech before Congress on February 20, 1950.[8]

He went on to make an explicit link between treachery and homosexuality. One person on his list, he said, was a homosexual and clear security risk who had been fired by State but then rehired; another homosexual fired from State was later found to be working for the CIA.

McCarthy's language was vague enough, elastic enough, to fit many groups—he practiced a philosophy of big-tent intolerance. Framing his crusade—in his mind, the crusade of all right-thinking defenders of freedom—in religious, moral, and character terms, he defined American values in a particular way, and demanded wartime vigilance in rooting out any deviance from those values. For McCarthy, homosexuals and Communists, together with the overrefined northeastern liberal elite, formed a tripartite affliction that would undermine those values and render the country vulnerable to the rising Soviet threat. Others soon rallied to his banner. Cliff Clevenger, born on a ranch in Lone Pine, Nebraska, later a Republican congressman from Ohio, argued that homosexuals in government would be protected by the "sob sisters and thumb-sucking liberals" at State.[9] This unholy trinity was made flesh in the person of Acheson, who embodied everything the crusaders reviled. Another Nebraskan, Senator Hugh Butler, summarized their impressions thusly: "I look at that fellow, I watch his smart-aleck manner and his British clothes and that New Dealism in everything he says and does, and I want to shout, 'Get out! Get out! You stand for everything that has been wrong in the United States for years!'"[10]

To counter the McCarthyites' claims, Acheson sent the antithesis of an elitist liberal sob sister to testify before McCarthy's committee. Deputy Undersecretary of State John Peurifoy was a counterpoint to Acheson in many ways. A Democrat to be sure, but a South Carolina low-country Democrat, from the town of Walterboro, population eighteen hundred. His mother died when he was six, and his father twelve years later. Peurifoy himself contracted pneumonia and was forced to drop out of West Point in his third year. With no degree, no family support, and no job, he headed west to Kansas City, worked in a supply room in a bank, moved to New York and worked as a cashier in a restaurant before heading to Washington in 1935. Eventually, using South Carolina connections, he became the elevator operator in the House of Representatives. Three years later, he landed a job at the State Department, starting as a low-level clerk, and working his way up quickly. In 1953, as ambassador to Greece, he earned a reputation as an anticommunist crusader, and in 1954, as ambassador to Guatemala, he emerged as the pistol-toting American enforcer who guided the CIA coup to drive the "communist infested" Arbenz regime from power and install generals friendly to American interests. And after troubleshooting (sometimes literally) in Greece and Guatemala, he was sent to Thailand to stamp out any emerging Communist subversion, and to quash any meddling by China.[11]

But in 1950, he and Acheson faced off against McCarthy, seeking to refute accusations that Communists and Communist sympathizers ran amok at the State Department. In fact, as early as 1947, Puerifoy himself had sought to revamp State's vetting and oversight policies—fearing that things had grown, as Republicans would later charge, too lax. After McCarthy's Lincoln Day speech, Puerifoy had cabled the senator immediately, wanting the names of the suspected Communists so he could investigate them. Square-jawed, nerveless, and good-natured—known as "Smiling Jack"—he sat across from McCarthy's committee, and, in the presence of correspondents from virtually all national press organizations, made every effort to demonstrate that State was actively engaged in rooting out the Communist infiltrators. He noted that, since 1947, State had dismissed 202 employees who had been found "undesirable." But not all were let go for harboring Communist sympathies. Ninety-one, he noted in his soft-spoken Carolina drawl, fell into "the shady category." He was asked to clarify. He paused and looked around, clearly uncomfortable with the subject he had just introduced. He then leaned into the microphone and whispered, "They were homosexuals."[12]

Peurifoy's testimony was an exercise in putting out fires with gasoline. Newspapers, heretofore uncomfortable even using the word "homosexual," characterized his admission as evidence of still more security issues at State. In response, Senator Kenneth Wherry of Nebraska brought the full investigative powers of the Senate to bear in an effort to root out the pink menace in government employ. Wherry grew up in Pawnee County, the son of well-off parents who owned multiple businesses as well as large tracts of farmland throughout the Midwest. Hyperactive, hyper-masculine, a World War I veteran and a chain smoker, he rose to the position of Republican whip in 1944, just two years after joining the Senate. His loud, blunt manner, and an ability, in the words of his home-state newspaper, to remain "unhampered by too much respect for his elders,"[13] peeved many of his senior colleagues. But the Capitol Hill secretaries voted him "jolliest senator."[14] In 1947, he was part of the conservative group on the Senate Appropriations Committee who wrote a letter complaining about then-undersecretary Acheson's "extensive employment in highly classified positions of admitted homosexuals, who are historically known to be security risks."[15]

Wherry, a man with finely tuned political antennae and a healthy dose of ambition, saw in Peurifoy's testimony an opportunity to capitalize on a potentially explosive issue. He quickly formed a subcommittee of two (Democratic senator J. Lister Hill of Alabama comprised the other half) in order ascertain the true reach of the homosexual coven in government. The Wherry-Hill committee filed an internal report which made several remarkable, if unsubstantiated, claims: First, that there were between thirty-five hundred and four thousand homosexuals working in government. Second, that Joseph Stalin had obtained from the Nazis a list of American homosexuals and had directed his agents to target gays in espionage operations.[16] The alleged Nazi list was nothing more than a far-fetched rumor, and the estimate of the number of homosexuals working in government came from a Washington, D.C., vice officer named Roy Blick, who later admitted to making up the number. Nonetheless, Wherry continued to press his case for purging homosexuals from government. He later told a reporter, "You can't hardly separate homosexuals from subversives."[17]

THUS DID GAYS BECOME not only eroders of American values, but threats to national security; soon their portfolio would be expanded to include menaces to children. *Coronet*, a monthly magazine that was, in the words of one critic, a *"Reader's Digest* that appealed mostly to sophisticated men,"[18] published a cover story titled "The New Moral Menace." Its author, Ralph H. Major, focused the fears of a nation on the heretofore unmentionable depredations of the homosexual male. The editors prefaced the article by acknowledging public discomfort with the topic: "In printing this article, *Coronet* seeks to demolish a long-standing taboo against a frank and factual discussion of homosexuality." The author then argued for the necessity of bringing the topic to light:

> Behind a wall erected by apathy, ignorance, and a reluctance to face facts, a sinister threat to American youth is fast developing. So little has been written about this subject that many people are unaware a danger exists, or even more significant, that homosexuality is rapidly increasing throughout America today. Amazingly few surveys have ever been made of this growing segment of our population. Yet each successive report, however inadequate, shows an alarming increase in the incidence of homosexuality.[19]

After recounting many harrowing (if specious) anecdotes of the seduction and ruination of young boys, the article quoted Eugene D. Williams, then special assistant attorney general of the state of California: "'All too often, we lose sight of the fact that the homosexual is an inveterate seducer of the young of both sexes, and that he presents a social problem because he is not content with being degenerate himself; he must have degenerate companions, and is ever seeking younger victims.'" The author then channeled McCarthy in warning that homosexuals could be anywhere: "While the appearance of most of these unfortunates may betray them to watchful persons, other sex aberrants look, act, and dress like anyone else. It is they who are the real threat. For, until an overt action is committed, their victims sense no danger." And, finally, the article implicated educators, detailing the seduction of one boy by his teacher at boarding school, and warning parents to "investigate your children's schools, camps, social clubs, and athletic organizations. Do not be afraid to ask frank questions of the adult leaders . . . Bring to their attention any reports . . . of homosexuality in such groups."[20]

Of course, in both the anticommunist and antihomosexual crusades, baser instincts were also at play: the whiff of political opportunity was in the air. As Republicans tarred Truman and the Democrats as soft on communism, so too did they attack the administration for harboring homosexuals—all of which was part of a more general effort to portray the Democrats as lacking the moral fiber, lacking the true American grit to face down the Communists. And as the witch hunt mentality gained steam, descriptions of homosexuality grew darker. In the House of Representatives, yet another Nebraskan, Arthur Miller, warned that "there are places in Washington where they gather for the purpose of sex orgies, where they worship at the cesspool and flesh pots of iniquity." He wondered, "How many of these homosexuals have had a part in shaping our foreign policy?"[21] In a letter to seven thousand party operatives, Republican National Committee chairman Guy Gabrielson wrote that the "sex perverts who had infiltrated our government" were "perhaps as dangerous as the actual communists."[22] By the end of 1950, the Wherry-Hill interrogations birthed a full-blown senatorial subcommittee investigation, this one chaired by Republican senator Clyde Hoey of South Carolina. Hoey's report deemed that "those who engage in acts of perversion lack the emotional stability of other persons" and were "not suitable for a position of responsibility."[23] Further, since they were "moral weaklings," lacking the character to resist when the reds came calling, they were obvious targets for Communist blackmailers. As the election of 1952 approached, Senator Everett Dirksen of Illinois recolored the pinkish threat, promising once and for all to eliminate "the lavender lads" from the State Department if Republicans were returned to the White House.[24]

Strip away the political opportunism, the demagoguery, and the witch hunt mentality, and there is, at the core of the McCarthy/Wherry/Miller crusade, a real fight over what it means to be American, particularly an American male. In their minds, manly traits of self-reliance, mastery of emotions, physical strength, toughness, and aggression were responsible for winning the World Wars and elevating the United States to preeminence among nations; the perceived squishiness at the heart of the East Coast liberal establishment ran counter to their ideal of American identity and put the country at risk. Further, they saw a clear link between citified, libertine intellectuals, communism, and tolerance for homosexuality. *Coronet's* article on the "new moral menace" not only raised the specter of hidden predators, but it also quoted the Kinsey report on sexual behavior to connect homosexuality and urban values: "There is a widespread theory among psychologists and psychiatrists . . . that the homosexual is a product of an effete and over-organized urban civilization."[25] The root of this conflict was not just political and cultural disagreement; McCarthy and others saw their opponents as symptomatic of the continuing decay of American masculinity. These concerns, first raised in the early twentieth century, perhaps allayed by victory in war, were amplified to new levels of emotional intensity by the threat of annihilation at the hands of the Soviets. The loss of rugged American masculinity belied an alarming moral weakness—one that, allowed to fester, would surely spell doom. McCarthy drew most of the attention. But he was only representative of a more broad-based and long-running effort to define—or perhaps reestablish—a particular vision of American values and traditional gender roles.

For these crusaders, any form of deviance was suspect. Defense of American values demanded constant vigilance. Gays in America took a particular beating, metaphorically and literally. A threat to national security, to American values, and to American children, they were hounded—perhaps with greater vociferousness than at any point in American history. The government purged them: in 1953, newly elected president Dwight D. Eisenhower signed Executive Order 10450, "Security Requirements for Government Employment," which required departments and agencies to investigate the background of any employee in a "sensitive position" (any job could be designated as such), and deemed as grounds for dismissal "any criminal, infamous, dishonest, immoral, or notoriously disgraceful conduct, habitual use of intoxicants to excess, drug addiction, [or] sexual perversion."[26] According to most estimates, between seven and ten thousand federal employees lost their jobs for suspected homosexuality.[27]

Law enforcement harassed them—governments enacted increasingly strict ordinances targeting gay men and women, and vice squads adopted increasingly aggressive tactics in pursuing them. In many states, liquor control boards—many of which could revoke licenses should bar owners allow their establishment to become a "disorderly house"—cracked down on gay bars, the presence of homosexuals being sufficient evidence of disorderliness. The medical community sought to cure them—doctors offered electroshock, aversion therapy, even lobotomies and castration as protocols for turning homosexuals into "proper" men and women.

And schools, for the most part, disowned them. The educational system's mission to instill proper character in their charges became not just a matter of moral concern, but of defending American values in a hostile world and protecting the safety of American youth. According to nearly every source of information on the matter, homosexuals pursued, recruited, enticed, and predated. The harm they could wreak in a school was self-evident—both in setting the worst kind of moral example, and in carrying children away to the dark side. Cities and states across America took ever-greater steps to root out gay teachers in their midst. In the 1950s, and into the '60s, active purges by school districts, with the backing of law enforcement, took on a McCarthyesque pall: teachers were accused, interrogated, and purged.

Perhaps the most notorious purge of teachers occurred in Florida, where the legislature empowered the Johns Committee (originally established in 1956 to investigate the NAACP) to root out "subversive and homosexual teachers."[28] Lead investigator Remus Strickland would conduct interrogations of teachers in courthouse rooms, police stations, or superintendents' offices. Teachers were questioned under oath, in the presence of Strickland, their district superintendent, and a law enforcement officer. While teachers certainly did not need to answer, and could by rights have counsel present, Strickland would warn them, "If you choose not to answer these questions, we can subpoena you . . . to a public hearing . . . where TV, newspaper, and radio people will attend . . . Now, do you want to talk to me and answer such questions as I might ask you?" Under threat of what amounted to blackmail, many teachers relented; they were compelled not only to admit to their own offenses, but also to name names. In some cases, teachers were brought in for questioning on the basis of student accusations such as "he minces around the school building," and "she walks like a man."[29] Perhaps over one hundred teachers lost their jobs as a direct result of the Johns Committee; no doubt many more quit rather than face investigation.

Other school districts did not engage in such hunt-and-purge tactics; they merely reacted swiftly to rumors of homosexuality on the teaching staff. Morals clauses in teaching contracts were ubiquitous, and most states and districts deliberately left the definition of immorality vague enough to allow administrators wide latitude in disciplining teachers. Homosexuals were considered immoral by their very nature, and suspected gays were expected to resign quietly.[30] For male teachers especially, even being single rendered one suspect. Gay teachers adopted a variety of survival tactics, all of which involved conforming to some degree to the dominant gender norms of the age—marrying (or at least bringing opposite-sex "dates" to social functions), dressing to fit proper hetero standards, avoiding issues of sexuality in school altogether.

As American societal institutions targeted gay adults, gay youth were also targeted—by peers, relatives, even teachers. Ostracized, exiled, mocked, and beaten, many fled school and home altogether. The stories gay youth tell vary little over the twentieth century. "I was relentlessly bullied from about fourth grade through high school," recalled one memoirist of his experiences in the 1950s. "One teacher, the high school athletic coach, called me 'his vegetable' because I was awkward, uncoordinated, and truly hated any activity even remotely related to sports."[31] In her book, *Growing Up Gay: The Sorrows and Joys of Gay and Lesbian Adolescence*, Rita Reed writes of her own isolation and fear in the 1960s: "There was no information, and no one spoke of 'it.' Since homosexuality was still considered psychopathological, it was best to know nothing . . . It wasn't safe to even think about it, so I didn't."[32] Some gay youth took a more aggressive stand toward heterosexual society. As a young man growing up in Kenosha, Wisconsin, in the 1950s, James Justen remembers learning to take care of himself:

> I ran with a pretty rough bunch of people, regrettably. My ex-lover used to fight golden gloves and I got my butt kicked at one time, and made up my mind I was going to learn to fight. And I spent a year learning how to fight. He taught me how to fight and defend myself. And if a problem developed it was going to be solved real fast. We just stood up for our own self and that was it. I guess we made up for the fact that we were gay by being strong enough to handle any situation that would come up.[33]

Events of the first half of the twentieth century brought a striking moral clarity in terms of who was fit to teach, and what could be taught. Moreover, in the 1950s, crusaders for this new moral vision embarked on a fevered effort to purge from schools what did not fit that vision. By falling in line with the witch-hunt mentality of the 1950s, schools clearly failed both gay teachers and students—not to mention American society as a whole. But it would be simplistic to expect schools to buck the tide when the medical community, government, law enforcement, and popular media all aligned in labeling homosexuality deviant and dangerous. Rare were any messages to the contrary.

One remarkable example of a more reasoned perspective on the perceived threat of homosexuality comes from the navy's 1957 Crittenden report. Its full title, *Report of the Board Appointed to Prepare and Submit Recommendations to the Secretary of the Navy for the Revision of Policies, Procedures, and Directives Dealing with Homosexuality*, explains its purpose rather clearly. With astonishing directness, the report laid bare the fallacious reasoning behind government policy toward gays: "The concept that homosexuals pose a security risk is unsupported by any factual data. Homosexuals are no more a security risk . . . than alcoholics and those people with marked feelings of inferiority who must brag of their knowledge of secret information . . . to gain stature. Some intelligence officers consider [that] a senior officer having illicit heterosexual activity with the wife of a junior officer or enlisted man is much more of a security risk than the ordinary homosexual."[34]

The Crittenden report represented a surprisingly enlightened approach to gays serving in the military. Perhaps less surprising—and more in keeping with the times—was the navy's decision not to publish it. The report remained buried for twenty years, until 1976, when Ensign Vernon Berg challenged in court his "other than honorable" discharge for homosexual behavior. Even in the 1970s, however, the report had little effect on the status of gays in the military. Despite its conclusions, the report recommended no substantive changes to military policy. "The service should not move ahead of civilian society," the report argued, "nor attempt to set substantially different standards in attitude or action with respect to homosexual offenders."[35] Homosexual soldiers would still be discharged, although thanks in part to Berg and air force sergeant Leonard Matlovich, who filed a similar suit in 1975, the military generally began to grant honorable discharges to homosexuals who were outed and dismissed.

AS OFTEN HAPPENS, the fever finally broke, and the frenzied pursuit of both Communists and homosexuals lost its intensity by the late 1950s. Clearheaded rationality even made an occasional appearance, as evidenced by the conclusions (if not the recommendations) of the Crittenden report. Although the moral hysteria of the early 1950s waned to some degree, in no way did homosexuality suddenly become acceptable in American society. In schools, clarity on the undesirability of homosexual teachers largely remained intact. Administrators and school board officials continued to reject the possibility that gay teachers could be good role models, but were less willing to expend time and resources—not to mention incur media attention—actively rooting them out. Fights over character and values in the classroom still flared—schools were not immune to the culture clashes of the 1960s— but as a specific issue, the "problem" of homosexuality receded to the background. Communities confronted the more incendiary conflicts brought about by court-ordered school desegregation, civil rights, the Vietnam War, and the sexual revolution. Questions about gay teachers and students were much easier to sweep under the rug than to address directly. But, of course, ignoring something does not make it go away. In the 1970s, grassroots efforts on both sides of the issue would force schools to address the issue of homosexuality anew. And while the leadership remained largely wedded to the view that homosexuality had no place in schools, activists in their employ began to bring homo-sexuality into the classroom.

Oranges, Banana Cream, and Beauty Queens

THE FIGHT OVER GAY TEACHERS COMES OUT OF THE CLOSET

A homosexual teacher who flaunts
his sexual aberrations publicly is
as dangerous to children as one of
the religious cultists.

—Anita Bryant, 1977

Thus always to bigots, Anita.
Thus always to bigots.

—Tom Higgins, after pie-ing Bryant
in Des Moines in 1978

AS THE COUNTRY BEGAN to loose itself from the straitjacketed gender and sexual roles of the 1950s, American views on homosexuality grew decidedly less hysterical. Certainly vice squads continued to make raids and arrests, and gay men and women were still hounded. But as the 1960s wore on, homosexuals lost their status as public enemy number one. Straight Americans, while not exactly accepting of homosexuality, could tolerate it—even if they did not want to see it, know about it, or recognize that gays walked among them. So long as gays remained in a separate world, or cloaked their gayness when they ventured out among the "normal" folk, many straight Americans could wrap their heads around a right to privacy that included the right to be gay. As long as everyone understood the rules—homosexuals would not flaunt their homosexuality in mainstream society, and mainstream society would tamp down the witch hunts—many felt the issue could be left alone.

The 1960s and early 1970s also brought some important changes in how institutions addressed the issue of homosexuality. The ACLU, which had played the role of disinterested bystander during the purges of the 1950s, claiming it saw no civil liberties issue at stake, now showed a willingness to defend teachers (and others) dismissed for their homosexuality. The National Education Association, the largest teachers union in the United States, offered similar legal support for teachers beginning in 1974. In 1973, the American Psychiatric Association removed homosexuality from its compendium of psychiatric disorders, and (as the joke went) millions of Americans were cured of insanity overnight. A year earlier, East Lansing, Michigan, became the first municipality in the country to pass a nondiscrimination ordinance that explicitly included homosexuals.[1] Other cities followed, slowly, and by the mid-1970s more than thirty cities had nondiscrimination ordinances. These victories were clearly significant, and demonstrated a budding recognition among activists that discrimination against homosexuals was a civil rights issue. But, in decades when Americans waged monumental struggles over racial equity and women's rights, the issue of gay rights was a relatively minor one, and the question of homosexuality's place in American society would flit in and out of public consciousness.

Despite some incremental progress, Americans either still viewed homosexuality with revulsion, or preferred to pretend it existed only elsewhere. Schools in particular avoided the issue almost entirely. After the purges of the 1950s, the "problem" of homosexuality receded from the minds of school leadership. Schools entered a period of uneasy coexistence with homosexual educators: while overt witch hunts were less likely, teachers who were discovered could still expect to be dismissed or asked to leave quietly. Clarity on the immorality of homosexuality largely remained intact, and the trope of predatory gay men seducing schoolboys still held sway in the popular imagination. Judging by their actions, administrators either believed this stereotype to be true, or knew that enough parents believed it to make administrating uncomfortable if they were discovered to be harboring homosexual teachers. Whatever their motives for doing so, most school leaders simply found it easier to avoid controversy, and gay teachers certainly found it easier to remain closeted. But confrontation was brewing—there were activists on both sides of the issue looking for a fight. Those seeking to actively root out homosexuality from schools rallied behind a beauty queen from Oklahoma; those seeking to bring homosexuality more openly into public institutions such as schools found a champion in a charismatic former army translator from New Jersey.

JOHN GISH WAS A POPULAR English teacher at Paramus High School who in the late 1960s and early 1970s became more and more active in the gay rights movement. By 1972, he had assumed the presidency of the local chapter of the Gay Activists Alliance and founded the Gay Teachers Caucus at the National Education Association. As a result, the Paramus, New Jersey, school board removed Gish from the classroom—a temporary measure on the way to firing him. Like most districts, Paramus was willing to tolerate gay teachers who maintained the fiction that they were straight and kept their personal lives hidden. And, as in most districts, administrators in Paramus felt well within their rights to dismiss teachers who failed to abide this arrangement. Unlike many teachers, and nearly all his predecessors, however, Gish did not accept the established rules of the game, and would not leave quietly. He vigorously opposed his reassignment, both through the media and in the courts. The school board gave Gish a temporary office job as curriculum coordinator but, to keep him away from students, banned him from walking the hallways when school was in session. Gish was also forbidden to use the cafeteria, an indignity that prompted him to announce to the media that he would go on a hunger strike. One week later, the school board backed down, allowing him to use the cafeteria and walk the hallways "filled with students who didn't really know who I was."[2] It was a small victory, far removed from Gish's ultimate goal of returning to the classroom. The district, hoping to prove he was unfit to teach, mandated that Gish undergo psychiatric evaluation—this at a time when the American Psychiatric Association still listed homosexuality as a psychiatric disorder. After contesting the district's right to require such testing, Gish hired his own psychiatrist, who gave him a clean bill of mental health. Unwilling to drop the issue, district officials insisted he be evaluated by a doctor of their choosing, who diagnosed in Gish "angry, paranoid thinking."[3]

Although a natural for the classroom in many ways—he is a performer, a storyteller with a keen sense of his audience—Gish was not drawn immediately to teaching. He attended Middlebury College in the late 1950s but left without a degree and joined the army. Despite its strong liberal arts reputation and a long-standing progressive streak— Middlebury was the first college or university in the United States to confer a degree on an African American student (Alexander Twilight, in 1823) and the first of the all-male private New England colleges to admit women (in 1883)—it was not a welcoming environment for a young gay man in the 1950s. Gish did not hide his sexuality as an undergrad, and became something of a marked man—targeted by some, shunned by most. He felt the army, of all places, might offer a safer home. The worst of the witch hunts had passed, and a gay man who kept his head down and followed orders would in all likelihood be left alone. He settled in as a linguist, translating dispatches from Mandarin to English. Still, Gish found the military an uncomfortable fit; he was perhaps unwilling to lead as closeted a life as necessary to remain unnoticed in the service. He left the army after several years, went home to New Jersey, and enrolled at Seton Hall. Shortly after graduation, he landed a job in the offices of tire manufacturer BF Goodrich. But public tragedy soon steered him toward teaching. "I was in the office when Kennedy was shot," he says. For Gish, President Kennedy's call to service resonated even more after the assassination. "It absolutely motivated me to get into education." He began taking night courses toward an education degree, and friends at a party told him about an opening for an English teacher at Paramus. Although he was just finishing coursework, he applied and began teaching in 1965. So it was that John Gish found his entrée into teaching at a gay cocktail party in New Jersey.[4]

Gish also became more of an activist—although openly identifying as a gay man in the 1950s, as he had done at Middlebury, surely constituted a political act. Beginning in 1971, he became more involved in the Gay Activists Alliance, the "gay goons"[5] who staged disruptive, surprise demonstrations targeting specific public figures or institutions in and around New York City. (One of their more notorious demonstrations involved pelting the house of Adam Walinsky with hundreds of eggs after the liberal New York politician called for the formation of a Liberals Against Gay Rights group.)[6] Over time, it became more difficult for him to keep his activism separate from his teaching. In early 1972, when the leader of the local branch of the GAA left under acrimonious circumstances, the membership turned to Gish. He reluctantly agreed to assume duties as president—well aware that such increased visibility would put his job at stake. If the school board became aware of his activism, "[I knew] I'd be fired instantly," he recalled. Nonetheless, he grew more and more outspoken. That spring, he drove to Atlantic City for the annual meeting of the National Education Association, the nation's largest teachers union, where he formed a one-man activist group: "I called myself 'the Gay Teachers Caucus.' Eventually, I met one other guy, Joe Acanfora, and he agreed to be cochair." As a student, Acanfora had been active in the Homophiles of Penn State (HOPS), and he had been denied a teaching certification in Pennsylvania on that basis. In 1972, he was hired as an earth science teacher in Maryland but later fired, as word of his activism at Penn State spread south.

As a two-member caucus with no official recognition, Acanfora and Gish simply sought to raise awareness for their cause. Standing on the front steps of the convention hall, handing out leaflets to a decidedly mixed reception, they gradually built a small network of supporters. "People came up to me," Gish recalled, "and would quietly ask, 'Is there anything I can do for you?'" But support was, initially, covert. "They would walk us down halls, up stairs," well away from the crowds, "to find a private room where we could talk." More experienced members of the NEA helped them navigate the organization's committee structure, get the attention of chairs and speakers, print more leaflets. But supporters remained largely behind the scenes, well aware of their likely fate if they linked their names to the Gay Teachers Caucus. The danger to one's career was immediate, but the benefits would be deferred—it was not until 1974 that the NEA added antidiscrimination language to its platform and began to support litigation efforts of teachers who were dismissed for their sexual orientation.[7]

Gish's work with the GAA and the Gay Teachers Caucus put him on a collision course with school administrators. Many of his colleagues were aware of Gish's activism; some voiced their support, while most did not bring it up at all. Not wanting to court public controversy, Paramus superintendent Paul Shelly warned Gish to keep a lower profile, and Gish finished out his last year as a teacher relatively uneventfully. Exams were given, seniors were graduated, and summer vacation commenced. However, he continued to speak out over the summer, arguing publicly that teachers should find ways to help gay and lesbian students cope in schools. School officials hoped that taking action against Gish over the summer months would draw little publicity. But this was exactly the confrontation Gish had sought, and he publicly contested his reassignment.

All along, Paramus officials insisted that the problem was not Gish's homosexuality, but his desire to be a "public homosexual." In their eyes, his behavior rendered him a disruptive and unhealthy element in the school. According to the Paramus superintendent, "A gay teacher who publicly makes his life style known, and then comes into the classroom, can create confusion, anxiety and so forth among children in that classroom. I don't think that the Board of Education, being aware of that, has to wait for that to happen before it acts."[8] Gish countered, arguing that by advocating for what the media of the day called "gay liberation," he was merely exercising his constitutional right to free expression, and doing so on his own time. "I do not advocate a gay lifestyle, and never have," Gish stated. "I have never publicly said that I am a homosexual."[9] Under questioning by school authorities, Gish stuck to a one-line refrain: "My sexual orientation is none of your business." The school board argued that Gish's actions—specifically, joining the GAA and founding the Gay Teachers Caucus—were "evidence of deviation from normal mental health."

Gish contested his dismissal, and after an exhaustive series of appeals that led eventually to the New Jersey State Supreme Court, the school board's actions were upheld. Gish never returned to the classroom. The case of John Gish, as captured by the paper trail of court documents, meeting transcripts, and newspaper articles, appears to be a straightforward example of teacher activism running afoul of a conservative administration. On one level, it is. Perhaps in anticipation of the outcry, and hoping to stave off controversy, school leadership sought to protect its community from what it saw as pernicious and immoral influence. Indeed, the administration decreed that any other teachers who joined the Gay Activists Alliance or similar groups would also be dismissed. (Gish recalls about twenty of his colleagues joining the GAA in response.) But in Gish's view, the dynamic at Paramus was much more complex. For one, his relationship with his superiors was genuinely warm and respectful. He had been an exemplary teacher, which administrators privately acknowledged and clearly appreciated. "[In hearings] we would share jokes; and on occasion we would bring each other coffee," he recalls. On his last day, after what seemed to outside observers like a long and acrimonious fight, Gish and his former boss had a quiet meeting to say goodbye and good luck. According to Gish, "There was never any ugliness—it was always very cordial."

Further, if administrators thought they were protecting their students from the influence of men such as Gish, they were sadly deluded. "Students have always known who the gay teachers are," says Gish now. "They would ask me sometimes [just to be funny], 'Oh Mr. Gish, are you married?'" Some may have been repulsed by his orientation, some were supportive, but Gish felt that most of his students typically knew—and really did not care much.[10] This is a perception echoed by Kevin Jennings, another former teacher, who founded the first Gay-Straight Alliance. "Teachers live in a glass closet at best," he wrote in his memoir *Mama's Boy, Preacher's Son*, "where students . . . can see in quite clearly, even if you never poke your head out."

Students' ability to recognize that some of their teachers were gay does not necessarily mean they were accepting of homosexuality—only that they recognized it as part of their world. Similarly, the fact that districts sought to rid themselves of teachers who were gay does not necessarily reflect animus toward gay teachers—only that administrators wanted to keep homosexuality out of their school communities. Perhaps they were motivated by antigay bias, perhaps by a desire to keep order and avoid controversy. A more charitable explanation is that their actions represented a misguided effort to inculcate the type of character in young men and women that society claimed to expect from their schools. To be sure, this involved an attempt to quarantine children from exposure to homosexuality, but also to avoid any discussions of teenage sexuality at all. And while administrators asserted their right to look out for the moral upbringing of their charges, students apparently did not share this concern.

Meanwhile, activists asserted different moral and legal rights—free expression and freedom from discrimination—that in their view trumped whatever values the traditionalists espoused. Over the course of the 1970s, the antidiscrimination movement would gain momentum, as more and more cities passed nondiscrimination ordinances that expressly included sexual orientation. However, these nondiscrimination ordinances did not necessarily signal support for open, "public homosexuals" such as Gish. Rather, these victories were a sign that at least some significant part of the electorate in at least some cities could recognize that homosexuals had a right simply to be. More specifically, they had the right to be left alone as long as they kept their head down and kept their homosexuality confined to their own private sphere. In a way, the ordinances reflect a desire to put the issue to rest—no witch hunts, but no public advocacy either, and no acceptance of open homosexuals in mainstream society.

STILL, NONDISCRIMINATION LAWS were an enormous step forward for the gay rights movement. Defenders of traditional values would fight back, and they found their symbolic leader, their Joan of Arc, in the person of Anita Bryant. Bryant positively radiated precisely those values the traditionalists cherished. She was a Disney princess come to life: small-town girl, Miss Oklahoma 1958, second runner-up in the 1959

Miss America pageant, unabashedly Christian, and possessed of a beautiful, powerful singing voice. Her signature song, "Battle Hymn of the Republic," was a particular favorite of President Lyndon Johnson; she performed it for him at a private White House dinner and sang it again at his burial. In the narrative of Bryant's upbringing, the character of young Anita is cast as a headstrong, precocious, and plucky young heroine, infused with a reverent "a child shall lead them" touch. As the story goes, she was born without a pulse, and the doctors were ready to pronounce her dead—until she was dunked in pail of ice, and came up breathing and wailing. When she was two years old, her grandfather, apparently impressed by her singing talent, taught her "Jesus Loves Me," which, at the behest of their pastor, she sang before the entire church community. At age eight, she asked to be baptized; told by her parents that in their church she had to wait until she was an adult, she stubbornly insisted, demanding, "Mama, can you show me anywhere in the Bible where it says how old I must be before I can be saved?"

Singing in church at age two, baptized at eight, and a regular on Oklahoma TV and radio programs before her teens, Bryant's career blossomed as if ordained from above. She won a national talent contest and signed a recording contract at age nineteen—all the while moving up the pageant ladder. She recorded several gold records—"Paper Roses" and "My Little Corner of the World" both reached the Billboard Top 10 in 1960—and married former DJ Bob Green, who shared her Christian values. He took over management of her career, and together they parlayed her talents and persona into a successful career as a touring celebrity and brand spokesperson—most notably for Florida Orange Juice, Coca-Cola, and Tupperware. She did USO shows for soldiers overseas with Bob Hope, who in later years called her the "house detective" after she expressed discomfort with the "hanky panky" among the stars on tour. A London *Daily Mail* reviewer of one of those overseas tours had this to say about her: "All over this vast continent are people who think of American as good, God-fearing, honest and nice to look at. Anita Bryant is all of these things. She stands for what people would like to believe is the heart of the United States. The lady is the folk heroine, an antidote to Watergate."[11]

She was, for some, an antidote not just to Watergate, but also to the cultural turbulence and shifting values of the 1960s and '70s. Although her recording career foundered as tastes shifted, she still represented American values as McCarthy envisioned them—a wholesome alternative to changing times. Her first foray into the culture wars came in the wake of Jim Morrison's now legendary performance at a Doors show in Miami in 1969. After nearly inciting a riot by failing to perform any music and asking the crowd, "Do you wanna see my cock?" before allegedly exposing himself, Morrison was indicted for "lewd and lascivious behavior in public by exposing his private parts and by simulating masturbation and oral copulation."[12] In response, religious teens organized a "teen-age rally for decency," at which Bryant performed—along with the Lettermen and other musical acts of a bygone era.[13]

By the mid-1970s, Bryant—though still a valued advertising commodity, still spokesperson for Florida Orange Juice and the Orange Bowl Parade, still a draw as a performer, and still possessed of her wholesome all-American charm—lived a relatively quiet family life in Dade County with Bob and their four children. However, when county commissioners voted to pass an antidiscrimination ordinance that included protection for homosexuals, she appeared before the commission to speak against the ordinance, and soon found herself at the forefront of a nationwide conservative movement.

Keeping homosexuals out of schools was, for Bryant, a moral duty—"a new Christian crusade." Of the Dade County law, she wrote, "The ordinance would permit known practicing homosexuals to teach in private schools and act as role models for their pupils, showing that homosexuality is an acceptable and respectable alternative to the life-style of the children's parents."[14] She argued that "a homosexual teacher who flaunts his sexual aberrations publicly is as dangerous to children as one of the religious cultists,"[15] and warned that "a particular deviant-minded teacher could sexually molest children"[16] (though she did acknowledge that gay teachers were not necessarily predators): "I'm not talking necessarily about molestation, in the physical. I'm talking about the psychological, which is more detrimental."[17] She further likened her concern over exposing her children to improper moral examples to her concern over proper nutrition: "If they are exposed to homosexuality, I might as well feed them garbage."[18]

Bryant's organization, Save Our Children, placed print ads featuring news clippings from across the country of shocking cases of sexual violence committed against children; she further noted that two big-city newspapers, the *Washington Star* and the *Chicago Tribune*, had run major investigative stories on child pornography and prostitution rings in their cities. Although her core message was one of protecting children from immoral influences, she also connected the crusade to a larger struggle over American values. There are, she said, "evil forces, 'round about us, even perhaps disguised as something good, that would want to tear down the very foundation, the family unit, that holds America together."[19] Her memoir argues that traditional families were under siege from "women's liberation programs—many of them fostered by women with lesbian tendencies," which "have weakened family ties and worsened [societal] problems."[20] She noted that "many leaders of the ERA and the NOW [National Organization for Women] support the militant homosexuals and their demands for special privileges."[21]

Television ads produced by Save Our Children contrasted traditional American pastimes with the gay lifestyle: Over footage of a high school marching band, a narrator intones, "The Orange Bowl Parade: Miami's gift to the nation—wholesome entertainment." As the scene shifts to what appears to be a pride parade, the narrator adds: "But in San Francisco, when they take to the streets, it's a parade of homosexuals—men hugging other men, cavorting with little boys." The narrator closes by warning that gay rights activists want to turn Miami into San Francisco East. Perhaps unsurprisingly, voters overturned the Dade County nondiscrimination ordinance in a landslide. Save Our Children held its victory party in the ballroom of the Miami Beach Holiday Inn. "Tonight," Bryant declared, "the laws of God and the cultural values of man have been vindicated. The people of Dade County and the normal majority have said enough, enough, enough!"[22]

AT THE BACK OF THAT sweaty ballroom stood a man who surveyed the adoring crowd with glee, who saw an energy, a commitment, and a fevered response that he had glimpsed only rarely in his career. John Briggs was a staunch conservative, a four-term California assembly-man before finally winning (on his third try) election to the state sen-ate in 1976. He was a politician whose ambition far outran his convic-tions—and, perhaps, his abilities. That he coveted either the governor's chair or election to the U.S. Senate was no secret in California, but as a first-termer from the Orange County enclave of Fullerton, he faced some difficulty building statewide name recognition. He first seized upon the death penalty as a way to raise his profile, and spearheaded an initiative that expanded the number and nature of crimes open to capital punishment. While voters overwhelmingly passed his Proposi-tion 7, legal experts predicted it would cause difficulty for judges and jurors—written in haste for the sake of political expediency, Briggs's law was ambiguous in the extreme. Indeed, Prop 7 led to a threefold increase in judicial reversals in capital cases,[23] and by some estimates cost the state hundreds of millions of dollars in additional legal fees annually until its repeal in 2011.

It was, however, Proposition 6 (soon known as the Briggs Initiative) that attracted greater notoriety, and on which Briggs pinned his hopes of statewide—even nationwide—elevation.

One of the most fundamental interests of the State is the establish-ment and the preservation of the family unit. Consistent with this interest is the State's duty to protect its impressionable youth from influences which are antithetical to this vital interest. This duty is particularly compelling when the state undertakes to educate its youth, and, by law, requires them to be exposed to the state's cho-sen educational environment throughout their formative years.

A schoolteacher, teacher's aide, school administrator or coun-selor has a professional duty directed exclusively towards the moral as well as intellectual, social and civic development of young and impressionable students . . .

For these reasons the state finds a compelling interest in refusing to employ and in terminating the employment of a schoolteacher, a teacher's aide, a school administrator or a counselor, subject to reasonable restrictions and qualifications, who engages in public homosexual activity and/or public homosexual conduct directed at, or likely to come to the attention of, school children or other school employees.

Briggs further defined "public homosexual conduct" as "advocating, soliciting, imposing, encouraging, or promoting of private or public homosexual activity directed at, or likely to come to the attention of schoolchildren and/or other employees." In one interview he stated, "What I am after is to remove those homosexual teachers who through word, thought or deed want to be a public homosexual, to entice young impressionable children into their lifestyle."[24] He borrowed much of his rhetoric from the Save Our Children campaign, framing the issue in terms of both morality and safety: "We don't allow necrophiliacs to be morticians. We've got to be crazy to allow homosexuals who have an affinity for young boys to teach our children."[25] For Briggs, though, it was not just the children who were in danger, it was also the American way of life: "Our whole society is based on the family unit— why would we want to put an anti-family group in the classroom?" In this way he sought to connect his crusade to a broader conservative platform of American values, much as his predecessors in the 1950s had done. "[There are] four institutions we worry about: the male-female relationship, the family, the Church, and the nation . . . the one threat to them is communism, but indeed the greater threat over a longer period of time is homosexuality, because we would breed ourselves right out of being a society if we allow this to become a viable lifestyle."[26]

BRIGGS DID EVERYTHING HE COULD to maximize publicity for Prop 6—not only did he introduce it from the steps of the San Francisco City Hall, but he also notified both local media and gay activists well in advance of his announcement. Throughout Briggs's career, it was an open question whether he was a true-believing crusader or just a politician trying to ride the waves of popular sentiment. Randy Shilts, journalist, historian, and gay rights activist, reported on Briggs's campaign from the beginning, and developed an odd friendship with him. Briggs himself acknowledged their relationship in an interview, saying, "Randy and I have known each other for a long time and I think he's an interesting fellow, a fine reporter . . . but I wouldn't want him teaching my children."[27] Shilts, too, found himself in an awkward position during the fight over Prop 6, noting that one friend accused him of "'bending over forward' to be objective about Briggs." But he remained convinced that Briggs bore no real ill will toward gay people, and quoted Briggs saying of his supporters, "A lot of these people are afraid of homosexuals. I think it's a misplaced fear, but they're afraid."[28] To his gay friend Shilts, Briggs justified himself thusly: "This is a political battle and in politics, anything is fair." To San Francisco politician Harvey Milk, who devoted much of 1978 to rallying activists to beat back Proposition 6, Briggs was "a cheap opportunist." "If he thought he could get more votes," Milk added, "he'd be a proponent of gay rights."[29]

Throughout much of 1978, the Briggs Initiative enjoyed widespread support in California—leading 61–31 in polling two months before the November vote. An editorial in the pro-gay-rights newspaper the *Advocate* stated, "We shall have waged a good campaign if the vote ratio is . . . less than 2–1."[30] However, public sentiment soon began to turn, and Hollywood star power helped close the gap. Rock Hudson appeared at rallies with other celebrities, and donated forty-nine dollars—one dollar under the mandatory reporting minimum for political contributions—to the antidiscrimination cause. Moreover, Briggs may have gone too far for many Californians, even those who might be inclined to support his cause, when he compared his opponents to "Good Germans": "I came to the conclusion that the reason for all the crimes . . . against humanity [during the Holocaust] was because nobody would stand up and do anything about it—not one single voice was raised in opposition." In California, he argued, "nobody will stand up and speak for children, and everybody is willing to stand up and speak for homosexuals."[31]

Further, the bill left many conservatives uncomfortable with the degree to which the state would intrude in citizens' private lives and its potential infringement on First Amendment rights. (That same year, Oklahoma enacted a similar law, but in 1984 the courts struck down the section that mandated firing teachers who advocated for gay rights.) Even California's Monsignor John O'Hare—who was, admittedly, less socially conservative than his colleagues and many in his flock, opposed the bill, insisting, "We just don't profit by peering in each other's windows."[32] And many of Briggs's opponents, who ranged from Democratic mayors to President Carter to conservative school boards and education commissioners (many of whom did not want the burden of having to weed out homosexual teachers), often compared him to McCarthy—which he and his supporters might have taken as a compliment.

In the end, a more prominent California conservative dealt the decisive blow to the Briggs Initiative. Ronald Reagan, former governor and Republican presidential aspirant, who made an appearance in support of Bryant at the Florida Conservative Union Dinner in 1977 (and brought her a birthday present of California oranges), released a statement in October 1978 calling the initiative an invasion of privacy. Then, in an editorial published a week before Californians went to the polls, Reagan offered a reasoned, conservative critique of the measure, calling it an unneeded expansion of government reach. He took pains to debunk the gay teacher as molester myth and the "gays don't reproduce, they recruit" canard. "Homosexuality," he wrote, "is not a contagious disease like the measles. Prevailing scientific opinion is that an individual's sexuality is determined at a very early age and that a child's teachers do not really influence this."[33] Thanks in part to the rational counterargument offered by Reagan, and in part to citizens' discomfort with the McCarthyite overreach written into the bill, the Briggs Initiative lost, 58–42.

BRIGGS'S DEFEAT may rightly be seen as a turning point; but in truth, the national crusade that Bryant had launched was already losing momentum. Bryant and Briggs had never been able to connect with a wider audience, and the fevered energy that had so attracted Briggs in the first place began to dissipate even before the California vote. While Bryant could still count on the goodwill of a devoted core of

supporters, her fight had disastrous personal and professional consequences. She topped *Good Housekeeping* magazine's "Most Admired
Women" list for three straight years, from 1978 to 1980. But a 1978 survey of junior and senior high school students for *Ladies' Home Journal*
named her the woman who had "done the most damage in the world."
(Adolf Hitler topped the list of men.)[34] Activists organized boycotts of
Florida oranges, and the Florida Orange Juice Commission eventually
dropped her as their spokesperson. She signed a contract to headline a
television variety show, but producers promptly canceled it after adver-
tisers expressed concerns. Protesters hounded her at appearances in
cities across the nation. In some cases, protests were not even necessary: a rally for decency in Indiana drew half the expected numbers,[35]
and a pro-family rally in Massachusetts was canceled after producers
could sell only seventy-eight tickets. When contestants in the Miss
National Teenager pageant voted Bryant "America's Greatest American," gay rights activists picketed the pageant in Atlanta.

Johnny Carson, among others, repeatedly targeted her: Was the
1977 New York blackout an act of God? "No," Carson quipped, "because
Anita Bryant never would've given Him time off." In another segment,
his alter ego, Carnac the Magnificent, predicted that "at the insistence
of Anita Bryant, all Muppets will undergo a sex test."[36] Repeatedly in
1977 and 1978, Carson portrayed Bryant as "a prudish, self-righteous
fanatic," in the words of one television critic.[37] Even Bob Hope, with
whom Bryant had toured in the 1960s and early 1970s, piled on with
a joke about how tough Jimmy Carter's year had been: "Yeah, he had
one of those rough periods—it was like Anita Bryant trying to get her
hair done."[38] As late as 1985, a TV show in Atlanta dropped her after
one appearance, because of "negative audience reaction."[39]

Even as Bryant's campaign first gathered momentum in 1977, an
activist in Des Moines, Iowa, helped turn it into farce, a taint the Bryant campaign could never quite escape. In an overcrowded pressroom,
amid flashes popping and news cameras whirring, Bryant sat behind a
table stacked with microphones and recorders, answering a question
about the pickets that now dogged her at every stop. Midsentence,
she was interrupted by a protester who hit her flush in the face with

a banana cream pie. Calling on years of experience as a performer, she was initially able to turn the tables on her attacker. "At least it's a fruit pie," she quipped. At her husband Bob Green's suggestion, she began to pray out loud for her assailant, to express forgiveness. But her voice began to quiver, the prayer trailed off, and Bryant dissolved into tears. The consummate performer—composed, confident, and in control—collapsed in utter defeat, her head bowed as she wiped cream pie off her cheeks, like a child on the verge of a meltdown. Bryant, the girl who could charm any crowd, appeared to be at a loss, unable to win over the national audience, no matter what she said or did. "Thus always to bigots, Anita,"[40] declared the stylishly dressed protester, Tom Higgins, as he was led away. "Thus always to bigots." Bryant, meanwhile, fought to regain her composure, and tried once again to play off the attack with humor. Licking banana cream off her fingers, she shrugged, "It's not bad."

Although a broad-based coalition of conservative leaders and politicians first organized opposition to Dade County's nondiscrimination ordinance, Bryant was the focal point for activists—willingly or not, she became the public face of the conservative movement. News reports referred to her as "America's most controversial woman," to the conflict in Dade County as "singer Anita Bryant" against the "homosexual community," and to those who volunteered for the Save Our Children campaign as "Anita's army."[41] Clearly, Bryant was no stranger to the spotlight, but the campaign did take a toll on her. Buffeted by the unrelenting pressure, she and Green divorced in 1980—which earned her the ire of many in her Christian base, and yet another line in Bob Hope's standup routine: Bryant and her husband split up because "she found out HE was one."[42] Nearly thirty years later, Green expressed both defiance and regret with regard to the aftermath of their effort to purge schools of homosexual influence: "Blame gay people? I do. Their stated goal was to destroy her career. And that's what they did. It's unfair." Regarding the entire campaign, he said, "It just wasn't worth it. It just wasn't. The trauma, the battling we all got caught up in. I don't ever want to go back to that."[43] Bryant herself expressed conflicted views on her crusade. In a 1980 *Ladies'*

Home Journal interview, she allowed that "the answers don't seem so simple now," but later, in 2010, she stated, "I did the right thing. I've never regretted what I did."[44]

NEITHER GISH NOR BRYANT succeeded fully in their aims, which is an apt illustration of 1970s American attitudes toward homosexuality. Despite the efforts of Gish and other activists, most straight Americans could not bring themselves to see homosexuals as similar to themselves, as "normal" Americans. Straight America remained hung up on the sex aspect, and remained sympathetic to Bryant's desire to protect her children from "immoral influences." But the fear and hysteria of the 1950s no longer resonated. The Briggs Initiative and Bryant's campaign overstepped. Many Americans could support a right to privacy that included the right to engage in homosexual behavior—as long as such behavior remained behind closed doors. Such a right did not include the freedom to "flaunt it" publicly, and certainly not in schools. Similarly, Americans could respect Bryant's spiritual conviction—as long as she did not flaunt it so publicly either. Conservative columnist William Safire may have summed up American ambivalence best when he wrote after the Miami-Dade vote, "Ease up, Anita Bryant. You were given a vote of confidence, not a flaming sword." He argued that for most voters, the choice was between "tacit toleration and outright approval of homosexuality," and further that, "As long as 'straights' are not forced to underwrite a homosexual sales message in the classroom, the straights have no right to penalize private citizens for their personal behavior."[45] Once seen as a perversion, disease, moral failing, or even a crime on a par with murder, homosexuality had become— for a wide enough segment of the American population—a civil rights issue, albeit still a private one.

Gish too overstepped, for his time and place. It is likely he could have remained in his job—and in his glass closet—indefinitely had he chosen to remain quiet on the issue of homosexuality. But society was not ready for openly gay activists in the classroom. Of course, deeming homosexuality as acceptable as long as it remained closeted did nothing to help gay youth navigate their school years. The most consistent theme in stories of growing up gay is that the feeling of isolation—of having nowhere to turn and no one to talk to—was the most terrifying and dispiriting aspect of recognizing one's homosexuality. The sense of being alone was overwhelming for many, and is a factor in the higher rates of suicide and substance abuse found among the school-age homosexual population. Straight America may have been comfortable with this don't-ask-don't-tell policy, may have seen it as a fair compromise, but its consequences for LGBT youth were torturous.

Gish—and Acanfora, and others—were trailblazers, and as trailblazers often do, they paid a price for getting out in front of public opinion. However, they also nudged society, and forced Americans to reckon with an issue they previously could safely ignore. Further, other gay educators could not help but notice that gay rights activists in other spheres wielded an impressive measure of political power once they accepted the risks of being publicly out—they put together a coalition to defeat the Briggs Initiative, and were able to essentially end Bryant's career as a public figure. So, while political action and court cases garnered headlines and public attention, the 1970s also saw a less visible, but perhaps more significant trend beginning in schools. Some within the educational community found unseen, less confrontational ways to address the plight of gay youth. Educators discreetly helped to educate mainstream Americans about homosexuality, to make it seem more normal and less threatening, and perhaps to send out a lifeline to those students coming to grips with their own sexuality in a climate of fear and isolation. This work was meant to escape the notice of school leadership, or to appear harmless and uncontroversial if it did not. But it would lay a foundation upon which teachers built more formal programs to support LGBT youth—which in turn became the basis for administrative policy, district mandates, and eventually state-level recommendations.

Homosexuality Enters the Classroom

SHINING A LIGHT ON THE PROBLEM

I try to be open-minded about this type of thing, but it's really hard because it's something I don't think is natural.

—Anonymous response to a survey from the 1980s about a gay speaker in a high school class

Some just needed an adult to tell them that they were OK.

—High school teacher Andrei Joseph, recalling the impact on gay students of bringing gay speakers to his class

I N A SMALL REGIONAL SCHOOL DISTRICT in the suburbs of Boston in the 1980s, a middle-aged social studies teacher appeared before the school committee to request support for addressing the issue of homosexuality at the high school. The committee met in a drab conference room in the administration building, which also housed preschool and kindergarten classes—on occasion, the children's artwork adorned the halls and entryway. By state law, school committee meetings are open to the public—though sparsely attended. It is in these meetings that the mundane business of running a school system occurs: budget proposals are discussed, recommendations are made, and congratulatory notes are added to the record—kudos for the success of the fall play or a band concert or athletic season. Citizens of the district are invited to make public comment, to which committee members respond patiently and politely, at all costs avoiding engagement with the petitioner beyond a nod and a thank you. Perhaps because school committee meetings are open and part of the public record, debate is generally civil, and committee members are cautious in what they say. Disagreement is almost unfailingly polite, and as a body, the committee seeks consensus before calling a vote. There is an earnest desire both to do right by the students of the district and to avoid conflict. School committee meetings tend to be boring, and it takes a great deal of discipline on the part of committee members to keep them so.

The district was what one calls "high-achieving," with a wealthy and engaged parent base, and students that were, for the most part, well behaved and relatively hardworking. To most at the school, it was a tranquil environment for teaching and learning. The teacher was one of the few who knew different. Though straight, he had tremendous affinity for those he considered marginalized, and was endowed with deep reserves of empathy and an ability to connect with all manner of students. Nor did he restrict his work to the classroom—his civil disobedience activity, in support of any number of causes, had earned him perhaps the longest arrest record in the history of the faculty. Though a Marxist—one of the few of the breed to survive with his ideological bearings intact—he maintained sincere friendships with the most conservative members of the faculty and administration. By virtue of his personality and biography he was what teachers and students alike called safe—which meant, if you had a problem, or needed help, or were not sure where to turn, he was your guy. And, on occasion, it meant that if he thought you were in trouble, he would bring it up with you before you were ready to talk to anyone. He was one of the few to whom some of the gay and lesbian teens at the school had come out, and he knew a little of what they went through.

That his petition even made it to the school committee's agenda represented a significant step. It goes without saying that not all on the faculty thought there was a problem, nor were all of his colleagues fully accepting of homosexuality. Thanks only in part to the teacher's activities, another staff member had dismissed the entire department as "those fags down in social studies."[1] Further, not all teachers who might be expected to support his work did so—there were some closeted homosexual teachers who preferred not to roil the waters. Finally, there was the district chain of command: his request first went to the

high school principal, and could not be forwarded to the school committee without her approval. The principal was an imposing woman
who first rose to her position with a mandate to restore order in a
school wracked by fights among the students and turnover among the
staff. A generation later, she remained—a rare feat for school administrators, where average tenure has been steadily decreasing. She
was also a stout Catholic who, at school dances, sought to maintain
proper separation between partners—"room for the Holy Spirit," as
the saying goes. Yet prior to becoming principal, she had been a guidance counselor, and retained her own reservoir of empathy. If she had
moral misgivings, or concerns about the potential controversy in her
building, she kept them to herself and forwarded his petition without
additional comment.

And so, under the heading of "new business" on the committee
agenda was the teacher's petition. The idea was simple: students and
teachers in the high school should be taught about homosexuality,
educated against common stereotypes, and encouraged to create a
supportive environment for homosexual students. Members of the
committee smiled and thanked him. Looks were exchanged. Silence
descended. It was an important issue, one member allowed. Of course,
gays had the right to do whatever they wished behind closed doors,
and it was important to be respectful of their rights. But was it an
appropriate issue for the school to address? Would parents be comfortable with their children learning about homosexuality? Schools also
had to be respectful of the community's rights. It was a tricky question, they agreed. Finally, the chair of the committee wondered aloud,
did it make sense to bring up such a topic, to invite such controversy
into the learning environment, if it was not an issue at this particular
school? To his knowledge, homosexual students were not a problem
at the school. Was anyone on the committee aware of any gay students in the schools? Once again, silence descended on the room.

Perhaps alone among those in attendance, the teacher[2] knew how
wrong the committee chair was. That fall, two students had come out
to him, confessed their terror at being found out, at being targeted
within the school, at being disowned by their families. With nowhere

to turn, they had come to him. He kept their secret, looked after them as best he could, and began his quest to help change the environment within the school. As it happened, one of those students was the child of the chair of the school committee.

AS THIS STORY ILLUSTRATES, teachers faced an uphill climb in creating support for LGBT students, not only because of antigay bias and a fear of controversy on the part of school leadership, but because of a general unawareness of the problem. Although the bitter fights of the 1970s had not resolved the issue of homosexuality in schools, most Americans could at least agree homosexuals had a right to privacy. But support for a right to privacy contained with it an expectation of secrecy. Rather than addressing homosexuality directly, Americans sought to distance themselves from it, to pretend that homosexuals were some exotic other, a society and culture apart from mainstream America. While school administrators at the district level are often genuinely unaware of day-to-day happenings in their schools—demands of the job are such that only extraordinary events reach their desks—their ignorance was also a cultivated state of mind. They needed to maintain the fiction that homosexuality did not exist in their schools, that it was a problem only elsewhere in society.

Further, administrative ignorance may well have had a generational component. A fifty-year-old administrator in 1975 would likely have been thirty before even seeing the term "homosexual" in the general media—it was not until the mid-1950s, and John Peurifoy's testimony before Congress, that mainstream outlets were comfortable even using the word. Nor would educators find useful information in academic literature. Homosexual youth were simply not a popular topic for researchers; grant money did not flow in that direction. A cover story in the *Journal of the American Medical Association* in 1972 did examine "youthful male homosexuality," and did find a remarkable preponderance of suicide attempts (31 percent of the subjects "had . . . made what they considered to be a significant attempt on their lives"), but the study skewed slightly older, with a mean population age of twenty.[3] In the mid-1980s, pediatric medical researcher

Dr. Gary Remafedi studied adolescent homosexuality and found high rates of verbal and physical abuse directed at adolescents who identified as homosexual, but his work was published in pediatric journals, and not until 1987.[4]

Administrators would not see LGBT students—let alone LGBT students in crisis—unless they sought them out. But administrators were not alone in ignoring their situation. Teachers, counselors, and other staff all contributed to that culture. A casual joke, a careless remark, even an inadvertent expression could reinforce a student's expectation or belief about the school community and plunge the student further into isolation. So too could inaction—a joke or taunt overlooked could mark a teacher as untrustworthy or unsympathetic. Gay youth could find support outside of schools; however, that meant that schools, the most significant social institution in most young people's lives, only exacerbated the divide between heterosexual and homosexual communities. Further, seeking help outside of schools underscores how disconnected gay youth felt from their schools. For schools to become part of the solution instead of part of the problem, schools would have to change.

Yet, in the 1970s and '80s—and in many cases, even today—school culture was not ready for such a shift. Gay adults shied away from outwardly supporting homosexual youth.[5] Safe places—a sympathetic ear, or at least a respite from harassment—were rare. Jokes about the drama club contain more than a kernel of truth, and are often tinged with sadness—for more than a few gay adults, theater was the only oasis in a hostile school. Teachers in particular felt vulnerable to the pedophilia accusation and constrained in their ability to offer support.[6] Peter Atlas, the first openly homosexual teacher at Concord-Carlisle High School—although he did not come out publicly until 1991—felt that gay students were reluctant to come out to him because getting "too close" to him might tip off their peers. "They came out to teachers they perceived as 'safe,'" he said.[7] Another teacher at Concord-Carlisle, in a letter supporting Atlas's decision to come out, expressed concern that students who worked closely with Atlas on theater projects might now be harassed by their peers, regardless of their sexual orientation.[8]

In such a climate, how could one address the pain and suffering of gay youth? Carefully. Very carefully. Still, a small cohort of teachers—composed of both gay teachers and straight allies—did seek ways to help their gay students. Their strategy—to the extent that there was an organized, articulated strategy—centered on the pursuit of three goals: First, become a "safe" person—someone gay students might be comfortable turning to. Second, find ways to bring homosexuality into the classroom, in nonjudgmental, nonconfrontational ways. Third, avoid controversy—or at least, do not invite too much of it. While these goals may seem modest today, they did represent important steps in keeping gay students safer. And if they seem timid, it made a great deal of sense for teachers to minimize administrative awareness and oversight of their actions. Administrators may have been reluctant to address the issue of homosexuality in schools, but only because they did not have to. If teachers raised the issue of homosexuality in ways that attracted too much attention, administrative indifference could have turned to suppression of any sort of action at all. As long as teachers could avoid getting themselves in the newspaper, head off any irate phone calls from parents to administrators, and generally keep from stirring up too much trouble for their bosses, they had room to try a variety of things. In the absence of any official school or district policy, teachers had some latitude to develop their own.

The first goal, becoming someone to whom students could reveal themselves fully, was deceptively difficult. Students have a remarkable capacity to don a mask and lock away all manner of fears, insecurities, and problems—while also desperately wanting help and support at the same time. Should they decide to open up, students might be reasonably confident of receiving support from peers, teachers, and family when dealing with many of the issues that teens face; and perceptive and sympathetic teachers—those capable of drawing a student out and encouraging a lessening of defenses—may find students beating a path to their doors. But homosexuality? If talked about, it was mostly disparaged. It was an easy taunt, a throwaway line, easily made and forgotten. For a teacher, gaining trust as a safe ally was exceptionally rare, and difficult. For teachers or staff to offer themselves up as an ally or lifeline typically required some positive action to demonstrate sympathy or at least a nonjudgmental disposition. Only then might students reach out. But this might take a very long time. When students' instinctual understanding of their environment tells them their survival depends on staying hidden—as was the case (and still is) for many LGBT youth—their problems will, in all likelihood, stay hidden.

Peeling back the layers on any high school will reveal a population visited by such a host of plagues and curses as might confirm a belief in a capricious and vengeful deity—as well as in the essential resilience of humankind. Moreover, such a deep look at a school population will impress any observer with the remarkable ability of individuals to don a mask, lock away all nature of problems, fears, insecurities, and pass through a day unnoticed. Depending on demographics, location of the school, and particulars of the community, the type and frequency of the problems may vary. But all can be found, often just below the surface, in any school. A look inside a school counselor's casebook might reveal a complete catalog of homelessness, substance abuse (among children, parents, or both), violent domestic environments, acrimonious splits, devastating diseases, poverty, suicidal ideation or other thoughts of self-harm, and other problems. It is telling that schools have developed a standard set of tools for evaluating a student's potential for self-harm (from minimal risk to round-the-clock watch to hospitalization) and for evaluating potential for harming the rest of the community (from minimal-and-probably-just-harmless-fantasy to keep-a-close-eye-on-him to sequestration, expulsion hearing, and hospitalization). Yet, to an outside observer, students walk the halls, attend classes, mill about the cafeteria, and all seems reasonably placid.

Perhaps the most obvious way for teachers to send such a signal was simply to address the many overt actions that turned schools into enemy territory for LGBT youth: the open taunts, offhand comments, and widespread bullying. Polly Bixby and Karen Grzesik taught at a semirural regional high school in central Massachusetts. They both cite the work of University of Massachusetts professor Pat Griffin— who wrote and taught extensively about empowering LGBT teachers to speak out in schools, to break down "the strict separation between personal and professional lives"—as enormously influential in helping them counter antigay slurs in their school. Bixby recalled, "Whenever I heard things [harassing comments from students or teachers], I addressed it."[9] How to do so was the tricky question. On one level, any admonishment of antigay slurs would be a clear sign to a vulnerable student that allies existed in the building. But, in the words of Cambridge teacher Al Ferreira, scolding students is "not education." Bixby, Grzesik, and Ferreira—as well as a host of other teachers—all sought less confrontational approaches. "Often, we would just ask questions," said Bixby. "'What do you mean by fag? What are you trying to say?'" The goal was both to engage students and to get them to think about their choice of words, about why they used particular labels as epithets. Students addressed in this manner might mumble an embarrassed response, mutter an apology with eyes fixed firmly on the floor, and—it was hoped—walk away not feeling so defensive, not subconsciously digging their heels in. It is important to note that there is no evidence that this approach worked. Still, it was hoped that engaging in this manner—addressing the offensive behavior without severing a personal connection with the offender—lessened the risk of dividing the school population into opposing camps of scolders and scoldees. It was, and remains, a method of changing school culture, one interaction at a time.

Bixby and Grzesik were, even in the early 1980s, open about their relationship, and like Arthur Lipkin, they were out before they had legal protection. However, they took a less confrontational approach than did Lipkin. "We never said, 'We're lesbian,'" recalled Bixby. "We just treated things as normal, and let people come around." By 1983, they were living together, and were perhaps fortunate to be working under a fairly enlightened administration. They were somewhat surprised when, shortly after they moved in together, both of their payroll checks began arriving at the same address—even though they had each kept a separate residence in order to maintain appearances of straighthood. When they discreetly approached the human resources director simply to express their gratitude, she replied, "I just thought it would be easier that way."[10]

Often, it was through working on the second goal—openly bringing homosexuality into the classroom—that teachers could most
clearly offer a signal to students. Writing in 1991, scholars Virginia
Uribe and Karen Harbeck claimed that "cultural taboos, fear of controversy, and a deeply-rooted, pervasive homophobia have kept the
educational system in the United States blindfolded and mute on the
subject of childhood and adolescent homosexuality."[11] While this was
true of systems as a whole, it was not universally true for every classroom, nor was it true for individual teachers:[12] by the 1980s, and in
some cases the 1970s, individual teachers had breached the "wall of
silence" to which Uribe and Harbeck refer. Teachers found multiple
ways to bring the outside world in, and to expose their students to
parts of gay culture. Bringing homosexuality publicly into the school
could be done any number of ways: a lesson plan, a book or reading
chosen with particular care, a validating discussion in health class.
The vast majority of these actions passed without comment, and with
barely a trace in the public record. But they may well have been crucial in keeping students safe. For a student coming to terms with his
or her sexuality, having even one person to look to might be a lifesaving difference—particularly when even family members may have
been kept in the dark.

In addition, for the most part, teachers adopted the strategy of trying to make homosexuality seem as normal as possible—the goal was
to counter stereotypes by making mainstream Americans see other
mainstream Americans, who just happened to be gay. And while it
might have been a stretch to say they developed a fully realized set of
policies, over the course of the 1970s and early 1980s teachers began
to interject subtle shifts into school cultures—all of which would go
largely unnoticed and largely unremarked on, but would gradually
build toward a fundamental shift in how schools would address the
climate they created for their LGBT students.

ERIC ROFES, teacher, writer, and activist, was a rare chronicler of efforts
to change school cultures in the 1970s. He taught elementary and middle school at elite private institutions in the Boston area in the 1970s

and '80s—this despite being told by his education professors that it would be impossible for an unmarried male to get a job teaching elementary school. He published a series of books with his students, most notably *The Children's Book of Divorce*. As a teacher in the late 1970s, he marched in the Boston Pride Parade with a bag over his head and a sign that read "Jack and Jill can come out, but their teachers can't."[13] After leaving teaching and turning full time to activism and organizing, he wrote a memoir of his years in the classroom. *Socrates, Plato, and Guys Like Me* recounts his efforts to assimilate into the largely conservative, heterosexual culture of the school, and his daily fear of discovery— sometimes prompted by such mundane concerns as his attire. ("How were my pants? Did they look too faggy today?") At one point, he was admonished by the rather old-school headmistress for discussing with his students aspects of his personal life that strayed too far from propriety—namely, the fact that he was not married and lived in a house with several other single men and women.[14] Yet he also notes efforts by other faculty members to broaden the horizons of both colleagues and students alike, such as an assembly organized by the drama teacher that included a mildly homoerotic performance by an outside theater group. Rofes recounts the conversation between staff members after the show, which highlighted both conservative and progressive views:

TEACHER ONE: I don't know why we are all freaking out about the show today. A little bit of culture isn't going to hurt the kids . . . And, Chucky, words like "fags" and "homos" aren't used much anymore. My husband has several friends who are . . . that way . . . and they seem to prefer being called "gay."

Chucky . . . looked just a little embarrassed.

TEACHER TWO: I suppose you're right . . . but these kids come from pretty conservative homes, and I doubt parents would approve of this . . . after all this is a private school and we're here to do what the parents want . . .

TEACHER ONE: Incorrect . . . We're here to do what we think is best for the kids, and if their parents don't like it they can take their kids and their money elsewhere.[15]

While it is striking that Rofes himself, a closeted gay man, remained silent, it is worth noting that the woman who chastised "Chucky" for his use of slurs was a closeted lesbian teacher, then in a heterosexual marriage. Rofes does not speculate on the motives of the drama teacher who arranged the performance—perhaps, in the interest of maintaining his own cover, Rofes was afraid to discuss it with him directly. However, the incident—mild as it may seem by present-day standards—represented an attempt to push at the conservative culture of a single private school: the theater teacher brought in a group to perform what would certainly be seen as controversial; straight teachers sought to process the performance in terms of their own views, which included fears about the community reaction. In this way, the teachers sought to shape their school's response—or at least what they thought the school's response should be—to a movement aimed at achieving broader acceptance of homosexuality in society. It should be noted, of course, that this effort achieved only limited success. Over the next two years, Rofes and his headmistress clashed over his sexuality, and in 1978 she declined to renew his contract. He went on to teach at another Boston area school—one progressive enough to support an openly gay teacher.

DR. WARREN BLUMENFELD, a longtime activist and educator, sought another way to expose the heterosexual universe to positive gay and lesbian role models. He began the Gay and Lesbian Speakers Bureau of Boston in 1972, at first working with universities, but later with high schools as well.[16] Blumenfeld trained speakers to cultivate a certain tone—as he says, "We didn't want to come across as defensive or angry." Further, he was sensitive to the particular audience in his choice of speakers: "We wouldn't send drag queens or 'Dykes on Bikes' to a high school."[17] His goal, it appears, was to present a relatively conservative, mainstream image of homosexuality for students' consumption. The Speakers Bureaus—which would make available LGBT men and women to speak publicly to classes—offered a way for straight teachers to provide positive gay and lesbian role models for their students, or for homosexual teachers to do so without risking exposure themselves.[18]

Of course, bringing in gay speakers did not always go smoothly. In an incident unconnected to Blumenfeld's bureau, Michael Roe, a straight teacher in Iowa City, was fired after bringing members of the Gay Liberation Front to speak to his eighth-grade sex education class.[19] In fairness to all involved, the Gay Liberation Front was on the fringe of the rights movement, advocating that most social institutions—in particular the family—ought to be dismantled and replaced by freer affiliations, and that the mainstream's adherence to heterosexuality was really just a matter of their inability to overcome their inhibitions.

Andrei Joseph, a sociology teacher at a suburban Boston school, recalled a wide range of disruptions when he brought gay speakers to his classes: students outside his class banging on the large windows that faced the hallways, people opening the doors and yelling or throwing things into the room, and people constantly peeking in—in his words, a "come see the monkeys in the zoo" attitude. Response from his administration was, at best, skeptical: "I did not ask permission," he recalls, "but I was asked to explain."[20] While there were complaints to the district school committee, and a meeting with the principal, he was not directed to stop. He explained to his administration, somewhat disingenuously, that exposing students to a variety of lifestyles and groups constituted an important part of any sociology curriculum.[21]

Any discernible impact from these early efforts would be difficult to measure. But samples from evaluations of Blumenfeld's Speakers Bureau events are illuminating:

I used to make fun of gay people . . . but after hearing what they have to say, I have more respect for them. I think that they have something wrong with them to be acting so unnatural but they seem to be human too, so I suppose I'll have to deal with them; hopefully as little as possible.

It was interesting to hear your point of view, I've never met a gay or lesbian before . . . I try to be open-minded about this type of thing, but it's really hard because it's something I don't think is natural.

I respect the fact that you can sit before a room full of people and talk about being gay. I am one of the many people in society that do not understand it or accept it, but you help me to understand it a little better.

I think it's fantastic that you could come into our class and stand up for what you believe in. I don't think it was necessary—I don't think it changed anybody's point of view . . . If your goal was to change people's opinions I don't think it was accomplished but if you just wanted to let students hear what you had to say—that's fine.[22]

These quotes were collected under the heading "Do We Make a Difference?" in the packet of instructional materials Blumenfeld created for prospective speakers, and there is no way to know if the authors of these anonymous evaluations were influenced enough by the speakers to reevaluate their perspectives on homosexuality. The quotes appear to answer a tentative yes to that question, while at the same time cautioning speakers not to expect sudden epiphanies from hostile audiences. Certainly teachers brought speakers into their classes as a way to make homosexuality seem "normal" and less threatening to their students—an effort at changing cultural attitudes. But Blumenfeld's goals went beyond simply helping to educate straight students. He felt that many homosexuals wished to share their stories as a way to affirm their identity to themselves as much as the audience.[23] And more importantly, he—and the teachers he worked with—intended the speakers as a show of support and a sign of sympathetic understanding for LGBT students. Joseph remembers students (whom he assumes were closeted) who would linger after a Speakers Bureau class, just to tell him, quietly, that they thought it was a great class. "Some just wanted to say 'thank you,'" he explained. "Some just needed an adult to tell them that they were OK."[24]

WHILE IT WOULD BE DIFFICULT to produce evidence confirming Joseph's assumption, gay youth often expressed the need for positive examples. Bixby recalls students that came back years after graduation—now out—to thank her and Grzesik for being role models.[25] Another teacher states that his decision to come out was driven largely by his own attempted suicide as a closeted high schooler. "I knew from my own experience that I was affected by closeted teachers who I knew were gay and what a difference it would have made for me if they had been out, if they didn't feel like they had to hide who they were," recalled yet another.[26]

When teachers began these early efforts, their primary aims were to offer some signs of support to LGBT youth, and to change conceptions of homosexuality and its place in society. They did so by curating a particular image of homosexuality that would be less controversial and more acceptable to mainstream society. Blumenfeld carefully chose which speakers would be sent to high schools. Bixby and Grzesik made every effort to appear and act "normal"—a word that keeps cropping up. And many noted attempts to push talk away from sex and sexual activity. In speaking to students and teachers, Bixby remembers being very careful about using even the most innocuous terms: "'Sexual orientation'—that gets people. Then it's all about sex."[27] Joseph recalls an early homosexual speaker in his class, who responded to a student question about sexual activity by saying, "What you do, we do. It's not about the bedroom."[28]

While teachers pursued an agenda that was progressive and potentially earthshaking for its time, their approach was as conservative and noncontroversial as possible. In part, this was out of a need to keep administrators uninvolved. Teachers did not attempt to use the institutional system to address the problems faced by LGBT students; in many ways, they saw the institution as part of the problem. One teacher notes that administrators at his school failed repeatedly to address the homophobic remarks colleagues directed his way.[29] Another recalled his headmaster's suggestion that he tell students that his wedding band was "a gift from someone you love" rather than divulge to them his homosexuality.[30] Further, until the passage of anti-discrimination protection—1989 in Massachusetts—simply being gay was risky enough for a teacher without also openly confronting the administration. Even Bixby and Grzesik, who worked in a remarkably tolerant environment, did not seek to change school or district policy early on. Teachers' work in the early 1980s was foundational and certainly saved lives, but it was composed of small steps—they could not be certain of support from administrators, parents, or even fellow teachers. But these steps added up; networks grew, and eventually teachers felt ready—either strong enough or fed-up enough—to force administrators and policy makers to become part of the solution.

Reforms Go Public

School is no longer an educational experience, but a constant struggle to survive.

> —Dr. Virginia Uribe, speaking at Phillips Andover Academy, April 1991[1]

If they have sufficient funds for that kind of program, they don't need any more money for any new programs.

> —California assemblywoman Marian LaFollette, on Uribe's Project 10

CAMBRIDGE RINDGE and Latin School is a large (by Massachusetts standards) urban public high school with a diverse (by Massachusetts standards) population. Its student body includes the children of working-class immigrants, of university professors, and of some of the oldest families in the country. It is home to many famous alumni, including Matt Damon and the Affleck brothers, Casey and Ben; the poet e. e. cummings; basketball Hall of Famer Patrick Ewing; and New York City mayor Bill de Blasio. Rindge's eighteen hundred students and two-hundred-plus staff are jadedly familiar with the entire list of luminaries. A name less known to students and younger staff is that of Arthur Lipkin, a former English teacher with an intimidating intellect and occasionally acerbic tongue. Lipkin was perhaps the first public school teacher in Massachusetts to come out publicly—although he wryly admits to a "pissing contest" over the matter with another former teacher.

When Lipkin first came out in 1980, there were no protections on the books for gay teachers. He did so as a political act and as a challenge to the leadership of the district. Administrators let him be—perhaps a reflection of Cambridge's generally liberal politics, perhaps a reflection of their desire to ignore and defuse a potential controversy—even as he repeatedly badgered them to address the issue of homophobia. Lipkin heard antigay remarks on a near-daily basis at school; often as not, faculty and staff were the offenders. He recalled one particular day when a school security guard chastised two boys wrestling in the hallway, yelling loudly that the two "homos" needed to stop. In Lipkin's recollection, the word "hung in the air." He stormed out of his classroom to confront the security guard, who responded by saying Lipkin should mind his own business—she hadn't directed the epithet at Lipkin, so, according to her, it was not his problem.

By 1987, he had had enough. When another teacher told a roomful of students that the boys who drop their pants in Lipkin's class would no doubt receive an A, Lipkin informed his administration that he was going home, and that he would not return until school officials could ensure a safe working environment for homosexual students and teachers alike. Yes, Lipkin was tired of fending off the abuse, but he was also a political activist with a long history of advocacy for a variety of leftist causes. His walkout was planned—he had made up his mind that he would use the next antigay incident to precipitate what he hoped would be a fundamental change in school culture. Coming out for him had been "a consciously political act," and the walkout was another. It had its intended effect; however, it also caused some consternation, even among his friends and close supporters.

Among Lipkin's colleagues were a number of closeted gay teachers. Periodically they met after work for drinks at the local Chi-Chi's, the Mexican food chain specializing in stomach-churning plates smothered in cheese and sauce, and giant margaritas. As teachers have done throughout history, they discussed the state of the school, gossiped about other teachers, effused over favorite students, bemoaned problem children and parents, and complained about the latest administrative idiocy. But the Chi-Chi's group also addressed other topics. As much as anything, they were a support system for one another—few others could empathize with their situation in the school, or help them navigate the tricky path their double lives entailed. In part these were venting sessions, in part just a chance to let the mask drop. But on occasion, they also talked about what—if anything—could be done to change conditions in school and society.

This was a difficult and fraught topic—particularly when it came to the school community. Teachers' views were intensely personal. They recognized that improving school climate involved more than merely trying to make changes in the workplace. Doing something involved risk: they might lose their jobs, or become such pariahs in the school community that teaching would be a practical impossibility. Some members of the Chi-Chi's group feared that any action they took would also mean unraveling the very fabric of their persona in the school, something they had worked very hard to create and maintain. Lipkin had assumed all these risks the day he came out. However, not all of his gay colleagues wished to be more open—they feared being tarred by the pedophilia stereotype and worried that colleagues would view them differently and students would avoid them. Difficult as it was, many had grown comfortable with the fiction of their double lives, had made their peace with the closet. Change seemed to them too wrenching to contemplate. Others—typically younger teachers—thought this stance cowardly. They believed that the only way to change their lot was through action. Older gay teachers thought the new generation had no appreciation for their history. The difficulties of being gay in the 1980s paled in comparison to the 1950s—the era of purges and electroshock therapy. Some had even been angered by Lipkin's decision to come out—he had not taken into account that his actions would affect them all, that the spotlight might shine their way as well. But what was the path forward without taking some action, without accepting some risk? Because it was such a divisive topic, it came up only occasionally, and often only sideways—a comment here, a silence there—before someone in the group changed subjects. They were, after all, one another's best—and sometimes only—support group.

Lipkin's walkout changed the conversation. Ended it, really. No longer was the question whether or not they should act. It was, now what? In one way, Lipkin put the ball squarely in the administration's court. His message was simple: leaders of the school district had a responsibility to ensure a safe environment for everyone in the building. However, it was also a completely novel idea to administrators; there was no blueprint to follow, no procedural manual. Firing Lipkin seemed out of the question—by 1987, Cambridge's nondiscrimination laws included sexual orientation, and besides, the likely fallout of trying to silence Lipkin seemed daunting, the kind of thing that might even cost administrators their jobs. But ensuring there were no more antigay slurs or jokes at Lipkin's (or anyone else's) expense seemed a practical impossibility. Many people were repulsed by homosexuality. Some would talk. How could they be stopped? More hall monitors and security guards? New rules about what could be uttered under one's breath or behind someone's back? What about someone making a joke in private, or to a group of like-minded others—was that permissible? Administrators, finding themselves in uncharted territory, stalled. A month went by. Lipkin retained a lawyer. Finally, at a meeting with the school superintendent, union representatives, and a lawyer for the teacher who had made the antigay slur, school leadership punted. They turned the question back to Lipkin. What was his solution?

Lipkin wanted the entire faculty and staff to undergo training on homophobia. But this request, which had been rejected in the past, now seemed insufficient in and of itself—a starting point rather than an end goal. And so the question became one for a group of like-minded faculty, union representatives, and staff, the core of which was the Chi-Chi's group. They looked around the country—was anyone else doing anything? Was there anyone they could ask? They were familiar with the Harvey Milk School in New York, but a separate institution would not make Cambridge Rindge and Latin School safe for gay students and faculty. The Washington Heights GIYS had long since disappeared, its example lost. But a group in Los Angeles was just starting to do work in schools, and while it did not perfectly fit what Lipkin and others had in mind, Virginia Uribe's Project 10 at least demonstrated that it was possible to support gay youth before they dropped out (or were kicked out).

FAIRFAX HIGH SCHOOL, in the Los Angeles Unified School District, sits on the edge of West Hollywood, just blocks from one of the epicenters of gay nightlife, Santa Monica Boulevard. From its earliest days, West Hollywood opened its arms to those living on the edge of the law. Although part of Los Angeles County, it was not part of the city, and thus not within the jurisdiction of the Los Angeles Police. In the 1920s, as the city of Los Angeles undertook efforts to clean itself up, casinos and strip clubs took root in West Hollywood. In the 1950s, as the LAPD gained a reputation for particularly violent and destructive raids on homosexual gathering spots, gay bars migrated there as well. By the 1970s, gay men made up roughly 30 percent of West Hollywood's population. When West Hollywood finally incorporated as a city in 1985, one of the first acts of its city council was to pass a domestic partnership law that granted same-sex partners hospital visitation rights and opened the door for the city to provide insurance benefits to same-sex partners of city employees. It was the second city in California to do so, behind only Berkeley.[2]

Despite its surroundings, Fairfax High School was just as unwelcoming for LGBT students as were schools elsewhere. In the fall of 1984, a student whom case officers called "Chris" enrolled at Fairfax High, his fourth high school in as many years. Openly gay and effeminate in manner, he was, according to reports, the butt of jokes by both students and teachers, and a frequent target of physical abuse by his peers. In November, he dropped out. That his absence was noted at all—being one of more than two thousand students—is somewhat surprising. That his case became an inflection point is a testament to the efforts of one of the school's science teachers, Virginia Uribe. "I kept asking about that student," Uribe recalled, "why he was no longer in school, why he was pushed out—other than he was gay."[3] Subsequent investigations revealed that Chris had been kicked out of his house when he was fourteen, and had lived on the streets for over a year. He eventually landed in a juvenile detention center, and then a home for gay and lesbian youth. He bounced from school to school, and at every stop incurred the wrath of his peers. Tired of being labeled a troublemaker for fighting back, tired of the punishment if he did not, he decided the streets seemed less risky than school.

This troubled Uribe, as did her colleagues' and superiors' apparent inability to see the problem. She started informal, unstructured, open counseling sessions at lunchtime—rap groups, in the parlance of the times—and soon found she was meeting a need. As many as twenty-five students would show up. She approached her principal about beginning a more formal counseling program, and he was supportive. Thus Project 10, the first in-school program seeking to support LGBT students, was born, and Uribe became a part-time science teacher and part-time counselor. The primary mission of the program was to provide a safe space for gay students, keep them in school, teach them about HIV and important precautions, and generally support those with nowhere else to turn. Uribe described the program's mission as "not only to keep kids in the classroom, but to keep them alive and claiming their right to be who they are."

By 1988, Uribe was training counselors at other schools, and with the support of the school board, Project 10 expanded throughout the Los Angeles Unified School District. It also became a target for conservatives in the California Assembly. The Republican caucus, led by Northridge assemblywoman Marian LaFollette, sought to freeze funding for any new programs in the district unless Project 10 was discontinued. "If they have sufficient funds for this kind of program," LaFollette declared, "they don't need any more money for any new programs."[4] Others demanded that parents be informed before Uribe spoke to students or Project 10 was implemented in their kids' schools. Even the Roman Catholic archbishop weighed in, calling the program "a camouflaged method to legitimize homosexuality" and a "blatant attempt at social engineering." "That's simply ludicrous," Uribe countered. "I'm just saying it's OK to be who you are."[5]

Much like the larger gay rights movement, Uribe's primary argument centered on the issue of rights and equality—ideas borrowed from the civil rights movement of the 1960s. "We are a public school system," she insisted, "and we should try to meet the needs of all of our students. We are talking about civil rights." But she also foreshadowed what would prove to be a much more successful argument—child safety. This was a nifty bit of political jujitsu, in that it flipped one of the most damning arguments social conservatives used against the homosexual community—that gays were a threat to kids—on its head. Instead, Uribe and others argued, gay students were under threat because of the bias and ignorance of the straight community. "We have reason to believe that gay and lesbian students are at much greater risk for alcohol and substance abuse, attempted suicide and dropping out," Uribe explained. "Loneliness and alienation are universal, and family disruption is almost universal."[6]

Uribe, who began her efforts in response to the plight of a single student, wanted to ensure that such students had a place to go, a safe haven where they could talk and find support. As she expanded her work, she trained counselors and teachers at other schools throughout the district to do the same. Although Uribe's approach was different, her goal was similar to that of the Harvey Milk School in New York—to get kids abused by the school system off the streets and back on track. At the time, this was perhaps the best that students in trouble could hope for—an oasis. School systems themselves were unable, or administrators generally unwilling, to do more. It was left to outsiders—in the case of Fairfax High School, a lesbian science teacher willing to go to bat for a marginalized, abused student who had been in her school for less than a month—and a few allies willing to help students in whatever small ways they could. Arthur Lipkin had a different goal in mind. He did not want to offer an offshoot from the mainstream school, or an oasis within it. He wanted to change the entire system.

EVEN IF THEY MOVED SLOWLY, administrators at Rindge were open to finding a way to get Lipkin back in his classroom. Faculty members—particularly a shop teacher from the Cambridge projects named Al Ferreira—played a key role as liaisons between administrators and Lipkin.

They also created a planning committee that put together what would be an unusual and momentous set of meetings for all faculty and staff. First, there would be an all-faculty meeting that would include a public declaration of support by teachers and administrators for LGBT members of the school community. Second, the school committed to holding smaller-group follow-up meetings to create some sense of common cause around supporting LGBT youth. But there were many doubts about the efficacy of such an approach—after all, teachers sit through mandatory training sessions on a variety of topics every year, with little impact on their outlook or pedagogy. Why would this one be any different? Or would it be terribly different? Would straight teachers rebel openly against the idea of supporting LGBT students and teachers?

There were no clear answers, and in the end, even Lipkin's most ardent supporters had less than complete confidence that this approach would work. There were, however, several points on which most could agree. First, that Lipkin was perhaps not the best spokesperson for the cause. Even Lipkin himself concurred: "I was viewed as a radical already," said the veteran of protests and marches for a number of different civil rights and antiwar causes. Furthermore, he had been hectoring faculty, staff, and students alike about their homophobia for years—quite likely, if he spoke, the school community would tune him out. To reach the student body, the movement could not be seen as just another lefty crusade. Lipkin needed speakers with what he termed "good cred"—teachers whom others would not dismiss out of hand, who had a chance of being heard. Second, the issue had to be made personal. Lipkin acknowledged his own tendency to turn to abstract questions of civil rights and equality; such an approach would likely not resonate with many in the audience. Third, supporters recognized the need to make homosexuality appear as unexceptional as possible— thus speakers had to be just regular, everyday folks who happened to have some connection to the LGBT world. Again, Lipkin—something of a loner with an intimidating intellect—did not fit that image.

Finally, the goal was not to scold. This was Al Ferreira's key insight: The problem, in his sense, was that "people didn't know what dialogue to have . . . they might hear [a homophobic comment] and say,

'Don't say things like that.' But that's not education, that's behavior modification."[7] In other words, teachers would likely resent being asked to police student behavior more closely. Teachers might react more favorably if the faculty assembly focused on giving them tools to become better educators—to help them address homophobia and protect LGBT students. Creating rules against antigay slurs and more vigilant enforcement against bullying were necessary, but on their own would not foster a more supportive school culture.

In the end the planning committee chose two speakers to address the faculty. One was a cafeteria worker whose son had died of AIDS. She spoke about the trials of caring for her son, and the difficulty in hearing the way students and some faculty disparaged AIDS patients and gay men. The second was Ferreira, who was, until that point, still in the closet. He spoke eloquently about how difficult it was to hide his identity, about the anger and sadness at having to exclude his partner of many years from his school life, of making his partner wait outside in the cold when he went in to a convenience store—because one of his students was working the register. "I felt a real rage inside," he said, "that this man, whom I loved more than anything, was someone I had to hide from students." He talked of the shame at hearing about a former student who felt such isolation and despair that he killed himself—which prompted Ferreira to wonder whether that tragedy could have been avoided had he been open about his own sexuality. Both speakers sought only to make a connection with their audience, not to admonish. They counted on a shared humanity within the school community to overcome what they assumed was a knee-jerk, unthinking antipathy. The event itself—perhaps the first of its kind in a public school—was a milestone in the relationship between LGBT students and their schools.

Aside from a desire to change school culture, and a willingness to go out on what was a very precarious limb, the two speakers shared one other important trait: a working-class background. This too was a conscious choice. In a community as diverse as Cambridge, class tension was a reality that had to be accounted for. Further, since the days of McCarthy, animus toward homosexuality was deepened by the belief that gayness was somehow an upper-class conceit. For many, homosexuality conjured up mental images of overly cultured, overly fashionable, European-sounding simpering types. Ferreira—the short, stocky, well-loved shop teacher who also happened to be a townie from the Cambridge projects—was anything but. In his own words, "It helped that I looked straight," and it was thought that he, as opposed to the more professorial Lipkin, might reach a wider spectrum of the school community. The approach appeared to work. Both Ferreira and Lipkin characterized the response of their colleagues as very supportive. Ferreira recalls a Catholic colleague who walked away from the assembly still believing that homosexuality was sinful, but very willing to work to keep all kids—even LGBT kids—safe.[8]

The faculty had been receptive to training on how to combat homophobia, and expressed a willingness to work on changing school culture. But would teachers confront students when they overhead antigay remarks? The actual practice of teaching involves making innumerable decisions each day; many involve deciding which student behaviors need to be addressed, and which can be overlooked. Teachers could easily tire of admonishing students to be more supportive. For school culture to change, students would have to do more to police their own, and LGBT students would have to become more visible in the school community.

Inspired by the faculty training, Ferreira posted a notice in the school's weekly bulletin, offering an after-school support group for LGBT youth and anyone else interested in discussing issues of gay civil rights. "I had no idea what to expect," he said. He only knew he wanted to start a group to help LGBT students, to ensure that no one felt so desperately isolated that suicide seemed the only way out. Ferreira also wanted his group to be recognized as an extracurricular club, something that was, in his words, "just like the . . . the student newspaper," something on equal footing with every other group in the school, part of the school's fabric. Inspired by the work of Fairfax High's science teacher-turned-counselor Virginia Uribe, whom they met after she spoke at Harvard University, Ferreira and his students decided to call their group Project 10 East.

Project 10 East was to prove instrumental in helping change the culture at Cambridge. Within their first year, Ferreira and his students helped organize an all-school assembly aimed at reaching the entire school community. Ferreira even reached out to the PTA to explain what his group was doing and why, and to invite parents to attend. Although the assembly itself would essentially be a repeat performance of the faculty assembly, the risks were considerably greater. Would speakers be shouted off the stage? Would parents raise an unholy fuss? The assembly was not a lecture, and not a scolding session—instead it was an attempt to explain to a largely straight audience what it was like to walk the halls as a gay teacher or student. And once again, reactions from the straight audience were largely positive, and parents were generally supportive. More important, never before had the LGBT students in the audience heard such a message—at least not in a school-sanctioned assembly, in front of the entire student body. Perhaps for the first time, many of them felt they belonged at the school.

Lipkin's belief about his school was, in the end, correct. Administrators, unwilling to risk controversy, had to be forced into doing something. They would not take on homophobia of their own volition. His walkout was consciously political, designed to precipitate a culture change in his school, but even he could not have foreseen the turn of events. Intentionally or not, his walkout precipitated Ferreira's speech and the creation of Project 10 East. But Ferreira was also proved correct: many people (at least in the Cambridge school community) would, in the end, be supportive. They just needed help knowing what to do. Even parent response was almost entirely favorable. Perhaps for this reason, administrators became full-throated cheerleaders for the work of Lipkin and Ferreira. Most fellow teachers were also supportive; many (as Ferreira predicted) would be willing to do more if they knew what to say or do. Shortly after the faculty training, Ferreira was asked by the school's physical education teachers to help them resolve the issue of a transgender student who was failing their courses. Having nowhere she felt comfortable changing, the student simply did not attend class. Working with the administration,

Ferreira and the phys ed teachers set up a secluded area—not just for this student, but for anyone who needed someplace safer—to shower and change. Ferreira even ran a workshop for elementary school teachers, who would not address the topic of homosexuality directly with students but who still wanted to be on the lookout for signs of harassment. Together, they devised a series of strategies for countering antigay bullying in the elementary schools.

WHERE THERE HAD BEEN NONE, now there were two. Just as Uribe's Project 10 expanded—she ran training sessions or helped set up programs at over a third of the public schools in the Los Angeles Unified School District—Ferreira soon found himself meeting with groups of teachers throughout the Boston area and beyond. Although Project 10 and Project 10 East were part of the same movement, there were differences between the two. Karen Harbeck, a scholar and lawyer who worked with both groups, characterized Uribe's primary mission as "protecting the [gay and transgender students] from the rest of the population," while Ferreira and Lipkin sought to integrate the LGBT students more fully with the rest of the population. Project 10 East was designed as an extracurricular group, not an intervention. Treating Project 10 East like any other club meant including information about it in the extracurricular pamphlets sent home to all parents, and setting up a Project 10 East information table at freshman orientation—in Ferreira's words, "right along with the ski club and French club"[9]— and that the group had its page in the yearbook. In treating the club like any other group in the school, administrators sent an unequivocal message to the entire community, a message no public school community had ever heard before: LGBT students were just like every other student in the building. And it echoed Lipkin's main point: not only did LGBT students deserve to be treated the same as other students, but schools had a duty to make it so.

Project 10 and Project 10 East used similar tactics to further their aims. While each made an argument about civil rights, they put significantly more emphasis on student safety. Doing so was part of a greater effort to move the issue from the abstract to the real and personal. As rhetorical tactics, these were successful—it is hard to argue against protecting a kid from bullying and abuse. A less-explicitly articulated part of this strategy, but one perhaps more important in the long term, was to normalize the idea of homosexuality in the minds of straight Americans. Or, more accurately, to present a very conservative type of homosexuality to straight Americans. Beginning with the earliest efforts in schools, teachers sought to portray LGBT students and teachers as fundamentally the same as straight students and teachers—as wanting the same things, living the same lives, engaging in the same practices.

The more radical political activists—people who had been on the front lines of the fight for gay rights—found themselves pushed to the background. To them, seeking the approval of straight America was tantamount to denying the uniqueness of their own culture, and to accepting, in some form, second-class status. If gay Americans had to act straight, talk straight, and dress straight in order to gain the acceptance of straights, the price was too high. For none other than Harry Hay, the founder of the gay rights movement in the United States, the assimilationist movement was a game of respectability politics—one that homosexuals would in the end lose. Assimilation, in his view, "was running us into the ground."[10] Hay (and others) sought a gay rights movement that was not about rights, but about liberation, not about acceptance by the mainstream, but acceptance on their own terms, as part of their own culture. Gay marriage and domesticity were fine; but so were promiscuity and a refusal to settle into what one writer called "a heterosexual world lost in strict gender roles, enforced reproductive sexuality, and numbingly straitjacketed social personae."[11] As the new, more muted, iteration of the gay rights movement pushed its more radical cousins to the background and focused on mainstream-oriented messaging, Hay grew impatient. He refused to march in the New York Gay Pride Parade because it sought to exclude the North American Man-Boy Love Association. Support for NAMBLA was of course politically and morally untenable for most; for Hay it was simply a question of refusing to bow to mainstream conventions. Hay believed that seeking to eliminate or silence some within the gay community for the sake of respectability was in the end little different from efforts to silence or eliminate the entire gay community. In other words, if one started to decide which parts of gay culture could be accepted by the straight world, one would find, in the end, that some arbiter in the straight world would deem every part of gay culture unacceptable.

Yet those working in schools took a significantly more conservative approach to furthering gay rights. They were, of course, significantly more conservative in general than Hay—but then, who wasn't? Hay was still a radical at heart—not only in his sexual politics, but in every aspect of his life. The Communist organizer risking life and limb on the docks forty years earlier had not been domesticated. Still, it is fair to say that the path to achieving cultural change within schools required being very careful about how homosexuality was presented. Thus, schools sought to counter not only stereotypes held by mainstream Americans, but also more libertine strands of gay culture promoted by more radical gay liberation activists. What began in the public schools in Massachusetts was as conservative a cultural upending as one could imagine. And at the same time this quiet shakeup began in the public schools, so too did teachers at tradition-bound New England prep schools begin to bring change to their socially conservative communities. And together, educators in both public and private schools would change state policy in Massachusetts.

Pulpits, Pink Triangles, and Basement Meetings

PRIVATE SCHOOLS JOIN THE MOVEMENT

Your cross may have been your salvation, and someday you may be happy you didn't have the burden of a "normal" life.

—Kevin Jennings, in a speech coming out to the school community at Concord Academy, 1988

ONCORD ACADEMY sits on Main Street, just outside the heart of Concord Center, just west of one of the town's many old cemeteries whose headstones date back to colonial times. As a school, it lacks the sense of self-importance and grandiosity of many of its prep school cousins in New England, and its campus reflects this slightly more humble character. There are no high stone walls or iron fences girding the perimeter, no imposing entry gates, no buildings of monumental grandeur. Along Main Street, the houses of CA blend seamlessly with the colonial residences that surround it—unsurprising, since the campus came into being with the purchase of one such private home in 1922. That single home—now the Haines House, after former house mother and director of maintenance Pamelia Haines—provided ample room for the fledgling all-girls school, as its first graduating class numbered only three. Change came slowly to CA: the school welcomed its first male students in 1971, and the campus gradually expanded as the school bought up more homes along Main Street and took over farmland rolling back to the Sudbury River. Still, CA remains small; not until 1948 did it graduate a class as large as twenty, and graduating classes are still under one hundred students. And the school's architecture has largely retained its simple New England colonial flavor, gray clapboard buildings with white trim and dark shutters, restrained and modest by design.

At the heart of the campus sits the chapel. As unadorned as the rest of the school's buildings, it bears the name of headmistress Elizabeth Hall, who envisioned the chapel as "a place for quiet in a crowded school." In the early 1950s, when Hall had only the vision but not the means to build it, a fellow teacher saw an ad in *Yankee Magazine* offering for sale, for the sum of $1,500, the Snackerty Brook Baptist Chapel, near Barnstead, New Hampshire. In the summer of 1956, faculty, staff, and volunteers set up camp in Barnstead, disassembled the chapel plank by plank, and transported it to Concord. By December, it had been reassembled on campus and repainted—just in time for Christmas services. Furniture and electricity would have to wait, but on the last night before the holiday, students, faculty, and staff gathered to sing carols and listen to readings by candlelight, seated on the floor or among the scaffolding that still climbed the chapel walls.

As at many prep schools, the chapel is still CA's primary assembly hall, even as the school itself has become ever more secular. Old traditions have been transformed, among them the chapel talk. A staple at many schools, chapel talks are an outgrowth of the morning sermons that used to begin school days at the religiously denominated prep schools. While formal church services have all but disappeared, chapel talks remain—a regular (if no longer daily) communal experience: chapel talks might be a personal reflection, a musical performance, or a poetry reading. At CA, each senior is afforded the opportunity to give a chapel talk on any subject of the student's choosing. In the words of current headmaster Rick Hardy, "the chapel is a vessel . . . that carries and holds the voices and stories of this community."

On a morning in November 1988, the speaker at chapel was not a student, but second-year history teacher Kevin Jennings. Jennings was young and popular, a sought-after adviser, and acknowledged by students and colleagues alike to be a compelling public speaker. Fully aware of his gifts, he was accustomed not so much to speaking before an audience as conducting it, as if at the head of an orchestra. He could play on listeners' emotions, bring them over to his side, take them where he wanted to go. His confidence rarely abandoned him. On this occasion, however, he imagined his audience turning on him, shouting him down, or sitting in stony silence as he floundered. It was his first-ever chapel talk, and while that might be a cause for anxiety in others, not so for him. He was a preacher's son, at home in the pulpit. His disquietude had a deeper source: as far as he knew—as far as anyone knew—he was about to do something never before done in the world of elite New England prep schools. He was going to come out in a public speech to the entire school community.

His speech was a source of apprehension for his head of school as well. Private schools face a set of pressures different from those of their public counterparts, and the headmaster at Concord Academy, Thomas Wilcox, had reason for concern. He was a tolerant person, had embraced diversity, and thought of himself as someone who had done much to support LGBT faculty at CA—he counted some of them as close friends. But he worried that Jennings's public coming out could put CA at risk, in a way that no public school would ever be. Public schools are viable because—save for the extreme fringe of the political spectrum—Americans believe they serve an important function in society. Barring a radical change in this belief, public schools will continue to educate American children far into the future. Further, across a spectrum that encompasses nearly all American ideologies (again, save for the fringes), it is commonly held that public education should be funded at a fairly consistent level. Some may argue for greater school choice, or expanded voucher programs, but in every year since 1987, states have spent between 20 and 22 percent of annual budgets on elementary and secondary education. Over that same period, the share of federal funds spent by states on education has fluctuated from a low of 8.9 percent in 2016 to a high of 12.7 in 2011; most years it has hovered between 10.5 percent and 12 percent.[1] Total expenditure on public education has risen consistently in real dollar terms over that same period. Different political parties, or factions within parties, may outline opposing visions of public education and funding levels for it, but in reality, spending on public education has consumed a fairly consistent slice of the budgetary pie.

Private schools work on a different business model, one reliant primarily on tuition, donations from parents and alumni, and, for the fortunate few, a sizable endowment. Funding for private schools is, therefore, considerably more variable. It is easier (and more common) for students to leave private schools—"lower transaction costs associating with opting to leave," in the words of education scholars—which makes them "more prone to the threat of a shutdown condition."[2] This threat has become particularly acute in the twenty-first century, as hundreds of private schools (most commonly Catholic schools) have closed their doors, enrollment has declined and is projected to decline further (even at independent schools), and the degree to which tuitions are discounted (through financial aid packages) has increased steadily—both in terms of the number of students receiving discounts and the average size of the discount.

The threat of shutdown is remote for well-established prep schools in New England, but it does point to the relative volatility of the private school market. While Wilcox probably did not fear the cataclysmic event of shuttering CA entirely, he recognized that there are many conditions between death and thriving. While the long-term viability of the school certainly bears consideration for a head of school, on a day-to-day basis he or she is more likely to worry about what might affect the school's reputation, what might lead to an erosion of the donor base, or what might cause a trickle of students and faculty to look elsewhere. Consultants for the National Association of Independent Schools, a trade association of sorts for private nonsectarian schools, describe ten markers of success for their clientele, among them market demand (the ratio of applicants to acceptances); measures of giving, from student families (including grandparents), alumni, and trustees; growing endowment; significant and sustainable financial aid awards; competitive faculty salaries; low student attrition rates; budget for professional development and technology;

and student-faculty ratio. Student outcomes—which could mean scores on standardized tests, or college acceptance rates, or participation in extracurricular activities[3]—are also on the list, though as a lower priority.[4] One might argue that these types of market pressures are more likely to work to produce successful student outcomes— almost as a by-product. After all, if one subscribes to the notion that the customer is always right, and if one believes that private schools must be more responsive to the needs and concerns of students and parents, then one would conclude that such a crucible improves student outcomes. This may be true. At the very least it is clear that, for a private school, perception—in the eyes of donors, alumni, and prospective students and their families—has tremendous influence on a school's success. In other words, branding matters.

In the 1980s, Concord Academy had a reputation as a strong academic school, committed to diversity and community—and possessed of a certain quirkiness that was hard to articulate, yet clearly present in its students. The school was, the words of then-headmaster Wilcox, a little bit "out there." (In many respects, it remains so. The school mascot is the chameleon, the school does not compute class rank and does not hand out any academic awards, and, at graduation, diplomas are handed out in random order.) The school had wonderful art programs and attracted students who did not quite fit at bigger, more successful, and more traditional institutions. It had an enviable record of academic achievement, and had earned a rock-solid reputation as a top-flight academic school that emphasized community, respected diversity, and provided students space to be just a little different. By any objective measure, CA was—and remains—a remarkable school.

And yet, to some in the prep school universe, CA was lacking . . . something. Those of a particular mind-set—certain donors, or prospective students and their families—could describe CA as "a wonderful school" without quite meaning it as a compliment. While some of its cousins trace their roots back to the 1700s, CA was still relatively young. It was one of the very few former girls' schools in the Northeast to transition to coeducation successfully without merging with an all-male institution. (Historically, mergers of single-sex prep schools

have typically been takeovers by the boys school.) It was not an athletic powerhouse—although it fielded over twenty interscholastic
teams, the school's noncompetitive ethos meant athletic success was
never a point of emphasis. And it was small, with little endowment to
speak of.

The pressure to grow—to cultivate a larger applicant pool, to
increase the endowment, improve rates of giving, and to hold on to
its current students—is certainly part of what one signs up for when
accepting a position as head of a prep school. For CA in the late 1980s,
such pressure was acute: Wilcox sought to maintain CA's enviable academic and arts reputation, but the school was also in the midst of a
campaign to boost the endowment and expand the campus. Doing
so meant appealing to a more mainstream slice of the applicant pool,
which in turn meant toning down the quirkiness, if only slightly.
Under such conditions, it is understandable that Wilcox was uncomfortable with Jennings's desire to come out publicly. He was well
aware of the teacher's homosexuality—Jennings had been up front
about his orientation during the hiring process. And there were plenty
of other gay faculty as well—all closeted to varying degrees—whom
Wilcox would support and protect if necessary. But when Jennings
came back from summer break wearing an engagement ring, it was
Wilcox who suggested he tell students it was a gift "from someone he
loved."[5] When Jennings first brought up his idea of a chapel talk, Wilcox asked him to wait, wanting time to consider the possible implications, and perhaps hoping to talk Jennings out of it. Jennings acqui-
esced, although he had intentionally scheduled his talk for October 11
to coincide with the first National Coming Out Day and the anniversary of the March on Washington for Lesbian and Gay Rights.[6] Some
of the straight faculty fully supported Jennings's plan. Some did not,
and in fact refused to attend when he finally did address the school.
Some of the gay faculty counseled him not to be so public, fearful that
the current supportive environment could easily vanish, that administrative backing would melt in the face of parental backlash. Even CA,
a school committed to diversity, was accepting of homosexual students and faculty only so long as they remained quiet about it.

No doubt Wilcox also worried that some students and faculty might choose to quit the school, that donations might dwindle or dry up completely, that the school's brand might be irreparably damaged. Yet Jennings's talk also risked magnifying CA's reputation for quirkiness in a way that further marginalized CA for that certain segment of the prep school universe. These worries, specific to CA, were piled on top of a more general and insidious fear: that of the historical stereotype around homosexual activity among men and boys at boarding schools. When fears of homosexuality first arose at the turn of the century, it was seen as especially pervasive in the single-sex climate of boarding schools: older boys initiating younger students, and, even worse, predatory teachers recruiting their charges. Thus did boarding schools actively seek to discourage any sort of behavior that might be perceived as gay. The predatory stereotype has never completely gone away, and likely always hung in the back of minds among the many who attended, taught at, or worked in boarding schools. Wilcox could support Jennings privately, and at the same time fear that others would react poorly to an openly gay—and very popular—male teacher at a boarding school. Yet, for all his concerns, Wilcox did not stand in Jennings's way. So on a crisp November morning, Jennings walked to the pulpit of the old chapel, took a deep breath, and began.

By all accounts, his rhetorical skill remained true. Many in attendance already knew the topic of his talk; those who did not would not have to wait long. In the first few lines, Jennings reflected generally on the power of words, then he got right to his point: "The word that . . . has shaped much of my life is the word 'faggot.' I have spent years dealing with what it means to be this thing that society calls a faggot, trying to find a foxhole of self-esteem in which I could hide from the incessant negative bombardment gay people face every day in the United States."

AT THIS POINT IN THE TALK, Jennings remembers thinking, "No one screamed, no one fainted, no one . . . fled the building, but, if I hadn't had their attention before, I could see I had it now." He continued to speak of the negative stereotyping gay men and women faced, but in his conclusion sought to broaden his message and relate his struggle to that of the entire audience:

> My topic today has not been gay rights . . . I've chosen my theme because we are all gay in some way . . . I am talking about a condition of the mind, an outlook on ourselves we all share. We all have a cross of some sort that we bear. You might fall into one of the easily targeted groups in our society . . . blacks are told they are inferior to whites, women that they are weaker than men, and so forth . . . hopefully you can see that it is not you that don't measure up but that the yardstick itself is warped.
>
> Perhaps your pain stems from a more private cause . . . However, in each of them, there is something that made you the special person that you are today . . . Your cross may have been your salvation, and someday you may be happy you didn't have the burden of a "normal" life . . .
>
> Treasure what makes you special, not what makes you like everyone else, and treasure what makes others different from you.[7]

That the preacher's son used the metaphor of the cross is perhaps not surprising, but it is striking, and a clear effort to invoke not just the suffering of Jesus but his charity toward those marginalized in his own time. Jennings further referenced the tendency to internalize the most negative impressions others may have. And while there was no appreciable impact of Jennings's talk on any of the markers of success for prep schools—no measurable change in donor support or market demand—a mob of students rallied to him, and colleagues gave him a strong expression of support.

For Jennings, the chapel talk was a catharsis, a smashing of the glass closet. It freed him to be himself. It also gave rise to a burning question: Now what? There were other gay teachers at CA, and much like Arthur Lipkin's and Al Ferreira's colleagues at Rindge, they held a variety of opinions on the advisability of being a publicly gay figure in high school education—particularly at a school with a number of boarding students. Certainly there were gay students at CA, and many teachers knew they struggled with their identity, with isolation and fear—the same issues and dangers as their teenage counterparts elsewhere. No matter how much CA encouraged diversity, it was not yet a place that openly supported and protected LGBT students. To what degree would the school—or its faculty—take that step? Privately, some teachers would seek to help a student at risk, often asking Jennings to counsel the student. While better than the traditional approach of turning a blind eye to the problem, it was not exactly a viable solution. Not all students' struggles were obvious, and turning Jennings into a one-stop counseling shop would have little outward effect on campus-wide culture. But the plight of LGBT students was not a problem school leadership actively tried to solve. CA, and Wilcox, faced a genuine conflict: by allowing Jennings to go forward with his talk, CA opened the door to both acknowledging and supporting gay teachers and students. But school leadership—not just Wilcox, but trustees and many faculty—feared that doing so would have potentially damaging consequences for CA. They were not ready to lead on the issue. Jennings's talk made him the voice of the LGBT community at CA; whatever the next step was, he would have to be the one to take it. So, now what?

The answer came from an unlikely source—a young, straight student who approached Jennings with the idea of creating a group for gays and straights alike to advocate for LGBT students at CA, and to be a vehicle for activism outside of school as well. Jennings, activist par excellence, the man widely credited with beginning the GSA movement, defers much credit to his students, not only for the founding of the club but for its agenda—first addressing homophobia, later advocating for the inclusion of sexual orientation in CA's nondiscrimination policy. While Jennings does not speculate on what led the student to seek him out, the timing—only weeks after his chapel talk—suggests his speech may have been the impetus. Moreover, Jennings had confronted the headmaster over the nondiscrimination policy earlier that school year.[8] It is possible that Jennings has valid reasons to frame the story in a way that emphasizes the role of students while diminishing his own: as noted earlier, teachers made a conscious choice to focus on student safety instead of a nationwide battle for gay rights. Making the issue about students, as opposed to an adult political battle, helped garner support. In addition, Jennings (like others, including Ferreira and Atlas) was cognizant of the still-prevalent perception that gays recruited children; as Jennings noted, "this claim was used to damn us as a community."[9] It may thus have been sensible to allow students to play the leading role. Without dismissing the students' importance in creating the Gay-Straight Alliance at CA, though, it is fair to state that Jennings was the primary driver of this reform, not only for his actions before the GSA was created, but because he was instrumental in spreading the GSA model to other schools and eventually to the Governor's Commission.

As it happens, at the same time Jennings sought to address the issue of homosexuality at Concord Academy, a group at another, more prestigious New England prep school was engaged in a similar effort.

PHILLIPS ANDOVER ACADEMY is only twenty miles northeast of Concord Academy, and yet the schools are worlds apart. Both are among the finest private educational institutions on the planet; their campuses and programs bespeak a wealth of resources most schools can only dream of. And yet, Andover exists on an entirely different plane. Samuel Phillips founded his academy in 1778, the first incorporated boarding school in the new nation. Paul Revere engraved the school's original seal (for the sum of two pounds and eight shillings), and John Hancock signed the original articles of incorporation. George Washington sent his nephews there. Additional alums include presidents George H. W. and George W. Bush; FDR's secretary of war Henry Stimson; landscape architect Frederick Law Olmsted; the founder of Harvard Law School, Isaac Royall Jr.; and actors Humphrey Bogart and Jack Lemmon.

It is not a school given to false modesty. Its chapel, in contrast to CA's, is an immense neo-Georgian edifice, a gift of Thomas Cochran—a man born to wealth who rose to become partner in J. P. Morgan. A childless widower, Cochran doted instead on his alma mater, spending nearly $10 million between 1923 and 1930 endowing faculty chairs and remaking the campus. He brought in renowned architect Charles

William Platt to design the imposing, barrel-vaulted chapel with its massive columns and engraved oak paneling. One writer reflected that in their zeal to design a campus for the ages, "It seemed as though neither Platt nor Cochran cared how much it cost."[10]

If there is a leadership group of leading private schools, Andover is in it. In 1931, *Time* magazine acknowledged Phillips Andover and its younger New Hampshire cousin, Phillips Exeter, as the "twin giants of prep schools in size and prestige." Indeed, Andover played an instrumental role in perpetuating WASP elitism in the early twentieth century, sending 74 of its 178 graduates in the class of 1930 to Yale. To a degree, it is insulated from some of the pressures facing schools such as CA—a $1 billion endowment will do that. Still, maintaining its position at the pinnacle of the elite independent school universe means at least being cautiously aware of potential controversies that could threaten that position. As a result, Andover, like its peers, had been content to pretend there were no LGBT students or teachers in its community.

The Phillips Andover GSA began surreptitiously. In the *Andover Daily Bulletin* of February 7, 1989, amid announcements about upcoming carnation sales for Valentine's Day, a dinner for the Chinese Club, an essay competition, and a change in practice time for the JV squash team, appeared a seemingly innocuous posting: "Discussion of gay rights, sexual preference, and related topics. Today, 6:45pm." The organizers intentionally gave little advance notice of the meeting to minimize the chance that opposing forces would mobilize against or disrupt it. The location of the meeting, in the basement of the academic administration building, was also chosen with care. "NOT an obvious location," in the words of one faculty adviser; not a place that saw much student traffic in the evenings."[11] The young woman who posted the announcement, a day student named Sharon Tentarelli, made her best friend come along, out of fear that she herself would be the only one in attendance.

Because her family lived in town, and Tentarelli did not board at PA, she was less cloistered than the students (and for that matter, the faculty) who lived on campus. Andover was not the totality of her community during the school year. She was part of a Quaker youth group that drew its members from all over suburban Boston, and counted among its leaders several young gay and lesbian counselors who could provide informational materials and guidance for her. At the end of her sophomore year, she got it into her head to attend the Boston Pride Parade. School would be out, her classmates would have gone home, and she could go by herself without attracting any attention. The pride festival began at City Hall Plaza, a massive, concrete, open-air bowl in front of the Government Center complex. Tentarelli rode the train from Andover into the heart of Boston, got on the subway, and finally ascended to the street at Haymarket Station. She walked up Congress Street, then up a flight of stairs to a spot that overlooked the plaza, and beheld something she never knew existed: "I looked out over this massive sea of gay people!" she recalled.[12] By the most amazing of chances, in that crowd of thousands, she ran into her English teacher. There was a very awkward greeting (neither of them was publicly out at school). Tentarelli, overcome by the whole experience, could only think to ask her teacher one of the many questions swimming through her mind: "How is all this kept secret?"[13]

She came back to Phillips Andover in the fall convinced of two things: first, that it was highly unlikely she was the only lesbian among the school's one thousand students; and second, that there was not any apparent safe space for her and others like her. She began a close examination of the faculty, looking for someone she could work with. Not wanting to force anyone out of the closet, she avoided approaching her English teacher. Instead, she found an ally through Andover's mandatory AIDS education program, which was ahead of its time for its open discussion of sexuality. One of the faculty members who led the program for juniors, a counselor named Cilla Bonney-Smith, had two important qualities as far as Tentarelli was concerned: First, she was clearly nonjudgmental and supportive. In her AIDS education workshops, Bonney-Smith talked about homophobia on campus—"a small step," according to another faculty member, "but at least the words gay and lesbian started to be heard on campus."[14] Bonney-Smith was, in a word, safe. Second, she was straight, which seemed important— gay teachers still had no explicit protections, and an effective support group would need support from the entire school community, not just LGBT students and faculty.

Tentarelli approached Bonney-Smith with her idea of forming a group; Bonney-Smith in turn approached faculty members she assumed would be sympathetic, and discussed the potential ramifications—for their careers, for closeted teachers, for student culture—if they moved forward. Within a few weeks, they were ready to proceed, and Tentarelli posted the meeting in the *Daily Bulletin*. She did not inform administrators, believing—as students often do—that it is best not to ask permission if the answer might be no. A handful of faculty members and a half dozen students showed up in the basement room for their first meeting. Tentarelli distributed the information sheets on homophobia that her youth group counselors had given her. Attendees read the handouts, and even talked about them for a bit. They brainstormed a little about what future actions they might take. But what had been envisioned as a serious discussion of homophobia on campus became something even more meaningful: a free and easy swapping of stories about roommates, classmates, and teachers. They bonded over their shared experience of being closeted and feeling isolated, and reveled in the fact that at last they had a place to talk openly and be fully themselves.

The meeting itself felt like a victory; still, it ended with a familiar question: Now what? Tentarelli took what was, for her, an even bigger and scarier step than starting the group: she published a letter in the school paper, outing herself ("yes, there are homosexuals at this school"), and inviting the entire community to the next meeting of the group. It was the first of many letters she and others would write, which became an important part of their presence on campus. Indeed, that constant presence was perhaps the group's key role in shaping Andover's public discussions of homosexuality and homophobia. For those who live in more enlightened places and more enlightened times, it is difficult to understand how significant such a small group could be. Alleviating feelings of isolation could have a profound impact on students' well-being. Faculty, too, felt more supported, more at home among members of the nascent GSA than elsewhere in the school. There were no publicly out teachers at Phillips Andover. Some were out to a few friends; others no doubt lived in the proverbial glass closet. But at one of the early meetings, faculty member Kathy Henderson disclosed her homosexuality to the group. "The GSA," she said, was "the very first safe place where I could reflect that part of me to straight people . . . the very first safe place I ever had as a gay person."

In the fall of 1989, the GSA applied for recognition as a sponsored school group, for which, according to Tentarelli, "you needed a faculty adviser, and you had to help sell doughnuts during the mid-morning break to raise money." They were now listed among the other clubs in the school directory—right between the chess club and the hand-bell choir. They had an institutional presence, and could be a voice for the LGBT community at Andover without any one student having to take that risk alone. They could be a voice for closeted students, and even for Tentarelli, the group was a source of strength. What might be terrifying or intimidating enough to silence an individual—whether teacher or student—could be within the realm of possibility for a group. At Andover and elsewhere, GSAs became political actors within the school system. When President George H. W. Bush (Phillips Andover '42) visited campus in November 1989, the GSA could protest with other student advocacy groups along his motorcade route. More important, when homophobic incidents occurred at school, the GSA could take appropriate action where individual students or faculty may have felt unable to respond.

The "Exonian incident" was perhaps the most egregious such example. The Exonian is a long-standing tradition where students—usually affiliated in some capacity with the student-run newspaper, the Andover Phillipian—produce a parody newspaper, spoofing their New Hampshire cousins at Exeter. It is published during the schools' mid-November rivalry weekend, when Andover plays Exeter in all sports, and is for the most part a typical bit of prep school japery. But in the fall of 1989, it struck particularly low notes. A letter to the editor spoofed a male student in love with his roommate asking for advice, to which the "editor" responded by calling the writer a "butt pirate" and "stool-pusher," and—in a perhaps-unintended show of support for gender fluidity—a lesbian. The letter concluded by suggesting that at least the writer must feel comfortable among the population at Exeter. Another letter made derogatory references to supporters of Massachusetts representative Barney Frank, then the only openly gay member of Congress. An article, written by "Dick N. Mouth," joked about NAMBLA members in leadership positions at Exeter, and quoted an Exeter senior named "Ima Phag."

The LGBT population was not the only target; the *Exonian* mocked women and various minority groups as well. Indeed, the authors' capacity to offend seemed limited only by the extent of their imaginations. The jokes were mean-spirited but probably not dissimilar to what could be overheard in the dormitories on campus, or, for that matter, in offices and at dinner tables around the country. However, as a publication purporting to represent the entire Andover community, it fell well below acceptable standards of decency. In the aftermath, officers of the *Phillipian*—which was technically not responsible for the *Exonian* parody but had allowed the authors the use of its publishing facility—were called before the entire student government to explain how the *Exonian* came to be published, and how the newspaper staff would ensure tighter editorial control in the future. Administrators strongly censured the authors. Most significantly for the LGBT population, editors and writers of the *Exonian* issued a statement in which they specifically apologized to the Andover Gay-Straight Alliance. Editors of the *Phillipian* also published an apology for, among other things, the "derogatory attacks on homosexuals" contained in the *Exonian*. Homophobic jokes were nothing new at Andover; apologies for making them were. It was an important step for the GSA, clear evidence that they had become "vocal and visible enough" that the community could not pretend no one had been hurt by the *Exonian*'s antigay invective.

Although the controversy blew over fairly quickly, in January 1990 members of the GSA—both students and faculty—published a letter in the *Phillipian* lauding the campus response to the pervasive ignorance and extreme stereotyping exhibited in the *Exonian* spoof. January also marked Andover's first-ever commemoration of Martin Luther King Jr.'s birthday. The daylong program on civil rights included an optional workshop, taught by Bonney-Smith, on homophobia. And in May of that year, as a direct response to the *Exonian* incident, the GSA sponsored their first "Awareness Week," an unofficial series of events, undertaken without official permission from the administration. They posted biographies and photos of famous gays and lesbians around the school, and placed a pink triangle in 10 percent of the student mailboxes. In a letter to the *Phillipian*, members of the GSA stated that the recipients of pink triangles were chosen at random; however, this was not entirely the case. GSA members took pains to ensure that students they deemed especially hostile—the loud makers of crude jokes, the mutterers of disapproval, the former friends who rejected them when they came out—all received a pink triangle.

Tentarelli spent her senior spring preparing for AP exams and trying to maintain her enviable academic standing—she was off to MIT in the fall. And, like any senior, she tried to soak up the last few months of her high school career, to cherish precious time with dear friends. Yet she found more of her time taken up by the GSA: she was the driving force behind Andover's first Awareness Week, and she arranged for Suzanne Pharr, author of *Homophobia: A Weapon of Sexism*, to speak on campus. And, of course, there was prom. Tentarelli wore a tux she had acquired on the cheap; her "date," a straight junior girl who desperately wanted to go to the prom, wore a dress. Two boys from the GSA attended as a couple, and one of their faculty advisers brought along her same-sex partner to help chaperone. The three couples sat together at dinner and no doubt attracted more than their share of sideways glances and whispers. Some prom-goers did not approve; clearly a much larger percentage did not know yet how to act around them. Some, after grappling with an issue they had never before thought about, became enthusiastic supporters. But none could disavow their existence. As Tentarelli looked toward graduation and college beyond, she left behind a dramatically changed campus, and a student group well prepared to continue what she started.

In the following year, the GSA sought to take more concrete steps toward making Phillips Andover a more welcoming place for LGBT students and staff. Most significantly, they advocated for a change in the school's nondiscrimination policy to include sexual preference—a step that would require approval by the board of trustees. The request worked its way from the GSA and its adviser, Bonney-Smith, to the head of school, Don McNemar, and from McNemar to the board. The proposal built support as it moved up the hierarchy. Students reflected on how important it was to have role models on the faculty who were not hiding their sexuality. Faculty members in turn reflected on the power of teachers who were publicly out—and acknowledged the risks such faculty would take, particularly with no explicit protections. McNemar recalls thinking it was a very small thing he could do, but feeling particularly struck by what a big difference it made for some closeted teachers. And he characterized the trustees as generally supportive, although he wryly acknowledged that "it took some discussion" to bring them to understand the importance of making the change.

The Andover GSA also hosted Virginia Uribe during the 1990–1991 school year. In addition to meeting with the GSA, Uribe ran a workshop for the faculty, one McNemar describes as very significant in changing attitudes among the teachers. "She helped us understand," he recalled—not only the plight of LGBT youth, but also the role that straight faculty could play in assisting these students. This was not always easy for teachers, who, with a wide variety of backgrounds, experiences, and personal beliefs, were not uniformly comfortable working with gay youth, nor were they universally accepting of the presence of a gay group on campus. To his credit, McNemar recognized his own past ignorance of the issue and sought to move his school in the right direction. The work of Tentarelli and the GSA made "clear what we needed to do," he said, but it was not clear how to get there. Uribe's workshop, he felt, helped move the faculty as a whole in the right direction, toward becoming more supportive.

The campus was not perfect, not suddenly a wholly welcoming community for LGBT youth. But in the GSA's two years of existence, the group could point to several notable achievements. They had an influential voice on campus. They had advocated for, and achieved, a change in the school's nondiscrimination policy. Gay Awareness

Week became an annual, school-sanctioned event. Several faculty members and a number of students had come out publicly. Antigay remarks were still heard, but were recognized as hurtful and beyond the bounds of acceptable behavior. When, for example, a small number of students booed an announcement by the new leaders of the GSA, multiple student groups denounced their behavior, and a quarter of the faculty signed a letter that called the booing "intolerable" and the "ignorance" behind it "very sad."[15] By 1995, Andover's GSA was thriving to the point where it could hold a dance, with the support of faculty and administration, well attended by gay and straight students alike, at which cross-dressing was encouraged as part of the fun.

Still, for Tentarelli, the most important impact of the GSA was on the members themselves. She recalled a story told by a younger student, of an airplane flight back to Andover after a school vacation. It was a stormy evening, and a turbulent flight, and the girl was stuck in a window seat next to a middle-aged man who, with no provocation (as far as she could tell), persisted with a continuous stream of antigay comments. Physically trapped, unable to respond to the man, and queasy from the effects of the turbulence, she grew more and more nauseated, until finally she got sick all over her homophobic seatmate. She never did confront him directly, but admitted to feeling a certain amount of pride at directing her vomit so accurately. And when she recounted the story at the first GSA meeting after the break, the whole group cheered and clapped for her. For Tentarelli, that became an important symbol, of the idea that a fifteen-year-old girl caught in a truly miserable situation did not have to be alone. She could come back to her group, tell her story, and together they would be a part of both its sadness and the joyfully appropriate outcome. The GSA was about support, about students (and faculty) finding a place—maybe the only place—where they could be themselves. Tentarelli often felt that one of the most important things about the GSA was, at first glance, one of its most trivial. "The GSA," she said, "gave us a chance to gossip about who we thought was cute, just like any other teenager did, without worrying about which pronouns we used."[16]

Teaching, Learning, and Moving up the Hierarchy

SCHOOL LEADERSHIP JOINS THE MOVEMENT

Schools never pay in the long run for doing the right thing. Supporting students and faculty in their decisions to come out, and providing support vehicles necessary to their thriving in our school communities as gay, lesbian, bisexual, or unsure people clearly seems like the right thing to do.

—Thomas Wilcox, headmaster at
  Concord Academy, 1981–2000

They were supportive. But . . . they moved a little more slowly than they might have.

—Don McNemar, headmaster at Phillips
  Andover, 1981–1994, on trying to bring
  his board of trustees around on helping
  LGBT students

S TUDENTS AND FACULTY at Concord Academy and Phillips Andover created a new relationship between gay and straight on their respective campuses in a relatively short amount of time. But it could very well have gone no further. The independent school world is rightly seen as somewhat incestuous, particularly in the Northeast. When faculty and staff change jobs, they tend to move within the same relatively small circle of schools. Many are prep school graduates themselves. Students and alumni tend to cross-pollinate—a student at Andover will have friends, siblings, cousins, or old middle school classmates at any number of similar institutions. Yet teachers often lead insular lives. Especially at boarding schools, the job can be all-consuming, the division between work and life all but erased. Dormitory parents and young single teachers live with students, and most other faculty members are required to be on duty in the dormitories several nights a week. Traditions around formal meals vary, but often faculty members preside over a table of students at dinner, and take most other meals in the dining halls. Some schools schedule evening classes after dinner, or have mandatory, faculty-supervised study hours. At many schools, half-day classes on Wednesday are a trade-off for half days on Saturday, and athletic contests—at most schools, teachers are also expected to coach—fill the rest of the weekend. If a teacher does not take care to do so, weeks may pass without leaving campus.

All of which is to say, teachers at one school may have very little sense of what is going on elsewhere. Although ideas do spread from institution to institution, the networks along which they travel may be as informal as a coach of one team speaking to another after a game. And even if teachers at one institution are aware of innovations at another, they may choose not to adopt them. There is no true governing authority for independent schools, no equivalent to the district- or state-wide department of education that can mandate particular policies for all independent schools. There are groups and affiliations through which administrators share ideas and concerns, but new initiatives at one school may simply be met with shrugs at another. In the case of how (or whether) to support LGBT students, it was entirely possible that the work at Phillips Andover and Concord Academy would be discovered by others only very slowly, or that administrators at other schools would decide that openly supporting LGBT youth was potentially calamitous and not worth pursuing. That the movement in support of LGBT students spread fairly rapidly was the result of work along two tracks: first, through a series of fortunate connections, teachers from CA and Andover began to collaborate; and second, administrators at CA and Andover sought to educate their fellow school heads and prod them to take similar action. Without progress on either track, it is possible the movement at private schools would have been delayed significantly, if not stymied entirely.

THE SPREAD OF GSAs outward from CA and Andover started with a simple recommendation from a long-serving figure in the prep school world. Richard Barbieri taught at Milton for about ten years, directed its summer program through a period of collaboration with area public school districts, served as executive director of the Association of Independent Schools of New England (AISNE), and became a sort of go-to fixer, serving as interim head of a number of schools over several decades. In the mid-1980s, he helped develop a new teacher training program at AISNE—independent schools rely on cheap labor, fresh college graduates without teaching experience or training, to fill out faculty ranks, and schools recognized the need for a teaching boot camp to bring their new hires up to speed. Barbieri, in turn, relied on relatively young, dynamic teachers—young enough to relate to college grads, experienced enough to offer some wisdom—to staff his training program. Sometime around 1987, a colleague recommended such a person to Barbieri, a teacher with several years' experience, an impressively engaging style, and a knack for connecting with young people: Kevin Jennings.

Jennings agreed to be a teaching mentor in Barbieri's workshops, but noted a problem with the program. Multiculturalism had become a major point of emphasis in education during the 1980s, particularly among the affluent prep schools attempting to diversify both their student body and faculty. Barbieri's training focused on issues of gender and racial diversity, but, as Jennings pointed out, there was no mention of sexual orientation. He suggested including a session on homophobia, and Barbieri, beholden to neither major donors nor a conservative board of trustees, nor concerned with either parental backlash or declining enrollments, agreed without a second thought. Reactions to Jennings's sessions were, according to Barbieri, "uniformly positive." Given that his audience was largely young, upper-middle class, white northeasterners educated at left-leaning liberal arts institutions, this may not be surprising. Still, such a response suggests that, for schools, the LGBT issue had found its time.

Barbieri also put Jennings in touch with Kathy Henderson from Andover, and the two GSAs began to collaborate. Prior to meeting Henderson, Jennings recalled feeling somewhat isolated: "There was no one to talk to, no one you could ask, 'How do you run your group?'"[1] In the fall of 1989, Henderson and Jennings conducted a joint session at one of the AISNE workshops, and the response "overwhelmed" Jennings. At that point, Jennings recalled, he turned to Henderson and said, "Hey, we gotta organize a group."[2] At first they formed an ad hoc committee under the AISNE umbrella; eventually they spun off as a separate organization with an independent board that included Jennings, Barbieri, and Henderson. Thus was GLISTN (the Gay and Lesbian Independent School Teachers Network—now GLSEN, the Gay, Lesbian, and Straight Education Network)[3] born. Although GLSEN today boasts more than thirty-five chapters, offices in New York and Washington, D.C., partnerships with numerous educational groups (including the nation's largest teachers union, the NEA), and a registration roll of over four thousand GSAs, it began in 1990 with just a handful of teachers, no clear plan of attack, and a serious need for outreach.

Outreach was a tricky issue. Most homosexual teachers were still closeted and justifiably still fearful of being outed. Attending a conference on supporting LGBT students, run by two of the very few openly gay teachers in the prep school universe, would have been a risk few teachers were willing to take. For their first conference on this topic, Barbieri deliberately listed it as a workshop on HIV/AIDS education, to provide cover for teachers afraid to ask administrators for permission to attend a "gay" conference. "It was all word of mouth," Jennings recalled,[4] and personal contacts within the independent school world—Jennings, Barbieri, and Henderson all had their own lists— mattered. In addition, fortuitous connections helped broaden GLSEN's reach. Arthur Lipkin learned that Jennings lived around the corner from him in Cambridge, and knocked on his door.[5] As it happened, Jennings was living with Bob Parlin at the time. (It was Parlin with whom Jennings had exchanged wedding rings the summer before Jennings's chapel talk at Concord Academy.) Public and private school networks began to merge, as Lipkin, Parlin, and others started working with Jennings and Henderson and attending GLSEN workshops. And then GSAs, too, jumped from the private to the public school realm.

The precise strands of influence in how particular schools came to support LGBT youth are difficult to trace, and it might be splitting hairs to differentiate between Jennings's GSA at Concord Academy and Ferreira's Project 10 East at Cambridge Rindge and Latin. Still, there were different understandings of each group's mission. Some recall

Ferreira wanting to provide a safe space for LGBT students, and therefore not encouraging involvement by straight students. Ferreira himself states that the group was created to "discuss gay and lesbian civil rights" and to provide support for students "if they needed that." Further, he never asked students about their orientation, to allow them the opportunity to define themselves on their own terms and in their own time.[6] In an article published in the Cambridge school newspaper in 1992, authors Elena Kari and Jessica Byers (Byers was the student leader of Project 10 East at the time) declared that the group was "open to anyone, regardless of orientation."[7] If there is a distinction between what Ferreira created and what the CA and Andover groups had in mind, it may be that Ferreira placed greater emphasis on student support, while Jennings favored a greater degree of student activism and involvement in educating the school community as a whole.

Whatever the differences, Parlin had been familiar with Jennings's ideas from the beginning, and wanted to bring the GSA model to his high school. "I just knew, this is exactly where we need to be heading at Newton South," he recalls. However, he remembers just as clearly, "I didn't know exactly how to get there."[8] He began by joining the school's Committee on Human Differences, set up to address diversity issues. After three years of work, he "finally maneuvered them around to talking about gay issues." But after agreeing to use an upcoming meeting to do so, members of the group backtracked. One guidance counselor stated there was no need because he "never had a gay student."[9] Others, including the school principal, agreed that there was no such "problem" at Newton South. Parlin countered by coming out to the committee—an unplanned act. He told of his own experience in high school to explain the risks faced by LGBT students.[10] The committee agreed to move forward with Parlin's request to address the issue of homosexuality, and used the summer of 1991 to plan their approach. They borrowed some tactics from the Cambridge program, in that they reached out to members of the community as well as faculty within the school. And they relied on the GLSEN network for training. The principal, Ernest Van Seasholes, addressed the faculty on issues of homophobia in September, followed by an all-faculty training workshop (presented by GLSEN cochairs Henderson and Jennings); breakout faculty discussions centered on a viewing of *Who's Afraid of Project 10?*, a brief documentary about Uribe's work at Fairfax High School and other LA public schools. The school administration made a public statement in the school newspaper in December 1991 about the importance of treating all students—and especially LGBT students— with respect, and, in January 1992, the school hosted a training session for the Newton South PTSA—again conducted by Jennings.[11]

The web of educators working on LGBT support grew, and connections formed across many lines. The advisers of the Andover GSA contacted Arthur Lipkin, who spoke at the school in 1990. GLSEN brought Al Ferreira to speak at their first conference, in 1991. He recommended that it be held on Sunday, to make it easier for public school teachers to attend—many, he felt would be afraid to explain to their administrators that they were taking a day off to attend a conference on LGBT issues.[12] Attendees at the 1993 GLSEN conference (held on a Monday) included a delegation from a nearby regional public school, Concord-Carlisle, which shortly thereafter began to set up its own GSA and conduct faculty training.[13] Teachers, dormitory heads, and coaches ran most of the workshops at the 1993 conference, with one panel featuring heads of school, and a few workshops run by college professors.[14] Ideas spread, often by personal connection from teacher to teacher. Only fragmentary evidence exists for these connections: a fax containing an outline of Al Ferreira's work, sent by Andrei Joseph at Concord-Carlisle High School to a teacher in Natick;[15] a note from Joseph on a list of support services for LGBT youth, "Does this match Parlin's List?"[16] Parlin himself recalls hearing from teachers at neighboring schools, asking about how to build a similar organization.[17] At Concord-Carlisle, Andrei Joseph and Peter Atlas turned to Ann Simon at nearby Lincoln-Sudbury High School—another early public school to take up the cause—as well as to Jennings for help in building their GSA.[18] Materials developed by Uribe and Jennings were used by other schools in their faculty training.[19] Pay stubs from schools in Acton and Wayland document training sessions conducted in their districts by Ferreira.[20]

As schoolteachers and administrators worked on the ground to change their schools' cultures, the higher education community had begun to create a body of literature on the subject. University professors had credibility in the publishing market, and therefore the potential to reach a wider audience. But before the growth of the GSA movement, it was not apparent that such an audience existed. One professor remarked that her research on LGBT youth was considered a professional dead end until the 1990s. In 1991, Karen Harbeck, then working at the University of Massachusetts–Boston, edited *Coming out of the Classroom Closet*, in which she cowrote, with Uribe, an introduction to the work of Project 10. In the same volume, Harbeck offered legal support—including precedents from case law—for teachers fearful of termination in places without explicit antidiscrimination legislation.[21] Pat Griffin, an education professor at the University of Massachusetts–Amherst, whom Karen Grzesik and Polly Bixby from Mahar Regional High School credit with informing much of their work,[22] contributed a study of ways to "empower" LGBT educators at all levels.[23] In 1992, Warren Blumenfeld, who in addition to his work with the Boston Speakers Bureau taught at the University of Massachusetts as well as Illinois University, published *Homophobia: How We All Pay the Price*, which included a model for conducting teacher training at the high school level.[24] Harbeck began doing training workshops around the country with Ferreira, and, in 1994, in the *Newsletter of the National Institute for GLBT Concerns in Education* (whose board members included Ferreira, Blumenfeld, and Uribe), she contributed a significant "Legal Leverage Tip"—namely, that the 1984 federal Equal Access Act, a piece of conservative legislation designed to facilitate the formation of student-based religious groups in public schools, could be used as a lever to create Gay-Straight Alliances: "The act applies to non-curriculum related groups, such as religious prayer meetings and dare I say—BGLT/Straight Alliances! If the school permits non-curriculum related clubs to meet, then under the Equal Access Act, all other-non-curriculum-related clubs must be permitted to meet as well. In order to qualify under the act, the group must be student-initiated and student led."[25]

Her advice had little impact in Massachusetts, where GSAs were part of state education policy by 1994. But it would prove instrumental in Utah, where an attempt to start a GSA at East High School in Salt Lake City led to a district-wide ban on all student non-curricular groups in 1997.[26]

GLSEN SPREAD ITS MESSAGE through training sessions, workshops, and by developing a network of teachers to share ideas. Teachers in both public and private schools brought those ideas into their communities. Meanwhile, school administrators found themselves navigating an uncharted and potentially perilous path as they became aware of the issues facing LGBT youth. Don McNemar at Andover and Tom Wilcox at Concord Academy looked for ways to offer support within their schools and bring the issue to the attention of their peers—all while trying to defuse potential backlash and negative publicity that might harm their schools' reputations. Both were open to taking action, but both also had other, more conservative constituencies to consider— particularly trustees and alumni.

In the early days of the GSA movement, leadership at Andover seemed more supportive than at CA—perhaps because they could afford to be. Their endowment was immense, and their donor pool more secure—with extreme privilege comes great luxury. "If you're coming from strength," McNemar acknowledged with a smile, "you have more opportunity to do the right thing." Or, as Barbieri put it, "No one's going to not apply to Andover because, 'Oh my god, they have gay people.'" Further, Barbieri remembers McNemar as someone "always anxious to prove that Andover was not above the fray, was willing to be in the mix" on difficult issues.[27] McNemar wanted Andover to be a leader, to use its position to push independent schools in a particular direction. Still, to the extent that McNemar made Andover a leader in supporting LGBT students and faculty, he did so by taking cues from the school's GSA. And, in turn, he had to bring his board of trustees around on the issue. They were, or became, "supportive. But," he says, again with a smile, "it took some discussion . . . They moved a little more slowly than they might have."[28]

Wilcox was, by his own admission, slow to act, and reluctant to let CA race too far ahead of other prep schools. CA was committed to diversity and, Wilcox believed, welcoming to gay and lesbian teachers. (Its reputation as such was part of the reason Jennings left Moses Brown School in Rhode Island for CA.) Further, Wilcox recognized that CA's diversity mission included LGBT students. "I wanted CA to be a place where gay and lesbian students could feel comfortable," and he believed it was (although he now readily admits that CA was not as welcoming as he thought at the time). "But," he says, "we didn't want to be labeled as 'the gay school.'" He recalls this with evident regret, but at the time, he felt it was a label CA could not afford. "People saw us as artsy, and way out," he says now. "Which we were. But [leading on LGBT issues] took us that much further out." Yet Wilcox, despite his wish to delay Jennings's chapel talk, didn't stand in the way. "I felt that telling him he could not speak would have gone against what we stood for," he says. As for the formation of the GSA? "I saw no real issue with that."

For Wilcox, the issue that caused the most conflict was the GSA's push to add sexual orientation to CA's nondiscrimination policy. The statement, seen by the school community as a hallmark of its commitment to diversity, featured prominently in admissions materials and the course catalog. Wilcox worried that including nondiscrimination on the basis of sexual orientation—before any other prep schools did so, when only one state, Wisconsin, had such protections—carried with it implications that he needed time to work through. Jennings, however, saw changing the statement as an important expression of principle, and if CA were to be labeled "the gay school," it should be a label worn with pride. Wilcox saw the reputational impact differently. He recalls a heterosexual student who reflected on the ways that CA's support for LGBT students changed him—he had become more open and tolerant himself. But, he told Wilcox, had his parents seen any statement of support for homosexuality in the school's literature, they never would have let him apply. Wilcox sought time to build greater consensus within the CA community, and a broader coalition of schools willing to address LGBT issues together.

Wilcox and McNemar started talking to each other, looking for ways to further their efforts to support LGBT youth, but also to push other schools to do the same. Again, change in the prep school world is often accomplished through such informal conversations and meetings. A sense of collegiality pervades; headmasters are, to some degree, rivals and competitors for the same pool of students and donations—which also breeds a sense of closeness. Few others understand the difficulty of the job and the pressures they face. While Wilcox recalls that some school heads "thought I was out of my mind" for offering such public support for LGBT students and teachers, he and McNemar were able to bring a few others along—slowly. Just as McNemar and Wilcox had needed an education on LGBT issues, they in turn needed to educate their peers. In 1992, at an annual meeting of the heads of school and chairs of boards of trustees for the most selective schools—a G20 for the prep school world—a board chairman remarked to McNemar that there were no gay issues at *his* school. McNemar recalls with some pride that his own board chair, David Underwood, jumped into the conversation, pointing out it was an issue at every school, whether people realized it or not. Wilcox, meanwhile, hosted the first-ever GLSEN conference at CA—and also expressed his hope that CA would not need to host again for a number of years, because other schools would step up and welcome GLSEN to their campuses. It was in this fashion, "encouragement and gentle criticism,"[29] that private schools moved haltingly to support LGBT students and faculty.

BOTH WITHIN THE private and public school universes, the way in which schools began to support LGBT youth represents an inversion of the traditional model of education reform. Typically, the thinking goes, initiatives begin at the top, and much is made of the need to achieve teacher buy-in if implementation is to be successful. However, the GSA movement began with students and teachers, who then worked to get their administrators to buy in. It is likely that school-based support for LGBT students was inevitable in some form and in some areas, but the movement began with the vision of individual teachers and students, who then persuaded school leadership to work with them. Heads of school who previously had evinced no interest in addressing the problem, and had taken considerable pain to avoid such controversies, began, with varying degrees of enthusiasm, to support the budding GSAs, and to provide them with space to continue their work.

How did teachers and students achieve buy-in? It is risky to draw any broad conclusions based on such a small sample size—individual personalities played a large role in how events unfolded at each school. At Concord Academy, Jennings took a more confrontational approach, as did Arthur Lipkin at Cambridge Rindge and Latin—although they both began with multiple efforts to nudge their administrators more gently. At Phillips Andover, students and teachers took a more understated approach, though they did not seek approval from the administration. But when they did approach the head of school, they found in McNemar something of an ally. Speaking some years after the formation of the Andover GSA, Bonney-Smith described him as "a fair and honorable man . . . he knew what was right, and was supportive."[30] Parlin, meanwhile, took a relatively patient approach, working within the established committee structure at Newton South for several years, eventually convincing others—including his principal—that the problems facing LGBT students required their intervention.

Could administrators have stopped the process if they wanted to? At public schools, the answer is, at least in theory, no. As Harbeck pointed out, schools were required to support all extracurricular groups equally, as long as they were student initiated and student led. However, Harbeck did not lay out her legal argument until 1994, and no one else had thought to apply the law in that manner earlier. Perhaps, in 1991, an administrator (and it is worth noting, a superintendent or school committee could have overridden a principal's decision) at Newton South or Cambridge could have tried to stop the movement before it gained momentum. At private schools, the reaction of their respective communities to Jennings's chapel talk and to the *Exonian* parody suggests that leadership at CA and Andover would have been hard-pressed to put an end to the movement, even if they had wanted to. Those wishing to stem the tide of campus activism and push homosexuality back underground were, it seems, out of touch with the community zeitgeist. Perhaps school leadership sensed this. For the most part, administrators did not try to halt the process; on the contrary, they worked closely with their teachers—relying on them in many cases—to further their schools' efforts.

The relationship between Wilcox and Jennings at Concord Academy was especially complex. Jennings clearly viewed Wilcox as someone determined to put up roadblocks, and he may have been correct. But there was a personality conflict as well. Jennings is by nature an activist and an organizer, and favors a direct approach. Boarding schools, on the other hand, seek to build loyalty, community, and consensus among faculty and staff. Their culture favors an approach to disagreement in which discussion and dialogue precede conciliation and resolution, or at the very least, a papering over of differences. If confrontation is unavoidable, it occurs behind closed doors. In the end, if differences prove irreconcilable, the problem is viewed as one of "fit"; perhaps, it is suggested, the unhappy party would be better off elsewhere. This approach is not universal, nor is it unique to boarding schools, but in a market where schools seek to exude tranquility and familial collegiality, a public airing of differences is frowned upon. Wilcox, well steeped in this culture, sought more conversation on the issue of the nondiscrimination statement, more time to bring the board of trustees around, and more space think through possible implications. Jennings and the GSA issued an ultimatum with a deadline, after which they would organize protests and class boycotts. As it happened, Wilcox was away from school, attending to a serious family matter, when the ultimatum was issued. He asked Jennings to wait until he returned and they could discuss the language of the statement. His request was ignored—a breach, Wilcox felt, of the communal norms he believed were important at a school like CA.

To Wilcox, Jennings's approach seemed unnecessarily provocative, designed to grab attention rather than resolve differences—which, Wilcox felt, risked harming the school. Wilcox wrote a brief introduction to an issue of the newsletter *Speaking Out: A Forum for Sexual Minority Issues in the Boarding School Community*, which contained a thinly veiled—transparent, really—criticism of Jennings's tactics:

Schools never pay in the long run for doing the right thing. Supporting students and faculty in their decisions to come out, and providing support vehicles necessary to their thriving in our school communities as gay, lesbian, bisexual, or unsure people clearly seems like the right thing to do . . . even if we incur short term giving losses due to the sensitivity of issues of sexuality. A greater number of donors and potential donors give to Concord Academy now and will give to us in the years ahead precisely because we are doing the right thing. Families come to and will come to our admissions office on the same premise.

It does hurt schools, on the other hand, if students and faculty become so excited about a militant agenda that they publicly challenge the school to engage in a series of practices that are only marginally related to the student and faculty experience.[31]

Jennings characterized Wilcox as overly intent on "building up the lacrosse team,"[32] of catering to a more traditional faction of the boarding school population. Wilcox felt that Jennings was using CA as a platform for a larger purpose.[33] Both impressions contain a grain of truth—Jennings left CA in 1995 to establish GLSEN as a private, nonprofit advocacy group, and Wilcox did endeavor to improve what he saw as CA's woefully substandard athletic facilities—but both are grounded in an apparent lack of trust between the two. Wilcox sought dialogue and consensus, and more gradual changes. Jennings was less patient, and viewed Wilcox's reluctance as an abandonment of students at risk. Despite their differences, Wilcox did position CA as a leader on LGBT issues among independent schools—even if it took a push from Jennings for him to step forward.

LOOKING BACK from a distance of nearly thirty years, Wilcox recognizes, "We learned so much." The question of how teachers and students achieved administrative buy-in does not lend itself to a simple answer, but the process was, in the best sense of the term, an education—in both directions. Administrators did need to learn about the plight of their LGBT students. In many cases, teachers and students were pleasantly surprised by their administrators' reaction, and came to view their bosses in a more charitable light. At Concord-Carlisle High School, teachers attempting to build supports for LGBT students recall many discussions about how to "neutralize" their principal, Elaine DiCicco. In the margin of the agenda for an early organizing meeting is scrawled a simple note: "Must deal with Elaine."[34] Yet only months later, the organizers wrote to DiCicco to thank her for her "sensitivity and exemplary bravery" in supporting their efforts to address LGBT issues.[35] At Newton South, it took Parlin three years to bring up his desire to start a GSA; yet he and others would soon laud principal Ernest Van Seasholes as a champion of LGBT issues, a man willing to advocate on their behalf with parent groups and the school committee.

The process of education continued, again flowing in many directions. McNemar recalls being particularly affected by a story related to him by a gay alum who, in the first week of his first year at Andover, heard an upperclassman in his dorm call another student a fag, while the faculty dorm parent did nothing. "At that moment," he related to McNemar, "I knew Andover was not a place I could truly be myself."[36] As alumni educated McNemar, he in turn sought to educate other, more conservative alumni. As word of Andover's support for gay and lesbian students leaked out, a particularly vocal claque of alums from the 1930s demanded a meeting to discuss what was, in their minds, a perversion of the Andover education. McNemar brought students and advisers from the GSA to the meeting, and let them do most of the talking. By the end, one of the older alums broke down in tears, unable to bear the thought that if his grandson were gay, he too would feel unwelcome and alienated from family and school.[37]

While administrators played a key role in supporting the GSA movement, they did have to be prodded. They had no true personal skin in the game, though one might wonder why gay administrators were not at the forefront of the movement. Certainly school leaders were pressured on all sides. Navigating the fears of the parent community and the attitudes of more conservative trustee boards was a delicate task—and the heads of school all received their share of irate letters and phone calls. But the pockets of resistance were surprisingly small, and the issue turned out to be less incendiary than anyone had imagined. There is a sense that administrators' fears were misplaced, that—at least in one segment of American society—this issue's moment had arrived. Still, schools had to move carefully. After Andover added sexual orientation to its nondiscrimination statement, and extended health care and retirement benefits to same-sex partners of faculty, Underwood, the chair of the board of trustees, stated that the school had "done enough for the present" and would take "a wait-and-see attitude before taking any further steps," to see whether other schools would follow suit.

With hindsight, heads of school largely recognize their own shortcomings on the issue. Even if, as Bonney-Smith avers, McNemar was an honorable man and knew what was right, he admits LGBT youth were not on his radar screen at all, and he left it to others to initiate any steps to support them. Similarly, Newton South principal Ernest Van Seasholes told Parlin that one of his greatest regrets was not having done more sooner for LGBT students.[38] Even Wilcox, who had perhaps the rockiest relationship with his teacher/activist employee, frankly admitted, "The world is a much better place for what Kevin has done."[39]

In a relatively short time, an issue that could not be talked about openly, that teachers could address only in oblique or camouflaged ways, had sprung into the light. Those who had sought small ways to support students, and those who had felt powerless as individuals, found themselves part of a larger movement. GSAs and other groups had demonstrable political power—they could bring change to school policy and culture in ways that individuals could not. Activism to address risks facing the high school LGBT community required an organizing force to direct the impulses that already existed among students and teachers—just as early LGBT activism in the United States required someone like Harry Hay and the founders of the Mattachine Society to begin the movement for gay rights. No doubt, in the generations prior to the formation of GSAs, students and teachers had often discussed the need to do something to improve conditions in schools—conversations that no doubt echoed Chuck Rowland's recollection of gay society pre-Mattachine, of gay men and women in the 1920s and 1930s, sitting in a bar somewhere, discussing hopes and dreams of a better future, saying to each other with a tinge of sadness, "we should get together and have a gay organization."[40] The Chi-Chi's group at Cambridge Rindge and Latin had many such discussions. Certainly the earliest high school GSAs, in New York City in the 1970s, are another expression of similar ideas that did not quite take off. And at Andover, there were whispers of an underground support group of gay students from before the advent of Tentarelli's GSA.

But getting from talk to action is difficult. Nationwide activism through the '50s, '60s, and '70s changed the environment in which schools operated, as did particular activism around Anita Bryant's Save Our Children crusade and the Briggs Initiative in California. While younger teachers and students in the 1980s grew up with a more activist mentality, forming an open, organized group still meant assuming significant personal risk. But once such groups existed, they lessened the risk for others. They provided not only a safe place where students and teachers could find support, but also means of acting without necessarily sticking one's own neck out—or at least, having one's neck be only one target among many. And as the early groups flourished, they showed other schools what was possible, and made the path easier at more conservative places with more risk-averse leadership.

The movement spread, faster than expected, and with less controversy than anticipated. Those responsible for the creation of the first supports for LGBT students won converts at all levels in many schools. Of course, a movement consisting of elite prep schools and affluent suburban public schools can hardly be considered widespread. Further progress would require winning over politicians and policy makers of all stripes, and prodding the institutional educational bureaucracy into action. By themselves, teachers could not do so. But in the early 1990s, political activists tapped into the energy of the LGBT movement in schools, and commenced changing statewide policy in Massachusetts.

Promises, Promises

THE MOVEMENT GOES POLITICAL

I'll be there for you.
>—William Weld, to members of the Gay
>Political Caucus, in advance of the 1990
>Massachusetts gubernatorial election

Do something for these kids.
>—David LaFontaine, lobbying coordinator
>for the caucus

EVERY I. I SECONDS a teen-ager tries to commit suicide,"[1] declared
the *New York Times* in an April 1987 article on suicide pacts and
suicide clusters. *Time, Newsweek, People,* and *Rolling Stone* ran
similar feature-length stories, most of them deep dives into the lives of
disaffected youth. Filmmakers also addressed (or exploited) the issue;
three made-for-TV movies were released in 1984 alone. The *Times* ran
through a laundry list of possible explanations for the spike in teen
suicide: "Easy access to instruments of death, such as drugs and guns
. . . faster-paced lives, the decline of organized religion," the fact that
"for many teen-agers a traditional family structure no longer exists."
Some, the *Times* noted, even blamed the new high-tech "playthings of
the 1980s: personal computers, VCR's, and stereos." "Perhaps the move
to a technocratic society and its inherent insensitivities to human emo-
tion have caused an increased sense of hopelessness," posited a trio of
researchers. Lacking any truly satisfying explanation, the article asked,
"Has self-destruction become the response to pressures that teen-agers
of every generation have faced?"

Others saw more sinister forces behind the frightening trend. In the 1982 blockbuster *E.T.*, the film's hero, Eliot, plays a role-playing game like Dungeon & Dragons to signify his status as a harmless, nerdy homebody. Shortly thereafter, though, the parents of a teen suicide in suburban Virginia filed a lawsuit against the makers of D&D, alleging that the game had caused their son "extreme psychological stress and emotional pressure." Their son's suicide, they claimed, was the direct result of a "curse" placed upon him by another player, "intended to inflict emotional distress."[1] The suit was dismissed, but its effect was such that a neighboring school district banned the game.[2] The teen's mother, Patricia Pulling, went on to establish Bothered About Dungeons and Dragons, an advocacy group devoted to the regulation of role-playing games, which maintained that games such as D&D encouraged "demonology, witchcraft, voodoo, murder, rape, blasphemy, suicide, assassination, insanity, sex perversion, homosexuality, prostitution, satanic type rituals, gambling, barbarism, cannibalism, sadism, desecration, demon summoning, necromantics, divination and other teachings."[3]

Rock music became another scapegoat. In two separate incidents, in 1985 and 1986, the parents of teenage suicides filed suit against Ozzy Osbourne, blaming the lyrics of "Suicide Solution," a song about alcoholism, for their sons' deaths. Noting that freedom of expression is protected by the constitution, courts dismissed both suits. But in 1990, the heavy metal band Judas Priest faced a similar lawsuit over a suicide pact by two of its fans. In a legal twist, the plaintiffs argued that the album contained subliminal messages, which could not be considered protected speech—they were "non-decipherable sounds below the conscious threshold of awareness" and therefore "not protected by the First Amendment." Further, the claimants alleged that "the band's 'cult-following,' suggestive artwork and hypnotic beat of the music aided in leading the young men to follow the 'commands' of the band." Judas Priest manager Bill Curbishley dismissed the claim as absurd. Why, he asked, would any band that makes its living on album and ticket sales encourage loyal fans to kill themselves? "I don't know what subliminals are, but I do know there's nothing like that in this music," he insisted. "If we were going to do that, I'd be saying, 'Buy seven copies.'"[4]

THE UPTICK IN SUICIDE RATES among teens (and media coverage of it) also led to a government response. The first congressional hearings were held in 1983, with the first bills introduced in 1984. As with much that Congress does, these efforts can be seen as a mix of politics, publicity seeking, and sincere efforts to address the problem. By 1985 President Reagan got involved as well. "Suicide is no longer a silent subject, but a recognized public health problem that can and must be addressed," he declared in a resolution designating June 1985 as "National Youth Suicide Prevention Month."[5] He also directed his secretary of health and human services, Margaret Heckler, to create a task force to address the issue. The Secretary's Task Force on Youth Suicide first met in 1985, convened three separate conferences on the subject, commissioned dozens of research programs, and published its four-volume report in 1989.

The Report of the Secretary's Task Force on Youth Suicide, issued in the first year of the George H. W. Bush administration, under the aegis of new HHS secretary Louis Sullivan, garnered relatively little attention on its release, and its general conclusions and recommendations were largely forgotten shortly thereafter. Still, it was a watershed publication, though perhaps not in the way originally envisioned. In the overview, amid a laundry list of factors that increased the risk of youth suicide, the authors inserted a single-word bullet point:

- Homosexuality.

Further elaboration came in the third volume of the report, in a chapter titled "Gay Male and Lesbian Youth Suicide," by Paul Gibson, a San Francisco–area social worker. He noted many of the health and safety risks faced by LGBT teens—familiar ground for those working with gay youth, but unprecedented for a government publication: "Many families are unable to reconcile their child's sexual identity with moral and religious values . . . gay and lesbian youth reported a higher incidence

of verbal and physical abuse from parents and siblings than other youth
. . . 45% of gay males and nearly 20% of lesbians had experienced verbal or physical assault in secondary schools. The shame of ridicule and
fear of attack makes school a fearful place to go."[6]

Two sentences in Gibson's chapter received the most attention:
"Gay youth are 2 to 3 times more likely to attempt suicide than other
young people. They may comprise up to 30% of completed youth suicides annually."[7]

Gibson targeted the educational system directly in his recommendations for addressing these risks: "Schools need to take responsibility for providing all students at the junior high and high school level
with positive information about homosexuality. Curriculum materials should include information relevant to gay males and lesbians
. . . a variety of gay male and lesbian adult lifestyles should be presented as positive and viable for youth . . . it is important for schools
to hire openly gay male and lesbian teachers to serve as role models."[8]
Schools, he concluded, had to create a safer and more supportive climate for LGBT youth:

> Schools need to take responsibility for protecting gay and lesbian
> youth from abuse and providing them with a safe environment . . .
> staff need to receive training on how to work with gay youth and
> handle conflicts involving gay youth. Teachers should feel secure
> in being able to defend gay youth against harassment . . . Coun-
> seling services that are sensitive to the needs and concerns of gay
> youth should be available to them. Special educational programs
> may need to be developed for those youth who cannot be incorpo-
> rated into existing school settings.[9]

Conservative politicians, ever attuned to the insidious creep of what
they termed the militant homosexual agenda, recognized the threat
contained in Gibson's chapter, and made a concerted effort to block
its inclusion in the final report. California congressman William
Dannemeyer presented newly appointed HHS secretary Sullivan with
a letter signed by thirty-seven Republican congressmen, demanding

that Gibson's chapter be removed or denounced for failing to affirm "traditional family values." Sullivan insisted that the report's views "do not in any way represent my personal beliefs or the policy of this department," and, noting it was written prior to his tenure, stated, "I neither endorse nor approve the report from the Task Force on Youth Suicide." However, in response to complaints by the National Gay and Lesbian Task Force about Sullivan's comments, a spokesperson for the department of Health and Human Services stated, "We are taking the recommendations of the task force to heart," and offered reassurances that, despite Sullivan's response to Dannemeyer, HHS had not rejected the report's "overall recommendations."[10] Since Gibson's recommendations were included only in the chapter on gay and lesbian youth suicide, and were not part of the report's overall recommendations, this statement was factually correct. On the issue of whether Dannemeyer pressured HHS into burying the report or curtailing its distribution, the spokesperson stated, "I am not aware of any effort not to distribute it." Sullivan's office also wrote back to Dannemeyer regarding his request to limit distribution of the report: "The department printed 2,000 copies of the report and has no plans to reprint. Distribution by the department of the complete report was, therefore, limited."[11]

Limited in its distribution or not, *The Report of the Secretary's Task Force on Youth Suicide* became a powerful tool for those working with LGBT youth. Gibson's argument was not new. Virginia Uribe had used much the same reasoning in 1984 to defend Project 10, and Dr. Gary Remafedi had done clinical research on suicide rates among gay and lesbian youth in the 1970s (which Gibson used to inform his report). While these lonely voices could be safely ignored by mainstream Americans, particularly those in positions of authority, the HHS report was another matter. In the words of one early activist, "It was the federal government. They [those who rejected the notion that the problem existed] couldn't pooh-pooh it."[12] To this day, Gibson's data on increased suicide risk for LGBT youth is still the most widely cited justification for in-school programs like GSAs.

Although conservatives disputed the data—and still do—counter-claims have failed to gain traction. This is partly because so much research now supports Gibson's original findings, partly because that number—homosexual teens are two to three times as likely than their heterosexual counterparts to attempt suicide—is such a simple and stark encapsulation of the problem, and partly because it fits a narrative that both sides already believed to be true. Even without statistical evidence, homosexual men and women were well aware of the elevated risks; many had experienced firsthand the pain of losing friends and loved ones to suicide. On the other hand, conservatives themselves had noted the greater likelihood of suicide among homosexuals, arguing that dissolute, perverted lifestyles led homosexuals and other deviants to seek an early death.[13] Eric Rofes, the gay teacher and writer, even spoofed this perspective in the title of one of his books, *I Thought People Like That Killed Themselves.*

For opponents of gay rights, the report represented the opening of a new front in their battle—and it placed them at a decided disadvantage. Conservatives had seized on the youth suicide issue, had blamed nefarious games and rock music, the general decline in traditional family structure, and the liberalization, secularization, and sexualization of American culture. At first blush the so-called suicide epidemic offered yet another opportunity to position themselves as saviors of American youth, crusaders in a campaign against the amoral, antireligious element in society that had run roughshod over traditional values throughout the '60s and '70s. Yet here, in a government report, were recommendations that the very institutions tasked with instilling those values, the schools, be used to underwrite a homosexual agenda—and do so in the name of protecting children from harm. Child safety had always been justification for purging homosexuals from schools. The report charged schools with ensuring the safety of homosexual children. How could one argue against protecting children? Or, as one LGBT activist put it, "Who could be for suicide?"[14]

Indeed, activists like Kevin Jennings came to credit the potency of this argument with much of their political success as they tried to expand the GSA movement statewide. "The effective reframing of this issue was the key to the success of the Governor's Commission on Gay and Lesbian Youth. We immediately seized upon the opponent's calling card—safety—and explained how homophobia represents a threat to students' safety by creating a climate where violence, name-calling, health problems, and suicide are common."[15]

Peter Atlas, who taught at Concord-Carlisle High School, notes, "When we talked about rights, that didn't go anywhere. But when we talked about kids' safety—well, who could be against that?"[16] Further, in the minutes of a 1992 Massachusetts Teachers Association conference organized by the teachers on the MTA Human Relations Council, "Affording Equal Educational Opportunity to Gay and Lesbian and Bisexual Students," under the question "What to Do?" teachers listed "Define the issue as *saving lives*" as the most effective way to build support.[17]

FOR ALL ITS EVENTUAL IMPACT on the debate, the HHS report did not by itself bring about any immediate, meaningful change for gay youth. Nor was it certain that it would. For activists, weaponizing the report required the right state—Massachusetts—but not for the reasons one might expect. It required the right political opportunity—in this case, a tight gubernatorial campaign—and a shrewd grassroots political strategy in bringing legislators around on the issue. But most of all, it required a ready-to-mobilize army to put a human face to the political fight: the students in the first GSAs at schools around the state, and the teachers who formed the leadership core of GLSEN. Together, circumstances conspired to make what had previously been a political dogfight—one that invited the worst kind of demagoguery and hate mongering—into an overwhelming political victory in which opponents of gay rights were rendered very nearly mute.

Massachusetts is rightly characterized as a liberal bastion, and at first glance, it does not seem surprising that the state led the charge in enacting laws and creating policy to support and protect LGBT youth in schools. However, progressivism in the Bay State is balanced by a conservative streak that dates back to its Puritan founders. Nineteenth-century abolitionists and suffragists found strong, early supporters in Massachusetts, but so too did the temperance movement. And as late as the 1930s, the New England Watch and Ward Society, founded in

1878 to root out a number of perceived societal ills—to watch and ward off evildoers—continued to hold such sway over what could and could not be published in the state that "Banned in Boston" became an honor badge that publishers affixed to books to increase sales in other cities.

Further, the state Democratic Party was built on a foundation of working-class Irish and Italian immigrants. Democratic? Yes. Liberal and progressive? Not always. The party consists of two wings, what one writer called "the older, pork-chop, brass-collar Democrats" and the liberal "intellectual wing . . . fascinated by lifestyles and experimental programs, often suburban and privileged."[18] While this intellectual, liberal wing clearly holds sway currently, it was not always so; in Massachusetts history, examples abound of the power of the socially conservative Democratic coalition. The clashes in the 1970s over school desegregation and busing in Boston were some of the most violent outside the South. The only female Democrat from Massachusetts elected to the U.S. Congress before the twenty-first century was Louise Day Hicks, an unabashed racist (or at least a craven opportunist) whose campaigns centered on her opposition to school desegregation and her stated belief that women like her could "no longer walk the streets in safety."[19] (The Republican Party, meanwhile, also had exactly one congresswoman in the twentieth century: Margaret Heckler served in Congress from 1967 to 1983, when President Reagan appointed her secretary of health and human services. It was she who commissioned the 1989 HHS report on youth suicide.) And antisodomy laws remained on the books in Massachusetts into the twenty-first century.

Because of the tension between its progressive and conservative wings, the Massachusetts Democratic Party often tried to downplay social issues. Institutionally, it was not equipped to lead on LGBT rights. Moreover, an economic downturn and a billion-dollar budget deficit put the progressives and their two-term governor (and failed presidential candidate) Michael Dukakis on the defensive going into the 1990 gubernatorial campaign. The pork-chop wing rose up and nominated Boston University president John Silber for governor. Despite his outsider status and impressive academic credentials—born and raised in Texas, he was a philosophy professor by training—the dour, acerbic Silber's rhetoric resonated with socially conservative Democrats. When asked at a primary debate about campaigning in Boston's predominantly African American neighborhoods of Roxbury, Mattapan, and Dorchester, Silber replied, "There is no point in my making a speech on crime control to a bunch of drug addicts."[20] Ben Bradlee Jr., then politics editor at the *Boston Globe*, called Silber "Archie Bunker with a Ph.D.,"[21] and *Globe* columnist Curtis Willkie labeled him "the sternest public figure in Massachusetts since Cotton Mather."[22]

Meanwhile, the Republican Party turned to a man whose family landed in Massachusetts well before Cotton Mather began the first great witch hunt in American history. William Weld went from Middlesex School to Harvard (the nineteenth Weld to attend), then to Oxford, and back to Harvard for law school. After a career as a federal prosecutor and in private practice, he turned his attention to the governor's office. In terms of temperament, he was Silber's opposite: effortlessly charming, comfortable and self-possessed in any setting, affable and insouciant. Intellectually, they were rare equals—Weld was a summa cum laude graduate in classics. He embodied the laissez-faire philosophy of the now largely extinct northeastern Republican ruling class. Limited, pro-business government was one of its pillars; the other was a very WASP-ish insistence on privacy and discretion in personal matters. That these Brahmins (Weld's family among them) also formed the backbone of the Watch and Ward Society in the nineteenth and early twentieth century is not as contrary to their values as it may seem; in their minds, it was possible both to limit the dissemination and influence of corrupting, immoral ideas, and allow one's private life to remain private.

Economic and fiscal issues loomed large in the campaign, but neither candidate could gain an edge with his respective platform. This should have given Silber a decided advantage, as historically the Democratic Party dominated Massachusetts politics. However, the decisive issues, the ones that could peel off enough voters on the margins to flip a close election, were personal and social—Weld's strengths. In contrast, Silber couldn't keep himself from antagonizing core Democratic constituencies. After alienating voters in minority communities, he took aim at another traditionally pro-Democratic bloc. In what was supposed to a be a puff-piece television interview, the type of sit-down designed to soften a candidate's image, Silber argued that working women neglected child-rearing duties. "There is no question," he stated, "that we have a generation of neglected children, we have a generation of abused children, by women who have thought that a third-rate day care center was just as good as a first-rate home." He further contended that feminism "denigrated" women who "decided to take their maternal responsibilities seriously."[23]

He also shunned the burgeoning gay rights movement, a group that had, since the Anita Bryant crusade, grown more and more politically cohesive and influential. In Massachusetts, the Coalition for Gay and Lesbian Civil Rights began submitting questionnaires to candidates for office beginning in the 1980s. They focused primarily on adoption and same-sex partner benefits, although the coalition also asked Boston school committee candidates about including positive LGBT role models in schools and AIDS education. During the 1990 campaign, the coalition requested a meeting with each candidate. Silber declined his invitation; Weld and his running mate, Paul Cellucci, happily accepted. While accounts of the meeting differ, it is clear Weld made a positive impression on coalition members. Asked about appointing high-level gay and lesbian staff, Weld replied, "No quotas, but no problem." Regarding how he would respond to incidents of gay-bashing, he said simply, "I'll be there for you."[24] "We started this process first being frightened by John Silber," gay activist and Democratic Party operative Andrew McCarthy acknowledged just before Election Day. "But we have found we truly like Bill Weld and Paul Cellucci. We trust them. We know they have compassion."[25]

The reactions of members of the coalition who met with Weld suggest that his responses to their questions were not the only reason he earned their support. His comfort in their presence and his seemingly uncalculated responses were partly the attributes of a consummate politician, and partly a reflection of his own deeply held personal convictions. One of his best friends, Mitchell Adams, with whom he roomed both at Harvard and after, was gay, and finally came out after they had been living together for a while. "He could never ever understand why or how anyone could care that I was gay . . . And he could never understand how it was anyone else's business but my own," Adams said of Weld.[26] Adams, an important fund-raiser for the campaign, would go on to marry Weld's chief of staff, Kevin Smith—little wonder that Weld could say that high-level homosexual appointees would be "no problem."

Silber's personal history is more complicated. His son David was gay, and died of AIDS-related complications in 1994. Silber spent countless hours caring for David as his health worsened. Though rumors swirled in the Massachusetts press that Silber had long ago disowned his son, David's last months were spent in his parents' Brookline home, in the company of his longtime partner, Marc Brody. Yet Silber also characterized homosexuality as "non-normative behavior," and, throughout his tenure at Boston University, he refused to add sexual orientation to the school's nondiscrimination policy.[27] Why this animus toward gay rights? Perhaps his general distaste for what he termed identity politics led him simply to avoid engaging with gay rights activists. Or perhaps he felt he could not afford to offend the conservative Democrats who carried him to the nomination in the first place.

In the end, it also appears he could not avoid conflating in his own mind the quest for gay rights with gay sex: in 2002, as interim chancellor of Boston University, one of his first acts was to disband the GSA at the university's high school affiliate, BU Academy. "We're not running a program in sex education," he declared. "If kids want that kind of program, they can go to public school and learn to put a condom over a banana. The last thing we want to do is introduce these kids to the importance of premature sex."[28]

It would be facile to argue that the gay vote alone swung the election to Weld; any number of equally significant voting blocs could claim responsibility. Weld certainly targeted the liberal vote. Speaking at an old abolitionist meeting hall in Boston, touting his ancestors' abolitionist cred, Weld extended a hand to the voters Silber had alien-ated: "When it comes to divisiveness . . . when it comes to setting groups against groups . . . when it comes to women and minorities being second-class citizens . . . when it comes to homophobia, when it comes to negative attitudes and thinly veiled hatreds of this sort, I'm going to be an abolitionist," he stated.[29] And as David LaFontaine, lobbying coordinator for the Gay Political Caucus, noted, "If we elect Bill Weld, we'll defeat the right wing in both parties with one brilliant stroke." Silber's campaign dismissed these efforts, arguing that liberal Democrats would "come home" by Election Day.[30] This prediction proved mostly correct: 58 percent of non-gay voters who self-identified as liberal voted for Silber. However, the efforts of LaFontaine and the caucus delivered the gay vote: of self-identified gay voters, 77 percent voted for Weld and only 16 percent for Silber; meanwhile, 74 percent of gay voters backed Democratic Senate candidate John Kerry.[31] It was, overall, an odd election: one-third of registered Democrats voted for Weld, while one-fourth of registered Republicans voted for Silber.[32]

It is true that Weld's actions bear the mark of political opportun-ism, but it is more accurate to say that the Republican's personal incli-nation toward social libertarianism made for good politics against a conservative Democratic opponent who was vulnerable on social issues. Rather than placing that part of his personal conviction in a lockbox throughout the campaign, Weld played it to great advantage. Had his appeal to LGBT voters merely been opportunism, surely Weld would not have expended much effort after the election to see that his promises were fulfilled. Although his legislative priorities lay else-where, Weld did use his executive powers to address gay rights. He appointed Mike Duffy, an openly gay Republican, to head the Mas-sachusetts Commission Against Discrimination. He named Mitch Adams revenue commissioner. According to Weld's adviser Marty Linksy, "We got needled a lot for being so gay-friendly." Still, Linksy says, "For Weld, the issue was a no-brainer—he was surprised at how big a deal it was. I don't think he was sensitive to how dramatic a change it was for some people."[33]

Most significantly, LaFontaine, who helped deliver the gay vote, gained the ear of the new governor, and made one request. He showed Weld a copy of the 1989 HHS report, and said simply, "Do something to help these kids."[34] Weld first sought to work through the Democratic-controlled legislature to create a commission to address the problems facing LGBT youth. But he was not about to battle the Senate over gay rights; a major fight over the state budget loomed in the coming legislative session. According to Linsky, the LGBT issue had "our interest and support, but not a lot of political capital."[35] But Weld still sought to fulfill LaFontaine's request. He created the Governor's Commission on Gay and Lesbian Youth by executive order, and named LaFontaine its chair. He went out of his way to publicize the creation of the commission, and posed with LaFontaine and several gay students for a photo op. He cited the alarming suicide statistic from the HHS report, and noted the prevalence of homelessness among gay youth. LaFontaine, for his part, stated that Weld stands "peerless as the most pro-gay governor . . . in the United States."[36] And Weld personally attended the swearing-in ceremony for the first commission, again referencing the staggering suicide and homelessness rates among gay teens. "We need to abolish the prejudice and isolation faced by gay and lesbian youth," he declared. "We need to help them stay in school so they can have healthy and productive lives."[37]

And just like that, advocates for gay youth had the imprimatur of the governor. Less than a generation earlier, they were ignored, dismissed, or threatened; most often, they worked in the shadows and actively avoided attracting too much attention. In a few cases, they had timidly sought approval from school administrators for their work; on very rare occasions, they risked open confrontation—and typically lost their jobs as a result. Only fifteen years earlier, Anita Bryant's Save Our Children campaign painted them as unwholesome and un-American, a cancer to be excised from society. Now they had an official, state-sanctioned commission—a real effort to save the children. However, its formation came with no guarantees. While the commission represented an unprecedented opportunity to affect state policy, it was clear that the governor's office—despite its belief in the basic goodness of their mission—was not going to go to bat for them in the statehouse. Weld still needed to hoard his political capital. According to Linsky, there would be "close to zero lobbying [of the state legislature] from our end."[38]

The risks for the commission were enormous. For good reason, the gay rights movement had been wary of addressing the problems of gay youth—the predatory stereotype was still present in most Americans' minds. Further, no politician at the state level—and certainly no Republican—had ever been so visible an advocate for gay rights. If the commission failed to produce a positive result, if public opinion came down on the other side, surely Governor Weld would be the last politician (at least for some time) to stand with them. Finally, it was possible that the commission would prove irrelevant: it could make its report, be thanked for its efforts, and ushered offstage—with no substantive results to show. The halls of government are littered with the carcasses of commissions and committees that had no perceptible effect on the communities they purported to serve. The gay rights movement had achieved a remarkable success. They had a heterosexual Republican governor advocating for them, and straight politicians talking about protecting homosexual children—not from homosexuals, but from the abuse they suffered at the hands of straight society. But that success also laid a potential trap—greater attention meant greater scrutiny, which meant that the work of the commission would have to proceed very carefully.

An Enormous Pressure to Succeed

FROM PROMISES, PROMISES TO A STATEWIDE POLICY

Teachers will be forced to teach about the homosexual lifestyle as normal and natural, which it is not.

—Nancy Sutton, executive director of Family First

We never thought of a gay person as an equal, lovable, and valuable part of God's creation. What a travesty of God's unconditional love. Had I viewed my son's life with a pure heart, I would have recognized him as a tender spirit in God's eyes.

—Testimony from Dorothy Remur, whose son committed suicide

THE WORK OF THE Governor's Commission was fraught with risk—of failure, of provoking a backlash, of irrelevance. But it also offered a great opportunity. On the one hand, the commission's task was simple—do something for lesbian and gay kids. The surface issue was clear, and the statistics made an irrefutable case for action: suicide rates were three times the national average, 28 percent of gay and lesbian youth dropped out of high school, and 26 percent were forced to leave home—"pushaways" or "throwaways" rather than runaways.[1] Never before had any state government made such a show of helping gay youth; activists usually shunted to the fringes felt they had a real chance to use the power of the state to make a significant difference for LGBT youth.

The commission also represented an unprecedented opening, a political moment. Its work could fundamentally alter the relationship between gay and straight society. To the extent that there is a single school system, it is the most far-reaching institution in American society. Nearly every child goes through it—roughly 90 percent of school-age children attend public schools. Parents, even grandparents, are connected to it. The commission represented an opportunity to do much more than support gay youth, to do more even than furthering the quest for equal rights. Many straight Americans had come around to the idea that gay adults had a right to equal treatment—if they kept to themselves and did not flaunt their gayness. As long as such a mentality prevailed, gay students could be consigned to a separate existence as well. Schools such as the Harvey Milk School, in New York, established specifically for LGBT dropouts, might have served as a model for educating those who could not make it in regular schools. But the commission instead proposed that all schools should support openly LGBT students and teachers. If schools did so, they would force something much different from acceptance of homosexuality by straight society; they would force interaction between gay and straight students and faculty. Heterosexuals would no longer be able to pretend homosexuality existed only elsewhere. LGBT life would become part of everyone's life.

If the commission succeeded. On one level, writing the report would be a straightforward exercise. From the moment LaFontaine approached Ferreira and Jennings to cochair the commission's education committee, its direction was clear; one suspects that much of it could have been written on the day of the swearing-in. At issue was the how, not the what: how to build such a compelling case for action that the majority of the public, their elected representatives, and bureaucrats who created and implemented educational policy could not help but support their efforts. For most Americans, this idea, that public schools should not only support LGBT students but help normalize homosexuality, was utterly radical. The goal of the commission was to flip prevailing attitudes so that the radical became mainstream, and the established orthodoxy—that homosexuality should be kept out of the schools—became extreme. To do so, the commission had to create among institutional actors—politicians, policy makers, administrators, and teachers—the will to change the way schools taught about homosexuality. If successful, the commission would bring about a fundamental shift in the values schools transmitted to the next generation.

Further, the opportunity presented by the Governor's Commission was the first of its kind. Never before had a sitting governor directed his administration to address the problems of gay youth. All members of the commission felt, in LaFontaine's words, "an enormous pressure to succeed." From the first days of the commission through the efforts to implement its recommendations in schools across the commonwealth, a single wrong step might have doomed the whole movement. If they succeeded, their work would blaze a trail for other states to follow. If they failed, the opportunity might never come again. Success would require not just building an objectively irrefutable case for action, but crafting an effective political strategy, and staging the right kind of political spectacle. All of which led to an important and fraught question: How could a group of mostly middle-aged men (two-thirds of the commission's members were male) successfully advocate that schools should be teaching kids about homosexuality? The predator stereotype was still deeply rooted in many minds, and the commission could not play into the fear that they were recruiting high schoolers to their lifestyle.

That the commission would even address conditions in schools marked something of a departure from the original idea. In 1990 and 1991, as LaFontaine lobbied state legislators to pass a law creating the commission, it was clear that bringing schools into the conversation would scare off much of the support he had cobbled together. When efforts to work through the legislature failed, Weld offered to create the Governor's Commission by executive order. ("I was not even aware he could do that," recalled LaFontaine.) A commission created by executive fiat—one that needed no legislative support—could take a bolder approach. The original vision, which focused solely on community-based health workers and support groups—BAGLY (the Boston Alliance of Gay and Lesbian Youth) and other AGLYs throughout the state—could expand to include work in schools. However, political activists such as LaFontaine were not connected to the teaching community. When he began pushing for a commission, he was not familiar with the work to support LGBT students in schools like Concord Academy, Cambridge Rindge and Latin, and Phillips Andover. A mutual connection put LaFontaine and Jennings in touch, uniting the political world with educational activists.

Jennings then recruited Ferreira, and LaFontaine had two experts in the kind of advocacy needed, two men who had already succeeded in changing mainstream opinion in their own school communities. Now the task was to take their message out of the progressive enclaves that had incubated their movement and to win over the urban, working-class residents of Boston and the more rural, conservative western two-thirds of the state. Although the audience would be much different, the strategy would be much the same: focus on the concrete damage homophobia wreaks on the lives of real people, and above all, put students out front as the face of the movement. The most effective lobbyists, the most effective advocates in pushing schools to support gay youth, would be gay youth themselves. Ferreira and Jennings, LaFontaine recalled, "brought the students into the work," and the students "became the deciding voices" in swinging public support to their cause. More than any other factor, it was the students who made schools the primary focus of the commission's work.

The commission scheduled a series of public hearings for November 1992, to be held at locations across the state. Ostensibly, the committee sought to gather testimonials to inform the recommendations it would make in its report. In reality, the recommendations were already being written, and the hearings were an exercise in political messaging. Six weeks before the hearings began, Jennings invited members of the GLSEN network—by that time, teachers in fifteen private schools and at least as many public schools were part of GLSEN— to a meeting on October 4 to "draft the first copy of the recommendations we will eventually submit to the Governor." In that same letter, Jennings asked for help in lining up students to testify. "We are looking for people," he wrote, "who can share their stories in a public hearing setting. We are particularly interested in stories about suicide and suicide ideation, problems of youth in schools, HIV/AIDS risk, substance abuse risk, harassment and violence."[2]

For LaFontaine, it was crucial that the Governor's Commission start with a public demonstration—something official that reflected the power of the executive office. Further, the commission had to be seen as "listening, rather than speaking." The adults could not be in charge. Jennings and Ferreira leaned on their groups—the Concord Academy GSA and Project 10 East—as well as the reach of the GLSEN network, to line up speakers who would be willing to share their stories publicly. This was no small task. Those who testified would be asked to share some of their most painful memories of public humiliation, of severe depression, of suicidal thoughts and attempts to take their own lives. Supportive parents would have to recount their heartbreak and feelings of helplessness in trying to protect their children from the abuse they endured at school. The throwaways and pushaways would speak about parents who threatened them and kicked them out. The testimony would be hard to hear and even harder to give; yet at the same time, it would be the decisive factor in building support for changing schools. The stories that students would tell, the reaction they would create, would turn a dry government report into an emotional imperative, a call to action.

Much of the testimony focused on the overall climate in schools—the types of behavior condoned or encouraged, and the ways in which conformity was demanded. "I had to be adamantly heterosexual and had to make dehumanizing comments about girls or else be labeled a faggot," one student recalled.[3] "I had to prove my masculinity by hazing the underclassmen. Others found pushing wasn't enough and so turned to Wiffle-ball bats. Once someone was rolled down cement steps in a laundry bag just for the fun of it." Another noted that "being anything but a . . . jock is socially unacceptable." Survey data from one school community—collected by a GLSEN member—reported that 97 percent of the student body heard antigay epithets, and half heard them quite often. Over 60 percent of the respondents said they would be "upset or afraid" if the peers thought they were homosexual.

In such a culture, it is hardly surprising (if no less disheartening) to hear of the consequences for those who strayed too far from the norm. One student testified about an incident she witnessed in the hallways of her school: "Two female students were standing in the hall with their arms around each other. Students began to encircle them and yell profanities, until a group of about thirty kids surrounded them." Another recalled, "One of my best friends . . . was only suspected of being gay. He was not, as a matter of fact. But at that suspicion, only that suspicion, he was beaten up every day at school. He was unable to attend classes many days." Yet another remembered the particular horrors of physical education: "Things had escalated where during gym class people would shove food and gum and other objects inside my clothing."

It is natural to ask, where were the adults? Could teachers or administrators not put a halt to such behavior? The answer is a murky combination of yes and no: in some cases, adults in the building were part of the problem. One mother testified that her son's friends told her they "often caught one of the male gym teachers walking with the jocks of the school, and the teacher was making derogatory hand signals towards [my son]." Often administrators simply failed to act. Another mother testified, "They (the school administration) told me that the gym class [my son] was attending consisted of a very tough group of boys, and they teased and tormented him terribly. The teacher couldn't control their behavior, so the only solution was to excuse [him] from the class. I requested that he be placed in another class. This never happened." And a fifteen-year-old revealed the degree to which biases could be ingrained in school leadership when he testified that an administrator told him, "'Well, you must have A.I.D.S. You're gay, aren't you?'"

Although teachers' silence should not be excused, many felt that they could not speak out. One student, a member of the Concord Academy GSA, stated, "I have spoken to teachers in schools on the issue of name-calling in the hallways and they feel they are not justified in going up to students . . . and saying, 'You cannot use that word.' And I ask them, if someone called an African-American student a nigger, would you stand around in your classroom and say, 'It's not my place to go out?'" One teacher argued in her testimony, "Today in school it's okay to hate gays and lesbians; it's actually encouraged by the behaviors and attitudes of faculty and staff. It's not a safe environment." Kathy

Henderson, one of the charter faculty members of the Andover GSA, noted that many teachers were uncomfortable enough with their own sexuality to refrain from intervening: "Most teachers, gay or straight, are afraid to speak up when they hear homophobic remarks. They feel it might put them at risk, that people might say, 'What are you, gay?' which remains a frightening question for most teachers to answer in the current climate." This fear was not unfounded: another private school teacher testified that after he confronted two students on their antigay biases by revealing that he was gay, he was fired, because, in the words of his administrator, he "'ruined those boys' lives.'"

There are, of course, many ways that a child's life can be ruined, and testimony before the commission offered example after example of the sheer loneliness and isolation that so many homosexual high schoolers felt: "I felt as though I was the only gay person my age in the world. I felt as though I had nowhere to go to talk to anybody," stated one student. "I was always an outcast at school," claimed another. "Books were my best friends. I ostracized myself from the rest of the world because I felt as if I could trust no one, not even my parents." A third student recalled his first years of high school, saying, "I couldn't see or find a community of people like me and so I felt I had no home anywhere, no place to relax and be myself." Another noted the adverse effect of his ostracism on his academic performance: "Feeling alone and isolated from the rest of the world, I managed to fail three of my five majors that year."

He might count himself lucky if the only casualty was his grade-point average. Many of his peers left school, foregoing their education altogether. "I was spit on, pushed, and ridiculed," testified one such dropout, or more accurately, pushout. "My school life was hell. I decided to leave school because I couldn't handle it." For others, such isolation had much more dire consequences: "My teachers and counselors labeled my confusion as rebellion and placed me in the category of a troubled discipline problem," said one female student. "But still I had nothing to identify with and no role models to guide me . . . I began to believe that I was simply alone . . . A few weeks into my sophomore year, I woke up in a psych hospital in Brookline after taking my father's camping knife violently to my wrists and hoping for success."

Another spoke of the tendency to internalize the abusive behavior of his tormentors:

> I just began hating myself more and more, as each year the hatred towards me grew and escalated from just simple name-calling in elementary school to having persons in high school threaten to beat me up, being pushed and dragged around on the ground, having hands slammed in lockers, and a number of other daily tortures . . . I went to bed every night praying that I would not be able to wake up in the morning, and every morning waking up and being disappointed. And so finally I decided that if I was going to die, it would have to be at my own hands.

A third expressed very similar feelings: "Who could I talk to? Through the last few years, I had been conditioned into believing gay is wrong . . . After three years of conditioning, I forgot all the things my mother taught me. I lost respect for myself and wanted to die."

Schools were not alone in placing upon their charges the near-unbearable "pressure of feeling so alone," as one student put it. Families were also complicit. "I got kicked out of my house in July," recalled one young man. "My mother went nuts and came at me with an iron and I ran downstairs and I locked the door and she called the police." A college student testified to a fateful interaction with his father: "Then came the moment of truth. My dad wanted an explanation, a reason for my disenrollment from the ROTC, and my very worst fears were realized when I suddenly became persona non grata in my own home." Some, for better or for worse, did not leave home but simply endured: "It cannot get back to my 12-year-old sister that I am anything apart from a carefree, heterosexual high school senior," stated one girl, "or as my father so eloquently put it, 'The heavens will fall in on your petty life.'" Little wonder that most students hid the truth of their orientation. "I still have to come out to my parents, but we have grown distant . . . and they hardly know me anymore. I'm afraid of what their reaction might be."

Taken together, the testimony offered a glimpse of the effect on the students whom schools were duty-bound to protect. In the final report, the commission tried to summarize the cumulative damage to students so completely cut off from friends, from family, and from the school community of which they are forced to be a part. The commission chose the words of psychiatrist John Maltsberger: "In the grips of aloneness the patient is convinced he will be forever cut off from the possibility of human connectedness; in suicidal worthlessness, the patient is convinced he can never merit the caring notice of anyone, including himself, again. The subjective result is the same; to be beyond love is to be hopelessly alone."[4] Or, as a student put it, "Not only does society shout at me that I am evil, but an inner voice whispers it as well."

Of course, many parents supported their gay children, and testified that they, too, had to come to terms with society's rejection. "My religious tradition taught me to believe that my son was a sinner," testified one father. "My medical support system taught me to believe that my son was sick; my educational system taught me that my son was abnormal; my legal system views my son and his partner in an unsanctioned relationship without legal rights and protections that are afforded my married daughter; my family, immediate and extended, provided no acknowledgement or support for having a gay relative in its midst; my major communication sources treated homosexuality as deviant." One mother spoke with deep regret and sadness: "We began to ask ourselves the guilt-based question, 'What did I do wrong?' After all, our Italian-American and Irish-American families were saturated with Roman Catholic doctrine and the cultural imperative of normality. Clearly we had failed and he was somehow defective," she lamented. "We began, perhaps worst of all, to live the lie . . . Lying breeds self-loathing, so you begin to avoid those to whom you must lie." Another mother remembered the day her son came out to her: "In the beginning, I was full of sadness and fear for our son and his partner . . . and along with my husband, wondered who would be supportive."

Some could only express deep sorrow at what they had lost, and regret for what might have been, had they been able to remove the blinders that religion or society or fear placed upon them. "We never thought of a gay person as an equal, lovable, and valuable part of God's creation," confessed Dorothy Remur, the mother of a teen suicide.

"What a travesty of God's unconditional love . . . Had I viewed my son's life with a pure heart, I would have recognized him as a tender spirit in God's eyes." Another expressed more anger than sorrow: "A wonderful child, with an incredible mind, is gone because our society can't accept people who are 'different' from the norm. What an awful waste. I will miss my daughter for the rest of my life. I'll never see her beautiful smile or hear her glorious laugh. I'll never see her play with her sister again. All because of hatred and ignorance."

There were important stories of salvation as well. Some expressed their gratitude for being lucky enough to attend a school with at least some measure of support. "I was constantly denying the feelings I had for other guys," recalled one. "In the process of hiding these feelings, I repressed all emotions. Concord Academy changed all this. It was the first place I encountered that was even slightly gay-positive." Another credited the support he received at Concord Academy with helping him through dark times: "I've spent more than one lonely night sobbing while downing shot after shot, and I've also planned out my suicide more than once. Fortunately I was not alone. There were gay students and gay faculty to whom I could go for help." A third similarly attributed her survival to Concord's GSA: "I never slashed, I never swallowed, I never jumped; I was much luckier than some of the people that we have heard today. As different as each episode was, the reasons for stopping short were the same. Every time, I was able to call on someone from the Concord Academy Gay/Straight Alliance, or someone who I'd come out to through the strength and support I received there, and call out for help." Another student, from a different school, said simply, "If not for the support I found in openly gay teachers at my high school, I would be dead today."

Attendees could hardly be faulted if, by the end of the hearings, they felt numb. Speaker after speaker shared stories of bullying, fear, depression, heartache, and loss. They stood at a podium facing the commission, while the media captured the scene from the well between the podium and the dais. Some could speak only haltingly of their experiences, some with heads down could only read verbatim their written testimony. Some could not speak at all and instead submitted their written testimony for the record. Supporters—in some cases family members, in some cases friends or teachers—filled the hearing rooms behind the podium. Long silences were common, as speakers choked back tears. They were not alone in that regard— members of the audience and members of the commission alike were often overcome as well, some in empathy for the sheer sadness and heartache expressed by a speaker, some because the testimony stirred up all too similar memories from their own childhood.

For many, the testimony was as much personal catharsis as it was engaging in the political moment. It was a chance to be heard in a society that had consistently ignored them and systematically isolated them. For those who had been bullied, testifying affirmed that their suffering had meaning—that they had endured such treatment so that future generations of gay youth would not have to. As student Chris Murther said of his best friend's suicide, "To know that no gay teen will ever have to go through what Richard and I went through would be the best memorial to his death."

Local newspapers and TV carried stories about the hearings— although typically buried somewhere in the middle of the newscast or the latter pages of the regional section. While the hearings were not headline news, coverage was significant: articles were sympathetic, and focused on the plight of the students and the loss of the parents. There were no criticisms of the lifestyle, no veiled references to teachers recruiting the younger generation. The tone remained respectful, neutral, and in that regard was evidence of a shift in societal attitudes—at least in the Northeast—toward the LGBT community. Members of straight society still appeared happiest to ignore the existence of the LGBT community in their midst, but could also, when it was brought to their attention, recognize injustice and sympathize with the victims. However, they would not necessarily be spurred to action; the efficacy of the hearings would be judged by their impact on school communities across the state.

AS 1992 GAVE WAY TO 1993, and the Governor's Commission prepared its report, activists mustered support in the halls of the statehouse to reopen another front in the battle for LGBT rights. For the third consecutive year, legislative sponsors introduced a bill in the Massachusetts

House of Representatives to amend the student civil rights law, which prohibited discrimination on the basis of race, color, sex, religion, or national origin, to include sexual orientation. The origin of this effort is somewhat complicated. It was the brainchild of the state Student Advisory Council (SAC), a body established in 1971 to give students a greater voice in forming state educational policy. (As such, it is part of the same trend toward greater student empowerment that gave rise to the first GSA in Washington Heights in 1972.) Students are chosen to represent their own schools at regional assemblies, then the regional assemblies in turn choose members who will sit on the state SAC, which elects one member to sit on the state board of education as a voting member. Overseeing the state SAC is one adult adviser—the legislative liaison—whose job is, in theory, exactly that: to advise and not direct. Although the SAC is recognized as a state agency and has the power to make recommendations to the state Department of Education, it does not have the power to make policy outright. At times in its history, its role appeared to be only to give students a token voice; at other times, its members have made a significant impact on policy.

One such time began in 1991, when the Student Advisory Council first sought to amend the student civil rights law. According to Phyllis Scattergood, then the legislative liaison to the SAC, members of the SAC had no connection to GLSEN or to the gay rights movement—they came to the issue on their own. Extending nondiscrimination protection to include LGBT youth seemed, to the members of the SAC, a logical step for a body interested in issues of student equity. In some ways, however, it was an unusual choice—amending state law was outside their purview. They were not experienced lobbyists—save for one student who, in the fourth grade, had pressed lawmakers to declare the corn muffin "Official State Muffin." (In an alarming but precocious act of political bribery, she baked corn muffins for all her legislators.)[5] The SAC had no real power beyond that of persuasion and had, by virtue of impending graduations, a transitory membership not necessarily suited to the long grind of the legislative process.

Nor, of course, can high school students file legislation. They did, however, find a willing sponsor and coauthor in State Representative

Byron Rushing of the Ninth Suffolk District. A man with a distinguished résumé as a civil rights activist, Rushing was naturally sympathetic to the aims of the gay rights movement. His district included Boston neighborhoods with significant (and politically active) LGBT populations, and by the 1990s he had long represented their interests ably. It is notable that even in 1988, when his opponent was the openly gay Michael Duffy (later chosen by Governor Weld to chair the Massachusetts Commission Against Discrimination), Rushing handily carried the gay vote in his district. He sponsored the nondiscrimination amendment to the student civil rights law in 1991, and again in 1992, rallying ample support and passing it easily through the House. But each year it disappeared in the Senate, buried under a blizzard of procedural arcana and never brought up for a vote. Going into 1993, the movement to support LGBT youth had met nothing but firm resistance in the Massachusetts Senate: the attempt to create a commission to address the plight of LGBT youth through the legislature had failed, and the effort to amend the student civil rights law appeared destined for a similar fate—and unlike Weld's creation of the Governor's Commission, state law could not be changed by executive fiat. The Senate had to be brought around, and the governor's office—despite its consistent support for action on gay youth—still had larger legislative priorities to address.

Activists on both sides were well aware that amending the civil rights law would be more than simply a cosmetic change. LaFontaine recognized the bill's potential to compel school districts to address instances of bullying and harassment. For students who felt they had no choice but to drop out, schools might well be required to provide alternative educational settings if they could not improve school climate—an expense few districts would willingly undertake. C. J. Doyle, director of the Catholic League for Religious and Civil Rights, articulated the fears of the opposition when he predicted, "The ultimate purpose here is to introduce homosexual programs into the schools."[6] He did not go far enough. The ultimate goal was the normalization of homosexuality by the schools. As the bill neared passage, Nancy Sutton, executive director of Family First, declared, "If

Weld is to sign this, he would be the biggest fool that ever walked the face of this earth . . . Teachers will be forced to teach about the homosexual lifestyle as normal and natural, which it is not."[7] For LGBT youth, it would be yet another recognition, an affirmation of the fact that they walked the same halls as their straight peers, but often faced a very different experience.

Members of the SAC prepared diligently for their lobbying campaign. They researched every legislator, worked with Rushing's office to track yeas, nays, and maybes. They honed their arguments by role playing, laying out their case for student equity and the furthering of student rights, and rehearsing how to address both positive and negative responses. If legislators had children in the public schools, the SAC brought in students from those schools. They flattered legislators, complimenting them on bills they had sponsored that had benefited their district or their schools. They practiced shaking hands. As some members of the SAC graduated, the veterans brought new members up to speed—in some cases having to convince them that LGBT rights was a worthy cause. Yet still, they could only watch as the Senate buried the bill in 1991 and 1992.

However, over the course of those two years, some nays began to waver, yeas became more forceful advocates, and a few maybes flipped to yeas. Although many of the original proponents in the SAC had graduated, the group persisted. Their 1993 campaign began with a phone call by Scattergood to Rushing's office, memorialized on a simple pink message slip: "re: getting bill out of Senate. Do you want the kids to do anything?" This year, the "kids" had reinforcements: thanks to the creation of the Governor's Commission, they had more state power advocating for their cause, and thanks to the networks developed by GLSEN, Project 10 East, and others, they had a much larger group of students ready to bring pressure on recalcitrant senators. Further, the new allies employed tactics from the Governor's Commission hearings. Lobbying in 1993 became significantly more public and much more difficult to dismiss. Where the SAC could focus on the issue of student equity and rights, LGBT students could testify to the stark impact on individual lives when equity was absent. GLSEN set as a goal that every senator would meet with a gay student from his or her district, to hear firsthand what equity would mean to them.

In a letter preserved in Rushing's archives, a young woman from the central Massachusetts town of Athol describes the manner in which she was targeted by a group of students, and the lack of support from school administrators. "I have been spit on," she wrote, and described "walking down the hallway to class and being followed by five or six boys chanting homophobic slurs and insults." She reported her experience to the dean of students, who, she wrote, "as far as I know, did nothing." A female student threatened to beat her up on the bus ride home; a boy on the bus yelled at the girl "to do it right, because he wanted to see blood." After she was attacked, she again reported the incident, and was told she was "partly to blame." Later that week, the same girl followed her home, this time with two accomplices. "They were screaming things like 'You fucking dyke,' and 'stupid lesbo bitch,' as they knocked me to the ground and repeatedly kicked me in the head and ribs."[8]

In his memoir, Jennings recalls a meeting between a gay student and a senator, who argued that his district had "good schools," ones in which teachers would surely address the problem quickly and prevent any recurrence should anyone treat students so poorly. In Jennings's recollection, the student began "in a quiet, low voice," and "related how he had once been picked up by a group of jocks in his school, shoved inside a locker that they then locked from the outside, and how he spent nearly an hour banging on the door of the locker until a custodian let him out."[9] For once, writes Jennings, the senator was speechless.

THE LOBBYING CAMPAIGN, much like the testimony before the Governor's Commission, illustrated the dark spaces in school communities that were hard to police, and difficult emotionally to confront. Students are skilled at finding the blind spots and shadows where they are beyond supervision; practically speaking, school authorities cannot be omnipresent. Yet they are not to be absolved entirely—administrators and teachers made choices about what they "cannot" address. Their personal moral beliefs may have colored their decision making, or they may have wishfully assumed that students were not capable of so cruelly targeting their peers. Or educators may have found it easier to pretend, as so many did, that there were no LGBT students walking their halls. The rise of LGBT groups in schools made these positions much more tenuous, and the lobbying campaign made the problem much more real. It is comparatively easy to view the dispute over LGBT rights as one of competing perspectives on morality, and to question whether schools were the appropriate venue for addressing the issue; this rationalization tends to fade away in the face of a teenager recounting the abuse she has endured because of her sexual orientation. As LGBT students became more visible, as the groups advocating on their behalf attracted greater numbers, their claim to equal treatment became much harder to dismiss.

The lobbying effort climaxed with a statehouse rally in Nurses Hall, a massive chamber dominated by a bronze sculpture dedicated to the nurses who served in the Civil War, bronze reliefs of distinguished Massachusetts soldiers from that war, and two grand marble staircases leading to a balcony ringed with marble pillars, above which hang murals depicting Paul Revere's ride, the Boston Tea Party, and other seminal events in the Revolution. Most days an awed quiet descends on the hall, broken only by footsteps echoing on the marble floor. But on October 13, 1993, it was the site of a boisterous rally, as students and teachers packed the hall, filled the staircases, and hung off the balconies. They waved signs trumpeting statistics on the dire risks LGBT youth faced or proudly celebrating their schools' newly formed GSAs. Addressing the crowd, Lieutenant Governor Paul Cellucci declared that the amended student civil rights bill would enshrine "one simple tenet—that every student is entitled to pursue a public education in an environment that is safe and free from discrimination." LGBT students again testified publicly to their mistreatment, and, although their stories were heartbreaking, the rally had the celebratory feel of a pride march.[10] The Senate still had not deigned to vote on the bill, but there was a sense of victory in the air, that the increased visibility of LGBT students, teachers, and their growing number of supporters gave them a newfound power that recalcitrant senators could not resist.

The Nurses Hall rally was followed up with another in late November, and in early December the bill was released from committee in the Senate and passed without debate.[11]

As 1993 came to a close, LGBT students and teachers could claim two watershed victories: passage of the amendment to the student civil rights bill and the overwhelming endorsement of the Governor's Commission Report. Perhaps most remarkable was the degree to which opposing forces were effectively neutered. Certainly, groups such as Family First and the Catholic League mounted a well-organized and full-throated opposition campaign, but they found themselves largely consigned to the fringes. Unable to gain any traction on the merits of their case, right-wing forces even tried to sabotage the commission by calling for investigations into alleged financial impropriety; their allegations were largely ignored or dismissed. Work that seemed at its outset fraught with risk for the gay rights movement was accomplished successfully without inciting a firestorm of reaction—indeed, with a minimum of public controversy of any kind.

It is clear that attitudes toward the LGBT community were shifting, not just in Massachusetts but across the country. In fact, 1987—the year the GSA began at Concord Academy—was the high-water mark (or low-water mark) for disapproval of same-sex relations; opinion polls show 75 percent of respondents thought same-sex relations were "always wrong." And 1994 was the first year a majority of the American public approved of gay high school teachers—although a majority still disapproved of gay middle school teachers. Further, the number of states with laws protecting LGBT citizens from employment discrimination grew from zero in 1974 (although the cities of Ann Arbor and East Lansing in Michigan, and Washington, D.C., had such laws in place), to nine by 1987, to nineteen by 1992. (Massachusetts did not pass such protections until 1989.) By 1993, the nationwide gay rights movement had become an effective political force, and both the work of the Governor's Commission and the lobbying for the student civil rights amendment were part of this larger movement.

However, the victories in Massachusetts were not simply a reflection of national trends. Even in 1988, 71 percent of Americans supported nondiscrimination in employment and housing—while 75 percent disapproved of same-sex relations. Support for LGBT rights might be indicative of the bedrock American belief that equality and freedom should be extended to all citizens; it did not necessarily reflect support for the LGBT community itself. Further, on questions of homosexuality in schools, there was still a tremendous amount of ambivalence. Activists in Massachusetts successfully navigated the risks inherent in the work of the Governor's Commission and effectively defanged the opposition by focusing on the humanity of the students they sought to support. They placed real people, as opposed to abstract laws and rights, in the spotlight, and created a well of empathy deep enough to overwhelm fears over bringing the proverbial gay agenda into schools.

Legal scholar Kris Franklin described what she calls the "Ellen DeGeneres effect" on American attitudes toward the LGBT community. When the comedian and television star came out publicly in 1997—an event memorialized by her cover shot for *Time* magazine, with the quote "Yep, I'm gay"—the American conception of what it meant to be gay shifted dramatically. Ellen's coming out marked, in Franklin's words, "a watershed in the way the straight mainstream media conceived of lesbians and gay men as simultaneously culturally meaningful and not intimidating." In other words, it became "impossible for the mainstream to talk about homosexual *behavior* without generating an image of *gay people*" (emphasis in the original).[12] Mark Driscoll, the executive producer of DeGeneres's hit sitcom, makes a similar point: "Ellen was so loved by audiences; she was so much the girl next door and so sweet. She was the perfect person to dispel people's fears about what a gay woman might be like."[13] In Massachusetts at least, a parade of high school students testifying to the ill treatment they had received in schools they were required to attend had a similar effect. It was humanizing in the extreme. If, when one talks about homosexuality, the image in one's mind is a girl being tormented by her classmates, or a seventeen-year-old weeping over the suicide of his friend, it is difficult to remain unrepentantly antigay.

Further, the hearings represented the continuation of a tactic begun by teachers who first sought to raise the issue of homosexuality in schools: minimizing the discussion of sexual intimacy and LGBT teens, emphasizing the difficulties they faced. In part, this likely represents both an awareness of the stigma of the predatory stereotype, and a conscious attempt to downplay the physical aspect of LGBT identity. "We were very aware of the stereotype," noted Al Ferreira about his early work with gay students at Cambridge Rindge and Latin.[14] In fact, two stereotypes played in the minds of straight society—that of gay man as predator, and that of gay people as exceptionally libidinous and promiscuous. Particularly in the 1980s, at the height of the AIDS epidemic, it was politically wise to minimize talk of sex. Even Uribe, who counseled students on safe sex practices and urged them to volunteer with AIDS patients, de-emphasized this aspect of her work with students. Andrei Joseph coached speakers at his school against discussing sexual activity, urging them to keep things "very PG." Testimony before the Governor's Commission further severed the link in some people's minds between gay identity and sex. These were simply teenage boys and girls, speaking haltingly and powerfully about some of their most vulnerable moments.

The manner in which the mainstream media covered events in Massachusetts further reflected this humanization. When the student civil rights bill finally passed the Senate, the *Boston Globe*'s coverage focused on two of the lobbyists, Brookline High School junior Sarah Longberg-Lew and freshman Anna Cotton. Any "controversy" surrounding the bill is addressed only in the seventeenth paragraph, and framed only in terms of the potential political price to be paid by Governor Weld for signing the bill.[15] (He did pay a price for his liberalism: Senator Jesse Helms blocked his nomination as ambassador to Mexico for, among other reasons, being a promoter of the "militant homosexual agenda." "If Weld goes to Mexico," said Helms, "he'll go as a tourist."[16]) Much like the *Globe*, the *Times* chose to emphasize the work of the student lobbyists and the mistreatment endured by gay students—photos accompanying the article were of student demonstrators and speakers.[17] The merits of the cause itself were no longer up for debate.

THE JOURNEY from the founding of the first Gay-Straight Alliance in Massachusetts in the late 1980s to the creation of a far-reaching state policy to support LGBT students in 1993 appears relatively short. Indeed, many of the students and teachers who were involved at the beginning expressed surprise at how quickly events unfolded. However, it is more accurate to think of this period as a singularly critical traverse in a long and unimaginably difficult road, a point at which activists turned the mainstream fear of predatory adults seducing children into recognition that mainstream society itself had long enabled straight bullies to target and abuse gay children. Efforts to support LGBT students did not begin in 1987, nor did they conclude in 1993. What is remarkable about the journey is not the speed at which the movement progressed, but the means by which activists effected such momentous change. Generations of LGBT youth had endured feelings of helplessness and isolation, had been beaten and taunted or rendered invisible; it took a type of strength rarely seen in high schoolers to turn this legacy, this apparent weakness, into power. Speaking publicly about their darkest, most vulnerable moments is something no school would ever ask of its students; yet LGBT youth chose to do so, and by making themselves the center of attention, they turned the spotlight on the moral weakness and fear in a straight society that did not stand up to cruelty and intolerance, would not reach out a hand in support, and willfully turned a blind eye to the suffering in its midst. In testifying to their own experiences, LGBT youth stirred empathy in those who had previously evinced none. They demonstrated a power to upend political norms, change the cultural conversation, and move government institutions. They built a wave of irresistible momentum that others would use in implementing the recommendations of the Governor's Commission, and in expanding the GSA movement nationwide.

The Massachusetts Model
Goes Nationwide

School-board authorities can and should be able to ban homosexual clubs and heterosexual clubs, especially if they fly in the face of community standards.

—Utah senator Orrin Hatch

They are not asking to have a club to talk about sex. They are asking for support and how to deal with their parents.

—Granger (Utah) High School student body president Asia Bevan

O N A WARM SPRING DAY in late May, thousands of high school students converge on the Boston Common. Some carry handmade signs, others wave banners and rainbow flags. Dozens of Gay-Straight Alliances make their presence known, and there is a friendly—and unstated—competition arising among many of them over which has the biggest, loudest, most colorful presence. As with any large gathering of high school students, hormones exert their inexorable influence. Boys and girls (and, more recently, those who acknowledge neither gender category) try to look cool, affecting a certain style of dress or an air of studied aloofness, seeking—with varying degrees of success—to embody some ideal of attractiveness just out of reach. Gaggles of teenagers whisper and point discreetly (so they think). Fits of laughter burst forth. Individuals dart in and out of the packs. On occasion, conversations are struck up. Less occasionally, means of contact are exchanged. Even more rarely, dates are formalized and relationships begun. In all, the gathering is a festival of youthful energy unshackled from the constraints of parents and norms of school behavior. It is the Boston Youth Pride Rally.

Much like the adult pride rallies, Youth Pride serves many purposes: it is a chance for old friends to reunite, an exercise in building and reaffirming the community, a political reminder of the power of the youth movement. It is also, if only for a day, a larger and more public realization of Sharon Tentarelli's dream: a chance for students to gossip about who they think is cute, without worrying about which pronoun they use. The brainchild of the Governor's Commission, Youth Pride began in 1995. Student organizers quickly rejected the event's original name—the Gay Youth Pride March—for the more inclusive Gay/Straight Youth Pride March, and then, simply, Youth Pride. In short order it became, to borrow the paranoid language of the opposition, a tremendous recruiting tool. Often, students from schools with no GSA would be so inspired by what they saw (much as Tentarelli was struck by her first gay pride march) that they would start one. More important, Youth Pride also serves as an antidote to the potentially oppressive focus on the risks faced by gay youth. LaFontaine, the original organizer of Youth Pride, remembers thinking, "I didn't want the emphasis on suicide to make youth feel that's what it meant to be a gay teenager." Youth pride is a celebration of what it can mean to be gay in an open and supportive society.

Youth Pride is also illustrative of the reach and success of the movement to support LGBT youth in Massachusetts. Although this effort was driven primarily by the previously untapped energy among teachers and students, it required some political organization and leadership to expand its reach throughout the state's school system. Even before the Governor's Commission's recommendations were wholeheartedly endorsed by both the Weld administration and the Department of Education, LaFontaine began organizing workshops to train faculty members, and Weld began orchestrating a means to fund what became the Safe Schools program without going through the legislature. In short order, over 250 schools participated in workshops run by the Governor's Commission, and GSAs spread from a few suburban public schools to hundreds across the state. Soon, many of the original activist teachers were fielding calls from schools all over the country, asking for help implementing programs or training faculty and staff. In many cases, GSAs were welcomed in school communities; in some, political fights brought greater nationwide attention to the movement. By the dawn of the twenty-first century, what began as an underground effort at a few schools had spread to every state in the country. But the movement's growth was not inevitable—organizers carefully strategized to maximize support and minimize controversy. Nor was its success absolute—while statistics bear witness to an improved climate for LGBT youth, many still face the same risks as in generations past.

The Governor's Commission published its report in February 1993, and in May, the state board of education voted to make the following recommendations based on the report: First, schools should include sexual orientation in their nondiscrimination policies (a step that was largely obviated by the amendment to the student civil rights law in 1993), and schools should extend anti-harassment policies to include students who are gay or are perceived to be gay. Second, school staff should be trained in violence and suicide prevention—particularly as it pertains to gay students. Third, schools should offer "school-based support groups for gay, lesbian, and heterosexual students," or in other words, create Gay-Straight Alliances, which "should have a faculty adviser and support from the school administration." Fourth, schools should provide counseling for family members, which might include extending "partnerships with community agencies to provide counseling services to gay and lesbian students and their families."[1]

In other words, schools were to become the locus of support for gay and lesbian youth. Although the Governor's Commission worked with BAGLY, PFLAG (Parents and Families of Lesbians and Gays), and other community-based groups, it quickly became apparent that schools could have the greatest impact—if they could be harnessed to the task. Further, activists felt that the commission should aim high while it had momentum and support—both of which could easily disappear. Convinced that such reforms would be controversial, the commission sought to focus its resources, energy, and political capital on schools while the moment was opportune. And the keystone for school-based support would be Gay-Straight Alliances.

The first issue was funding. While the members of the commission were volunteers, sustainable programs would require funded positions. Officials at the Department of Education who would direct implementation of the recommendations, trainers who would conduct workshops for school personnel, and teachers who would serve as faculty advisers for new GSAs all would (and should) expect compensation for their work. More than a few well-intentioned reform efforts have foundered owing to a lack of consistent and adequate funding. However, additional money would not be forthcoming from the legislature; unless alternative sources of funding could be found, the Safe Schools program would be cannibalizing other Department of Education programs—not a good way to build support with school administrators.

The Weld administration got creative, diverting $450,000 from a voter-approved cigarette tax increase, $33 million of which the legislature had already earmarked for the Department of Education. The increased tax revenue was supposed to be allocated exclusively for antismoking programs, which included, in the words of education department spokesman Alan Safran, "comprehensive health education." The Department of Education reasoned that efforts to change school climate in ways that reduced suicide risk and substance abuse among gay teens certainly amounted to comprehensive health education. The Republican minority leader in the House, Peter Forman, called this interpretation "a pretty long stretch," if not "an outright fantasy." He may have had a point, as the voter-approved law stated that money could go to comprehensive health education, "provided that such programs shall incorporate information relating to the hazards of tobacco use."[2] While the Department of Education was mum on whether its training workshops or GSA materials would include antismoking pamphlets, the diversion of funds raised surprisingly little controversy from anyone but conservative opponents of the Safe Schools program.

The money was used primarily for three purposes. First, the Department of Education created two full-time positions to oversee the Safe

Schools program and direct its implementation. Initially, it must be noted, the department was somewhat reluctant to get involved in the work of the Governor's Commission. This may have been due to skepticism on the part of officials to take on any program initiated by those outside the administration. It is also certainly possible that homophobia—latent or overt—on the part of Department of Education administrators may have played a role. In addition, there may have been some administrative reluctance to court the controversy that would surely accompany the Safe Schools program. However, the department hired two exceptional administrators, Kim Westheimer and Jeff Perrotti, who oversaw the implementation of GSAs in hundreds of schools, and a tripling of the Safe Schools program budget in their first eight years.

A second portion of the program's initial budget went to fund grants for schools interested in starting GSAs or hosting staff training sessions on LGBT support and school climate. In terms of engineering a grassroots spread of the GSA movement, the grant-making process was an inspired approach. Rather than mandating that schools create GSAs and training programs, the Department of Education solicited grant proposals from schools across the commonwealth. Most of the grant requests came from individual teachers and counselors who wanted to start GSAs. The process would often involve teachers selling their administrators on the idea; certainly this sales job was made easier by the fact that the school would be receiving money from the state if the grant were approved. Moreover, because teachers were seeking out the program, rather than the state imposing the program on schools, efforts to organize GSAs and train faculty and staff were much better received than typical Department of Education programs.

The final piece of the budget went to organizing and staffing workshops and training sessions at schools. These served two different purposes. The Governor's Commission held fifteen workshops throughout the state for teachers who wanted to start GSAs or work to change school culture. LaFontaine estimates that over 250 schools participated in these. The second purpose was to train entire schools or districts—to try to get teachers, administrators, and staff on board with the work of those who were starting a GSA. A number of teachers got involved as trainers, among them Bob Parlin. Parlin, according to LaFontaine, was the essential voice, the one who could talk to other teachers and "make them believe it could be done." His success at Newton South was, in many ways, the template for what the Safe Schools program was trying to achieve: he had brought the principal on board, created a GSA, hosted dances and other events at school with high levels of gay and straight participation, and worked with the school committee to change district policy—all without fireworks, all in a way that generally fostered agreement and defused tension. "We were desperate to have him present," recalls LaFontaine. "If it hadn't been Bob [presenting], I don't think [the training sessions] would have worked."[3] More important, without the funding to pay presenters, the commission could not have maintained an ongoing program that kept Parlin and others involved.

Parlin was not the only faculty trainer. In most cases, workshops would pair a gay and a straight teacher, to emphasize the importance of the G-S part of the GSA. Andrei Joseph from Concord-Carlisle often worked with Al Ferreira; occasionally they would switch roles, mostly to point out the folly of stereotyping another person's sexual orientation, partly just for the fun of it: Joseph would play the gay teacher and Ferreira would pass as straight. GLSEN, now a wholly independent nonprofit organization, also conducted training workshops geared toward private school educators. As individuals and groups, they also found themselves fielding calls from across the nation. Sometimes teachers or even students would call just looking for advice; sometimes schools brought them in to conduct a workshop for the entire school community. Ferreira would often travel with Karen Harbeck, a member of the commission and a university professor. While Harbeck would bristle and fume at antigay remarks, Ferreira could speak gently to hostile audiences, looking to shift perspectives, always seeking to lower the temperature in the room. The model pioneered in Massachusetts—establishing Gay-Straight Alliances, seeking to train entire school communities to combat homophobia and antigay harassment—spread throughout the country, much in the same way it evolved originally: from teacher to teacher or student group to student group, by word of mouth, convincing administrators to go along, and occasionally fighting openly with school leadership when they did not.

ONE OF THE lengthiest and most public fights began in Salt Lake City in the fall of 1995, when seventeen-year-old Kelli Peterson formed a Gay-Straight Alliance at East High School. The school principal, R. Kay Petersen (no relation), supported the formation of the club, and that may very well have been that, were it not for the sudden interest of city and state officials in protecting Kelli Peterson and others from clubs that might "create an unsafe atmosphere for children." However, as Harbeck was quick to mention when students and teachers reached out for advice, the federal Equal Access Act stated plainly that schools could not choose which student clubs were allowed to meet; it was all or none, under penalty of losing federal funding. The Utah state attorney general concurred. In January 1996, an alarmed state school board met in secret (in violation of state open-meeting laws), concerned that a GSA signified the beginning of a slide toward rampant homosexual activity—and perhaps worse—in its schools. Board member Grant Hurst wondered, since GSAs were permitted, could students form a neo-Nazi club? Was the school forced to tolerate a "recruiting ground" such as the GSA operating under its roof?[4] The board's own attorney, Doug Bates, tried to calm the board's worst fears: "It's a knee-jerk reaction for a lot of straight people to think if you're gay, you are promiscuous and predatory," he stated, though he agreed that "the school could stop a homosexual recruiting club," if such a thing existed. However, he insisted, "the purpose of [the GSA] wasn't to assist kids to proselytize other kids, it was to allow kids who think alike to come together and talk."[5]

Bates largely failed to bring any semblance of rationality to the debate. Utah senator Orrin Hatch, one of the original sponsors of the Equal Access Act, dismissed the Utah attorney general's opinion as "crazy," insisting that "school-board authorities can and should be able to ban homosexual clubs and heterosexual clubs . . . if they fly in the face of community standards." He argued that the act should not "force public officials to accept every conceivable group," that "[it] was never intended to promulgate immoral speech or activity." He further pointed out that the act had provisions for banning clubs to protect the "well-being of students." When asked how banning the GSA did so, he replied, "Just plain morally." Utah's Republican governor, Mike Leavitt, also weighed in: "I just don't think it's an activity we ought to be promoting in our schools." When asked by reporters whether this constituted an antigay position, he stated, "I don't feel that way as far as people are concerned. As far as the activity and . . . the lifestyle, I'd like it not to be promoted." Kelli Peterson refuted their reasoning quite simply: "It's not a technique club. We do not talk about sex and I don't think anyone is interested in talking about it. Our club is more about stopping the suicide and the drug use and the dropping out of school."[6]

The state board passed a resolution calling for the banning of the GSA, and the Salt Lake City Board of Education voted 4–3 to disband all student clubs rather than allow a Gay-Straight Alliance in its schools. Mary Jo Rasmussen, school board president, voted against the ban. "This is just not a student-friendly policy," she said. "I can't express how this decision bothers me to my very soul."[7] Board member Karen Derrick defended her vote in favor of the ban as a vote in favor of states' rights: "This has nothing to do with homosexuality. It was a vote on whether or not the federal government is going to dictate from Washington, D.C. what is going to happen in schools in Salt Lake City."[8]

"I am taking this as a declaration of war," declared Kelli Peterson. "Now, I want to see clubs like this at every high school in the state of Utah." Speaking at a rally, Erin Wiser, a fellow member of the East High GSA, expressed a similar desire for acceptance and tolerance: "We are not an epidemic. We are different and we don't know exactly why. And this is America, where the rights of the minority are protected."[9] For the most part, students opposed the adult interference in their extracurricular life. According to one press report, "hundreds of students—only a small fraction of them gay—marched on the State

House" to demand the reinstatement of student clubs.[10] Student opposition to the GSA was comparatively minor: an antigay petition at East High School garnered only a few dozen signatures, while students at another high school attempted to form a group they called SAFE (Students Against Faggots Everywhere). They could recruit only a handful of classmates, and the group proved to be mercifully short-lived.[11]

Another Utah district, Granite, followed Salt Lake's lead and banned all extracurricular clubs when students at Cottonwood High School attempted to form a GSA. Once again, students protested—making a statement against adult interference as much as one in support of LGBT youth. Asia Bevan, the student body president at another district high school, said of the students seeking to set up the GSA, "They are not asking to have a club to talk about sex. They are asking for support and how to deal with their parents." For Bevan, "the most important thing in high school is belonging." Henry Alvarez, the student body president at a district middle school, articulated a similar sentiment: "Some kids aren't good in athletics or math. Being a member of a club makes them feel good about themselves and gives them the encouragement they need that they might not get from home." But McKell Withers, the principal at yet another Granite District school, dismissed such notions, stating that many non-curricular clubs "detract from the educational mission of the school," meeting only once or twice a year so students "can have something to put on a resume and can get their picture in the yearbook."[12]

The Salt Lake City ban, which allowed curriculum-based clubs—those that had a direct connection to a course that was (or would be) taught—to continue while prohibiting non-curriculum clubs, caused a great deal of confusion, and added several layers of red tape for Utah school administrators. Presciently, Salt Lake board president Rasmussen urged caution: "We have to be really careful to not circumvent the intent of the law . . . If we say, 'Put the chess club in math class, and Young Democrats and Republicans in social studies to keep those clubs,' then we are opening ourselves up to lawsuits."[13] State education attorney Bates seemed resigned to the inevitability of legal action: "What we don't want is a lawsuit over every different kind of club. We want to structure a rule so we can get the issue fairly litigated and get it over with." The state sought to establish guidelines for what types of clubs could be allowed, and in April 1996, the state legislature passed a law that enabled districts to ban clubs that "materially or substantially encourage criminal delinquent conduct, promote bigotry, or involve human sexuality."[14] Despite Kelli Peterson's protestation that students had little interest in talking about sex in a school club with a faculty adviser present, the law was clearly designed to ban GSAs (and, it must be noted, any potential neo-Nazi clubs percolating in the district).

In March 1998, backed by the ACLU, the Lambda Legal Defense and Education Fund, and the National Center for Lesbian Rights, students at East High School sued the Salt Lake City School District. The lead plaintiffs were sixteen-year-olds Ivy Fox and Keysha Barnes, and it was clear to them that school administrators approved of clubs that certainly appeared to be non-curricular but promoted traditional values. The Key Club, the Future Homemakers of America, and the Future Business Leaders of America were all allowed to continue their activities, while the GSA was not. In response to the lawsuit, Karen Derrick, now president of the school board (and apparently no longer worried about decision makers in Washington, D.C.), claimed the decision to limit clubs "was an economic issue, not a gay-lesbian issue." According to her, "It became impossible for us to sponsor every club students brought to us."[15] So as not to provide further ammunition for the lawsuit, all clubs in the district had to resubmit applications for approval as curriculum-based, and only two continued to operate at the start of the 1998–1999 academic year. GLSEN stepped in to support the East High GSA, and re-formed it as a community-based group, paying East High School six dollars per hour to rent space in the evenings. The Key Club was the only other club to take this approach.

As the suit made its way through the courts, media attention and national pressure focused on Salt Lake. Articles about the ban appeared in newspapers on both coasts. National television news programs came calling. And GLSEN, seeking to raise its national profile, decided to hold its inaugural national conference in Salt Lake City. After the ban went into effect, the small Utah chapter of GLSEN grew tremendously—from the handful who founded the group to over fifty members, with over a hundred more on its mailing list. Other western and midwestern chapters sent large delegations to the conference in support of their Utah colleagues. At the conference, Utah GLSEN members profusely, if sarcastically, thanked the Salt Lake Board of Education, expressing the belief that no individual or group in Utah's history had done as much for gay rights. In a more sincere vein, GLSEN honored East High principal R. Kay Petersen, who consistently supported the students in the East High GSA, with its Pathfinder Award for pioneering leadership on issues of gay rights.[16]

Although she had graduated from East High in 1996, Kelli Peterson became a symbol for gay and lesbian youth across the country—not an easy thing for an eighteen-year-old to be. Her image mattered, especially in straitlaced Utah. "It's a lot of pressure to be perfect," she admitted. "I have to dress a certain way. There's a lot of pressure to present this normal, mainstream . . . gay kid." All of this while trying simply to survive life as a regular student—sometimes, it seemed, literally: there had been death threats against her at East High, and she spent more time than she would have liked in the principal's office—for her own safety. Petersen, the principal, was a constant ally. "He made the high school experience safe for me," she recalled. "When I was being harassed, I told him who was doing it, and it ended." He called her house regularly just to check in, and consistently supported the GSA and its mission—even in the face of hundreds of calls for his dismissal. Despite her best efforts, Kelli Peterson graduated from East High with a feeling of failure: "The biggest disappointment is the realization that I could not change everything. I could not make people think these are normal teen-agers who needed help." Still, she maintained a firm belief that in the end she would prevail, and that the ban "is going to be Salt Lake's most embarrassing moment."[17]

While this last statement is certainly arguable, Salt Lake was forced to reverse course as legal pressure mounted. "Clubs have officially made a comeback in Salt Lake City Schools," declared the *Salt Lake Tribune* as the 2000 school year opened. It took a third iteration of the original lawsuit to lift the ban. When another student club—this one dedicated to studying historical events and sociological issues from a "gay-positive viewpoint"—was denied, despite having clear connections to both history and sociology courses offered at the school, U.S. District Judge Tena Campbell granted an injunction allowing the club to meet. The school board, rather than appeal this decision, rescinded its ban on student clubs.

Students reacted with tremendous excitement, preparing applications to form meat-eating clubs and lawn chair repair clubs, as well the more traditional ski clubs and chess clubs. Board president Derrick continued to insist that the ban was not a gay issue but, abandoning her earlier arguments, no longer claimed it was an economic issue. Nor did she aver that states' rights were at risk. "I don't see this as a primary gay-lesbian issue. I see it as an issue of clubs," she stated, noting that kids had missed out on important opportunities. One board member dissented, reaffirming his opposition to clubs that condoned homosexuality by insisting that "the value [of clubs] does not outweigh the potential harm that can come." Students, as is often the case, took a broader view. East High student body president Nate McConkie spoke out in favor of allowing all clubs, including GSAs: "It's not a matter of lifestyle. We want to create an environment where we love students and accept them for who they are."[18]

IN 1972, the prototype for Gay-Straight Alliances burst into being during a turbulent period at a large, multiethnic urban school in New York City. Before the decade was out, that first GSA, the Gay International Youth Society, had ceased to exist—its example lost, an opportunity missed, and lives no doubt lost as a result. But, by the late 1980s, GSAs sprang up again, and this time, the idea began to spread, even if slowly. In the early 1990s, it was still possible to count the schools with GSAs quite easily, probably on one hand. But their moment had arrived. With political support in Massachusetts, they proliferated. GLSEN, too, began to expand its reach nationally. Teachers and students reached out to colleagues in Massachusetts on their own, and events in Utah only served to focus greater attention on the movement, which then spread across the map, into nearly every state and (as of 2018) at least seven other countries as well. GLSEN now has thirty-seven chapter offices across the country, while another umbrella organization, the GSA Network (which in 2016 changed the meaning of its initials to the more inclusive Gender Sexuality Alliance), boasts registered state-level networks in forty states. If there is a single marker of a school's support for its LGBT (now LGBTQ) students, it is the existence of a GSA.

GSAs did not begin with a vision of far-reaching networks supported by nonprofits that raise millions of dollars annually. Students and teachers had no greater plan than wanting to talk to others who understood, others who looked out at the school community and saw a culture that ranged from apathetic at its most benign to violently antagonistic at its most malefic. Those who formed the first groups were primarily seeking, and offering, support—or, in the words of high schooler Asia Bevan, "belonging." Emboldened by the support they found, strengthened by the simple fact that they discovered that they were no longer alone in the hostile world, students and teachers in the GSAs turned a critical eye on their schools and sought to change them. GSAs continue to be the place students turn to for support, but they have become so much more. They are an important symbol, a rallying point, and a vehicle for political action in their communities. It may take unknowable reserves of courage for an individual student to stand up to school administrators, unwelcoming teachers, or the vast numbers of straight peers. A GSA makes doing so easier. Groups can advocate for individuals who can't do so by themselves; they have a power that individuals cannot muster on their own.

Although evidence suggests that more can be done to support LGBT students, the impact of GSAs is evident. The GLSEN school climate surveys, conducted every two years, paint a mixed picture of LGBTQ[19] students' experience in schools today, more than twenty-five years after the movement started. According to the latest data, 77 percent of students at schools without GSAs hear antigay comments "often or frequently," compared with 59 percent of students at schools with GSAs. Statistics regarding negative comments about gender expression are similar; 46 percent of students at non-GSA schools reported hearing them "often or frequently," compared to 36 percent at GSA schools.

Students are less likely to report feeling unsafe at GSA schools (50 percent vs. 66 percent), and less likely to miss school because they feel unsafe (26 percent vs. 38.5 percent). Students are less likely to report being harassed, victimized, or assaulted because of sexual orientation or gender expression at schools with GSAs. And students at schools with GSAs are more likely to report that there are "many" or "some" supportive staff members, and are significantly more likely to feel accepted by their peers, and connected to the school community.[20]

Over time, GSAs have become more of a fixture in the educational landscape. In 2001, only 25 percent of students reported that their school had a GSA or similarly structured support group; in 2015, that number was up to 54 percent. Over that same period, incidences of reported harassment and violence have decreased across the entire population of LGBTQ students. Further, more LGBTQ students report that their school has at least some supportive staff members, and more students feel accepted by their peers. Although recent years have shown a slight uptick in antigay language at school, it is too early to know whether this is simply a blip or a bit of statistical noise; over the longer term, trends all point to more positive school climates for LGBTQ students in their school communities.[21]

One can read these numbers either as a heartening measure of the impact of GSAs, or as a clear warning that the levels of harassment are still unconscionably high, even at schools with GSAs. Certainly the survey demonstrates that no magic cure exists to end all antigay harassment and violence. Further, the penetration of GSAs throughout the nation is far from complete. While 54 percent of students surveyed reported that their school had a GSA or a similarly structured support group, the number is higher for high schools (61 percent) and for secular schools (55 percent of public high school and middle schools; 61 percent of secular private schools of all ages).[22]

The distribution of GSAs across the country is uneven. In the Northeast, 70 percent of all students report that their schools have a GSA, compared to 61 percent in the West, 53 percent in the Midwest, and 37 percent in the South. Further, 63 percent of students in suburban or urban districts attended schools with GSAs, while only 31 percent of rural students do. One might well ask the chicken-and-egg question: Are GSAs simply the effect of more tolerant populations, rather than a partial cause for populations becoming more tolerant? It is no coincidence that the first GSAs sprang up in more progressive areas of the country; however, it is also true that GSAs have changed school climates, and GSAs have succeeded in what were once hostile environments. Salt Lake City, which elected its first gay mayor in 2016, is but one example. Certainly it would be foolhardy to draw a direct line between the creation of a GSA and the election of a gay mayor twenty years later; however, it is also fair to assume that attitudes and behavior learned in school are carried out into the world.

While evidence points to only partial success at ending anti-LGBTQ violence and harassment, other statistics highlight the impact of GSAs on individual lives. The GLSEN survey notes that LGBTQ students who report lower rates of victimization and harassment also report higher grade-point averages and are more likely to be considering attending college. If GSAs do reduce antigay activity in schools, they are also at least partially responsible for LGBTQ students performing better in school, and earning for themselves a wider array of opportunities when they graduate. Statistics pointing to decreases in harassment are best interpreted as fewer kids bullied, beaten up, or afraid to walk the halls each day.

As too many personal histories illustrate, the notion of a lifeline is not hyperbole. A 2011 study demonstrated that the presence of GSAs in high school correlated with lower levels of depression in adults ages twenty-one to twenty-five, and further noted that GSAs seemed to create a buffer between low levels of harassment and lifetime suicide attempts—that is, even for students who experienced some levels of harassment in high school, the presence of a GSA reduced the likelihood they would attempt to kill themselves. It is important to note that GSAs did not appear to create a similar buffer when levels of harassment were elevated—high levels of harassment are associated with significant risk of suicidal ideation and attempts later in life, GSA or not. However, to the degree that GSAs reduce overall levels of harassment, fewer students face such conditions.[23] For those students who were targeted and found a lifeline in the GSA, or for those who have never been targeted at all because of the existence of a GSA, the significance of this movement is beyond debate.

Both anecdotal testimony and statistical evidence show that GSAs help keep LGBTQ kids alive. In addition, a 2014 study of students in British Columbia points to an even more remarkable effect: GSAs help keep heterosexual kids alive as well. According to the researchers, "Heterosexual boys in a school whose GSAs had been in existence for more than three years were about half as likely as those in schools without GSAs to attempt suicide."[24] As the researchers point out, this outcome should not come as a complete surprise. Youth who do not conform to traditional notions of gender identity might become targets as well. Kids who "look" or "act" gay get harassed. (Bullies have a way of picking the most hurtful words available, and in some places the epithet "gay" stings like no other; if one's goal is to cause pain, effectiveness is prized over accuracy.) Because GSAs provide a way to advocate for more inclusive school policies and stronger action against bullies, they can reduce overall levels of harassment. They offer a community of support to all students.

For generations, LGBT students and teachers were seen as the weakest and the least. Together with straight allies, they built a coalition of strength that has fundamentally altered not only schools, but the very essence of the relationship between the LGBT community and American society. Statistics cannot tell the full story. When students leave school, they carry what they have learned into the world, to friends, families, and into the lives they create as they grow into adulthood. No direct measure can capture the precise impact of the GSA movement beyond the schoolhouse door, but its effect should not be ignored. When schools make a conscious and affirmative effort to support their LGBT community, the country cannot remain unchanged.

Now What?

Increasing . . . [the] likelihood of contact remains a key challenge.

—Gordon Hodson, a researcher at Brock University in Ontario, Canada, on getting intolerant individuals to associate with those they find objectionable

People don't want to sit next to you in class; they don't want to work with you on group projects because [they think], "oh, you're funky."

—A Massachusetts high school student who identifies as transgender

N 1992, an editorial in the Boston gay weekly *Bay Windows* proclaimed, "Gay rights has become a mainstream issue, with a majority of Americans committed in principle to most of what is on our wish list." However, the author cautioned, "In spite of support for gay rights, the fact remains that the underlying lifestyle still makes a great many people very uncomfortable. We are probably more or less in the same position as Hare Krishnas."[1] While almost certainly overly optimistic in its estimate of support for gay rights, the author's analysis was, in the main, quite perceptive. For most Americans, support for gay rights did not mean acceptance of gay people. The country was not wholly on board with gay participation in mainstream American institutions. Work in schools was only just beginning. Fights over marriage, adoption, and the military still loomed. Since 1992, though, Americans have become steadily more accepting of the LGBT community as equal partners in society. The process has not been simple or straightforward, and progress has not been universal, nor does it seem irreversible—views have shifted, but the issue is not settled. Still, the degree of change fought for—and won—in a single generation has been astonishing.

In 1960, historian Bernard Bailyn defined education as "the entire process by which a culture transmits itself across the generations."[2] In 1954, Justice Earl Warren made much the same argument in his majority option in *Brown v. Board of Education*, calling education "the very foundation of good citizenship . . . a principal instrument in awakening a child to cultural values . . . and in helping him adjust normally to his environment."[3] Schools are not the sole means of cultural transmission or awakening—families, communities, churches, and media are certainly important as well—but in an era of compulsory public education schools have assumed a role of special significance. Different groups hold competing values and have battled throughout history for control over schools' educational mission and the character of educators—which explains the occasional outbreaks of hysteria over homosexual teachers. However, schools are not merely conduits of societal values. They also seek to shape them. Teachers and administrators act as gatekeepers, promoting values they deem to be salutary, and quarantining values they deem harmful. Further, students are not mere sponges; they filter what schools seek to transmit, and have some ability to change the values of schools themselves. Despite these limits on the capacity of schools to instill the proper kind of values, they are widely seen as responsible for doing so, and educators are assigned the task of guarding students' character and virtue.

Traditionally, this job included protecting children from the "threat" of homosexuality. Teachers working to support LGBT students flipped this notion of protection on its head by advancing the perfectly reasonable argument that it was homosexual children who were in most dire need of protection. LGBT students became the most effective advocates for their own cause, and were able to create empathy for their plight in ways that adults could not. Together, students and teachers built a reservoir of support, not least among their peers and colleagues, and these new values began to spread throughout the community. Events in Salt Lake City offer a clear example of this reverse osmosis: parents and politicians may have been afraid of homosexuality insinuating its way into schools; students often just shrugged. In the name of protecting children, adults leapt to the nuclear option of eliminating all clubs, while students were less concerned with the "scourge" of homosexuality, and more interested in the need for all students to find their own group, their own place in the world.

The societal impact of the work in schools has been largely underreported and underestimated. In schools, gay rights were not something one could support merely in the abstract. For straight faculty and staff, gay rights meant working side by side with openly gay teachers—or teaching, supporting, and protecting openly gay students, closeted students, and even straight students who were targeted just for seeming gay. For straight students and their families, it meant coming to terms with a gay peer as a lab partner or teammate, or a gay teacher at the front of the classroom. In schools, there would be no supporting gay rights and avoiding gay people. Gay rights activists have fought long and hard in many arenas to push the country toward an equality that is rightfully theirs; it would be intemperate to suggest that the GSA movement is primarily responsible for the shift in straight American attitudes about homosexuality. Yet schools have done more than simply build greater support among straight Americans for gay rights. They have fostered greater acceptance of the LGBT community as full and equal members of American society.

Social science researchers have amassed a large body of evidence to describe how schools can wield such influence. Although the idea predates his work, Gordon Allport coined the term "intergroup contact hypothesis," which posits that contact between members of one group with members of another reduces prejudice between the two. The list of caveats and qualifications is quite extensive, but the basic premise has held up over nearly seventy years of research: contact reduces prejudice. However, in applying this hypothesis to contact between gay and straight populations, several specific concerns have arisen. As researcher Thomas Pettigrew wrote, "prior attitudes and experiences influence whether people seek or avoid intergroup contact, and what the effects of contact will be."[4] Put more simply, intolerant people are likely to avoid people or groups they believe to be gay, and gay people are likely to avoid people they perceive to be intolerant. Contact is more likely to occur with straight people who are already accepting of gay people. Therefore, skeptics argue, contact is not the cause of greater acceptance, but the result.

In response, researchers have sought to clarify how the contact effect works on those more likely to hold antigay views. Two psychologists at the University of California–Davis, Gregory Herek and Eric Glunt, studied a variety of factors in addition to contact that might affect individuals' acceptance of gay men, including religion, attendance at religious services, political ideology, educational attainment, gender, and geography. They concluded that even among groups that traditionally hold negative attitudes toward gays, contact made a significant difference. "Interpersonal contact," they wrote, "predicted attitudes toward gay men better than did any other demographic or social psychological variable." Another researcher, Gordon Hodson of Brock University in Ontario, found that "contact benefits were often statistically stronger among prejudice-prone persons." In other words, those who are most likely to avoid contact are the ones most likely to benefit from it. (As Hodson explained, less prejudiced people seem to benefit less from contact because of a "ceiling effect"—since they were already more likely to be accepting, their attitudes toward homosexuals could only improve so much.) However, despite the clear benefit of contact for those who preferred to avoid it, Hodson noted, "increasing . . . likelihood of contact remains a key challenge."[5]

Even in schools with GSAs, LGBTQ students are not seamlessly integrated with the mainstream straight population. In schools, more often than not, like associates with like. Many teenagers, still self-conscious about their own identity, still concerned about their own social status, reflexively avoid those who seem different. One current transgender high school student observed, "People don't want to sit next to you in class; they don't want to work with you on group projects because [they think], 'oh, you're funky.'"[6] This undercurrent of avoidance is hard to shake, even as schools become more and more institutionally supportive of LGBTQ students. Supreme Court Justice

Antonin Scalia's dissenting opinion in *Lawrence v. Texas* (in which the court struck down antisodomy laws as unconstitutional) essentially made a claim for this right to avoidance. "Many Americans," he wrote, "do not want persons who openly engage in homosexual conduct as partners in their business, as scout masters for their children, as teachers in their children's schools, or as boarders in their home. They view this as protecting themselves and their families from a lifestyle they believe to be immoral and destructive."[7]

By their very existence, GSAs reject this claim, and argue instead that antigay views are immoral and destructive, that they enable the targeting of LGBTQ students and allow schools to ignore the problem. Where politicians, school officials, and administrators engaged in a sort of wishful avoidance by assuming no gay students attended their schools, GSAs shattered these comfortable notions. Where officials practiced overt avoidance by seeking to keep GSAs out of schools, students and teachers forced their way in and illustrated the sheer foolhardiness of avoidance as a strategy. This is education at its most elemental: one might hope that people know better than to reject an entire class of individuals based on uninformed assumptions; again and again, history shows otherwise. Education is perhaps the most powerful tool in reducing such mindless biases. GSAs have done more than simply protect LGBTQ students from harm, more even than pushing schools closer to accepting LGBTQ students as full and equal members of the community. They have not solved the problem of homophobia completely; division and discomfort still exist. But they have encouraged greater connection between groups, and helped broaden those minds most in need of broadening. Even when GSAs are little more than a lonely outpost in a hostile world, they can have a profound impact well beyond their own membership, and well beyond the schoolhouse doors.

BOTH IN THE NATURE OF ITS IMPACT, and the process by which it came to be, the movement to create in-school supports for LGBT students is not a typical school reform. It is not a massive structural change along the lines of the charter school movement, court-ordered desegregation, or, to go back even further, compulsory public education. Nor is it simply a tweak, such as a purportedly new teaching style, the implementation of new technologies, or changes in curriculum content. In its own way, it has been revolutionary—yet almost unnoticeably so. GSAs are not magic cure-alls for intolerance, but where they become active, they force changes in school culture, which in turn influence the values of everyone connected to the system. The creation of a GSA is a deceptively small change—a simple addition of a single extracurricular club. But more momentous change tends to follow in its wake. Phyllis Scattergood, liaison to the Massachusetts Student Advisory Council, which lobbied to include sexuality in the nondiscrimination clause of the student civil rights law, recalls a politician who told her, "Gay marriage doesn't happen [in Massachusetts] without the student rights bill."[8]

One could argue that changes in school culture are really only reflections of changes in the society of which schools are a part. Seen from this perspective, the creation of GSAs is not so much a reform, but an aftershock—the result of society becoming more tolerant and open, itself the result of several generations of activism by the gay rights movement. There is probably some reciprocal feedback between schools and society—the gay rights movement creates individuals willing to advocate for change in their schools; and changes in schools then influence changes in larger society. In the case of supports for LGBT students, advocates in the schools were seeking change that was, at the very least, uncomfortable for the leaders of those schools. Moreover, teachers were creating supports for LGBT students well before political activists were ready to take up the cause. The change that teachers and students created in their own schools not only outpaced reforms in other areas of society—it accelerated them.

That such a fundamental shift began with those ostensibly at the bottom of the educational hierarchy should cause some rethinking of how change comes to schools. There is a pernicious canard that insinuates itself into any discussion of schools, that has become so ingrained in the popular narrative that it is very nearly an assumed part of the dynamic of educational reform—namely that teachers, wedded to old habits, fearful of change, are significant obstacles to innovation in education. This view holds that school leaders and policy makers attempt to implement important and progressive changes, but teachers often stand in the way. In fact, this view has birthed a fashionable trend in educational research: inquiries into how to achieve teacher buy-in for school reforms. The GSA movement demonstrates an utterly different process of reform. In this case, progressive teachers and students sought to implement significant change, while conservative and fearful administrators, policy makers, and politicians resisted. In order to achieve success, teachers and students had to achieve buy-in by school and government leaders.

It is likely that other, similar examples of bottom-up reform exist. Martin Linsky, who moved on to Harvard Business School after serving in the Weld administration, has done extensive research on the idea of leadership. He makes an important distinction between those in positions of authority—in his model, those who are responsible for providing "protection, direction, and maintaining order"—and those who are leaders. According to Linsky, leaders are those who are able to close "the gap between reality and . . . aspiration"—those who push organizations, communities, or societies toward some shared goal or better version of themselves.[9] Of course, one's position in a group hierarchy influences one's ability to effect change within it; often, those in positions of authority have the power to thwart those below them who would exercise leadership. The teachers and students who led the GSA movement had space to do so because the problem they wished to address—supporting LGBT students—was not one those in authority wanted to touch. (Even now, at schools that profess to embrace their LGBTQ population, leadership does not always lead: one transgender student observed that even at his school, which has an openly gay administrator, "The school views it as the responsibility of the individual rather than the administration and teachers to make the school a safe place.")[10] Issues with high visibility—in the education world, standardized testing and charter schools come to mind—attract the attention of those in authority, not to mention large sums of money from both governments and non-state actors. Issues at the margins—and in the 1970s, '80s, and '90s, the problems LGBT students certainly were considered marginal—are practically invisible to those in authority. On low-visibility (not to be confused with insignificant) issues, those outside the authority structure have opportunities to exercise leadership in identifying problems, and generally setting the agenda for solving them.

Schools do not operate with a traditional hierarchical structure. Students and teachers have more room to effect change in their schools. Teachers in particular are often quite good at addressing the problems directly in front of them, and typically have space to do so. One might ask if this is how the first instruction for English-language learners (formerly known as English as a Second Language, or ESL, instruction) began, or the first programs for inclusion of students with special needs. Did ideas born of necessity in under-resourced classrooms and schools form the basis for what later became official policy? These are tantalizing questions; no doubt, finding the historical evidence to answer them will be difficult. Too often, the work of teachers and students in classrooms goes undocumented, while politicians and policy makers tend to leave more extensive paper trails. Still, if for the moment one assumes that many significant reform efforts begin at what is traditionally considered the low end of the hierarchy, a different understanding of school leadership emerges.

Unfortunately, current trends in education may limit teachers' opportunities to exercise such leadership. Many school districts seek to tie teachers' pay or advancement to measurable improvement in student outcomes. In principle, such an approach makes sense. Pay-for-performance is a bedrock foundation of a free-market system. However, economists Susan Helper, Morris Kleiner, and Yingchun Wang have found evidence that strong incentive-based compensation systems may produce suboptimal results if pay is based on "types of performance that are easily observable, even when important dimensions of performance are hard to measure and observe." They further note that achieving better manufacturing outcomes, specifically increased product quality, is often the result of workers increasing "effort on hard-to-observe tasks, such as [making] suggestions for process improvement, and avoiding hard-to-detect shortcuts."[11] In other words, pay-for-performance makes sense only if organizations can identify exactly what good performance means.

In education, it has proven frustratingly difficult to create metrics that capture any outcome deeper than a test score. If school districts base teacher evaluations or compensation on such limited metrics, they risk creating overly constrictive economic incentives for teachers, who would be encouraged to direct more time and energy toward test preparation, and away from potentially more productive endeavors. For teachers, hard-to-observe tasks might include developing innovative lessons or courses, helping new teachers improve their practices, and supporting students who face any number of health or behavioral risks. There are clear long-term benefits to providing time and space for teachers to engage in these tasks, but the benefits may defy quantification, particularly in the short term. To the extent that compensation or employment is based on easier-to-measure outcomes such as student test scores, potentially more beneficial hard-to-measure tasks will get crowded out. Teachers will have limited incentive to innovate, invent, or lead.

Encouraging the type of grassroots reform work that built the GSA movement will require both teachers and administrators to reimagine their roles in fostering innovation. Administrators should be encouraged to take on a more facilitative role, providing time and space for teachers to solve problems. Teachers will need to inhabit a more entrepreneurial frame of mind, be more willing to take on risk, and more willing to work to change their school communities. This may seem like a step away from the core of the educational mission, which is to teach. However, the essence of teaching is exactly this type of work: advocating for constructive change, ensuring support for all students, and fostering the growth of students into citizens that contribute positively to society. How one achieves these goals depends on time and place and student. In this regard, teaching is an ever-changing profession, and successful teaching requires constant problem solving. "Leadership," in the words of Linsky and his colleagues Ronald Heifetz and Alexander Grashow, "is an improvisational art."[12] Teaching is much the same. Improving educational outcomes—both easy-to-measure and difficult-to-measure—is a matter of enabling teachers to approach their profession with a leadership mentality. Teachers must find spaces in the educational system where they can lead, or create room where it doesn't already exist.

Some problems affect only a handful of students; some impact multitudes. Sometimes solutions seem small and inconsequential; only on occasion do they appear to have grand significance. The movement to support LGBT students in schools began in different places with different people all trying to solve a problem most educators did not (or would not) recognize. In some cases, teachers began down this path over concerns about a single student. In others, simple conversations over time eventually led to action. In all cases, their focus was decidedly local. Thoughts about a larger, national impact came later; the great political battles of the age were far from their minds. Teachers and students were simply seeking to change the small and often quite personal community that makes up a school. In education, major reform can begin with such small steps. The important thing is to encourage the beginning.

Acronyms and Abbreviations

ACLU	American Civil Liberties Union
AISNE	Association of Independent Schools of New England
BAGLY	Boston Area Gay and Lesbian Youth
BGLT	Bisexual Gay Lesbian Transgender
CA	Concord Academy
CGY	Committee for Gay Youth
GAA	Gay Activists Alliance
GIYS	Gay International Youth Society
GLBT	Gay Lesbian Bisexual Transgender
GLISTN	Gay and Lesbian Independent School Teachers Network
GLSEN	Gay, Lesbian, and Straight Education Network
GSA	Gay-Straight Alliance
HHS	Health and Human Services
HUAC	House Un-American Activities Committee
IPLGY	Institute for the Protection of Gay and Lesbian Youth
LGBT	Lesbian Gay Bisexual Transgender
LGBTQ	Lesbian Gay Bisexual Transgender Queer/Questioning
MTA	Massachusetts Teachers Association
NAACP	National Association for the Advancement of Colored People
NAMBLA	North American Man-Boy Love Association
NEA	National Education Association
SAC	Student Advisory Council

Notes

INTRODUCTION. THE PATH TO REFORM

1. Anonymous interview with the author, November 11, 2013.

2. Alcohol, Drug Abuse, and Mental Health Administration, *Report of the Secretary's Task Force on Youth Suicide* (Washington, D.C.: U.S. Department of Health and Human Services, 1989), 3–112.

3. Governor's Commission on Gay and Lesbian Youth, *Making Schools Safe for Gay and Lesbian Youth: Breaking the Silence in Schools and Families* (Boston, February 25, 1993), 8.

4. Governor's Commission, *Making Schools Safe*, 8.

5. Peter Atlas, letter to the editor, *Concord-Carlisle Voice*, October 1992, 4. In Concord-Carlisle High School Spectrum club archive.

6. Kevin Jennings, telephone interview with the author, November 23, 2013.

7. Joseph G. Kosciw, Emily A. Greytak, Mark J. Bartkiewicz, Madelyn J. Boesen, and Neal A. Palmer, *The 2011 National School Climate Survey: The Experiences of Lesbian, Gay, Bisexual and Transgender Youth in Our Nation's Schools* (New York: GLSEN, 2012), 58.

8. See Larry Cuban, *Inside the Black Box of Classroom Practice: Change without Reform in American Education* (Cambridge, MA: Harvard Education Press, 2013).

CHAPTER 1. OUT OF THE SHADOWS AND INTO PARADES

1. Quoted in Eric Marcus, *Making Gay History: The Half-Century Fight for Lesbian and Gay Equal Rights* (New York: HarperCollins, 1992), 50, e-book.

2. Marcus, *Making Gay History*, 14.

3. Jim Kepner and Stephen O. Murray, "Henry Gerber (1895–1972): Grandfather of the American Gay Movement," in *Before Stonewall: Activists for Gay and Lesbian Rights in Historical Context*, ed. Vern Bullough (Binghamton, NY: Hayworth, 2002), 24–34.

4. John D'Emilio, *Sexual Politics, Sexual Communities: The Making of a Homosexual Minority in the United States* (Chicago: University of Chicago Press, 1998), L343, Kindle.

5. Barbara Gittings, quoted in Marcus, *Making Gay History*, 18.

6. There are allusions to this in multiple newspaper pieces and first-person accounts, but I have been unable to locate any corroborating documentation that these practices were in fact carried out.

7. Will Roscoe, "The Radicalism of Harry Hay," *Gay and Lesbian Review*, December 1, 2013.

8. Quotes from Jonathan Ned Katz, *Gay American History: Lesbians and Gay Men in the U.S.A.* (New York: Avon Books, 1976), 616–30.

9. Roscoe, "Radicalism of Harry Hay."

10. Marcus, *Making Gay History*, 24.

11. Among the many sources in his HHS report, Gibson cited Roesler and Deisher, "Youthful Male Homosexuality," published in the *Journal of the American Medical Association*, February 21, 1972.

12. Marcus, *Making Gay History*, 55.

13. Marcus, *Making Gay History*, 225.

14. Anonymous flier, High School Gays United, 1972, in Coll. 28, "The Project 10 East Collection," History Project, Boston, archive.

15. According to work by Gary Remafedi, "Those less than 18 years of age experienced higher rates of psychiatric hospitalization, substance abuse, high school drop-out, and conflict with the law than did older participants." From "Adolescent Homosexuality: Psychosocial and Medical Implications," *Pediatrics* 79, no. 3 (1987): 1.

16. Tom Miles, undated (and unsourced) news clipping, History Project archive.

17. Undated clipping from *Gay Community News*, Boston, History Project archive.

18. Andrew Elder, "Timeline for Massachusetts Youth Pride Online Exhibit," History Project, Boston, archives.

19. Hetrick-Martin Institute, "About Us," http://www.hmi.org/about/our-mission-history/.

20. Marcus, *Making Gay History*, 282.

21. Larry Rohter, "New York Offering Public School Geared to Homosexual Students," *New York Times*, June 6, 1985.

22. Rohter, "New York Offering."

23. "George Washington Goes Gay," quoted in Stephan L. Cohen, *The Gay Liberation Youth Movement in New York City* (New York: Routledge, 2008), L3854, Kindle.

24. Virginia Uribe and Karen Harbeck, "Addressing the Needs of Lesbian, Gay, and Bisexual Youth: The Origins of Project 10 and School-Based Interven-

tion," in *Coming Out of the Classroom Closet: Gay and Lesbian Students, Teachers, and Curricula*, ed. Karen Harbeck (New York: Harrington Park, 1992), 10.

CHAPTER 2. FEARS OF A PETTICOAT REGIME: CHARACTER AND EDUCATION IN THE UNITED STATES

1. Willard Waller, "The School and the Community," reprinted in *The Structure of Schooling: Readings in the Sociology of Education*, ed. Richard Arum, Irenee Beattie, and Karly Ford (New York: Sage, 2015), 83.

2. Jonna Perrillo, "Beyond 'Progressive' Reform: Bodies, Discipline, and the Construction of the Professional Teacher in Interwar America," *History of Education Quarterly* 44, no. 3 (2004): 337.

3. "Wants Teachers to Be Hygienic Models," *New York Times*, November 22, 1935, quoted in Perrillo, "Beyond 'Progressive' Reform," 337.

4. Henry S. Curtis, *Recreation for Teachers* (New York: Macmillan, 1918), 13, quoted in Perrillo, "Beyond 'Progressive' Reform," 341.

5. T. Minehan, "The Teacher Goes Job-Hunting," *Nation* 124 (1927), 606, quoted in Waller, "School and the Community," 81.

6. Jonathan Turley, "Teachers under the Morality Microscope," *Los Angeles Times*, April 2, 2012, http://articles.latimes.com/2012/apr/02/opinion/la-oe-turley-teachers-under-scrutiny-20120402.

7. Quoted in Joseph Alva Baer, "Men Teachers in the Public Schools of the United States," PhD diss., Ohio State University, 1928, https://etd.ohiolink.edu/pg_10?0::NO:10:P10_ACCESSION_NUM:osu1225222285, 109.

8. *New York Times*, October 14, 1911, 12, col. 7.

9. Frank Oheley, "The Job of Being a Dad," *Hamilton Evening Journal*, November 10, 1925, 9, quoted in Baer, "Men Teachers," 108.

10. E. F. Chadwick, "The Woman Peril," *Educational Review* 109–19, February 1914, quoted in Baer, "Men Teachers," 127.

11. Walter Small, *Early New England Schools* (Boston: Ginn, 1914), quoted in Baer, "Men Teachers," 4.

12. Quoted in Baer, 5.

13. Walter Small, *Early New England Schools* (Boston: Ginn, 1914), quoted in Baer, 3.

14. Baer, 24.

15. Baer, 205. In the nineteenth century, administrators could pay men a higher wage with the understanding that they might need to support a family; over time, many states adopted equal pay laws, which didn't so much raise women's salaries as drive men's down.

16. Salmon Chase, quoted in Doris Kearns Goodwin, *Team of Rivals* (New York, Simon & Shuster, 2005), 38.

17. Baer, "Men Teachers," 51–69.

18. Baer, 51.

19. Quoted in Jackie Blount, *Fit to Teach: Same-Sex Desire, Gender, and School Work in the Twentieth Century* (Albany: SUNY Press, 2005), 65.

20. Baer, "Men Teachers."

21. Baer, 130.

22. Robert Beachy, "The German Invention of Homosexuality," *Journal of Modern History* 82, no. 4: 829–31.

23. Arthur MacDonald, "Moral Stigmata of Degeneration," *Monist* 18, no. 1 (January 1908): 112, http://www.jstor.org/stable/27900088.

24. Jay Hatheway, *The Gilded Age Construction of Modern American Homophobia* (New York: Palgrave Macmillan, 2003), 6.

25. Edward Stevenson, *The Intersexes: A History of Similsexualism as a Problem in Social Life*, quoted in Blount, *Fit to Teach*, 39.

26. Quoted in Blount, 75.

27. Blount, 77.

28. Willard Waller, *The Sociology of Teaching* (New York: Wiley, 1932; reprint, Kindle version), loc 2611.

29. Waller, loc 2611.

30. Waller, loc 2622.

31. Waller, loc 8116.

32. Waller, loc 2641.

33. Waller, loc 2111.

34. Waller, loc 5579.

35. *Report of the Special Committee on the Matter and Methods of Sex Education*, American Federation for Sex Hygiene, 1913, 12, https://babel.hathitrust.org/cgi/pt?id=uc1.31175035152951;view=1up;seq=5.

36. *Report of the Special Committee on the Matter and Methods of Sex Education.*

37. *Report of the Special Committee on the Matter and Methods of Sex Education*, 3.

CHAPTER 3. POSTWAR HYSTERIA: THE RED MENACE AND LAVENDER LADS

1. For a more in-depth look at this dynamic see John D'Emilio, *Sexual Politics, Sexual Communities* (Chicago: University of Chicago Press, 1998).

2. "Soviet Atoms Gains Laid to US Laxity," *New York Times*, September 26, 1949.

3. Ted Morgan, "Judge Joe: How the Youngest Judge in Wisconsin's History Became the Country's Most Notorious Senator," *Legal Affairs*, November/December 2003, http://www.legalaffairs.org/issues/November-December -2003/story_morgan_novdec03.msp.

4. Richard Hofstadter, "The Paranoid Style in American Politics," *Harper's Magazine*, November 1964, 86.

5. To be fair, losses in the Soviet Union had been greater, by orders of magnitude. But the American mentality probably saw little beyond its own borders.

6. Quotes from Joseph McCarthy, "Speech at Wheeling, West Virginia, February 9, 1950," http://www.advances.umd.edu/LincolnBirthday/mccarthy 1950.xml.

7. Jack Anderson, "Kissinger: One-Man State Department," *Washington Post*, October 18, 1974.

8. Joseph McCarthy, speech to the U.S. Senate, February 20, 1950, *Congressional Record*, vol. 96, part 2, 81st Congress, 2nd session (February 3–March 4, 1950). He claimed to be quoting a U.S. intelligence officer.

9. *Congressional Record*, vol. 96, part 4, 81st Congress, 2nd session (March 29–April 24, 1950), H5402, April 19.

10. "The Red Menace: McCarthyism and His Trip to Nebraska; Nebraska's Response to McCarthy," Nebraska Studies.org, http://www.nebraskastudies. org/0900/stories/0901_0112.html.

11. Flora Lewis, "Ambassador Extraordinary: John Peurifoy," *New York Times*, July 18, 1954; and "Peurifoy's First-Name Diplomacy Succeeded in Hard Assignments," *New York Times*, August 13, 1955.

12. Rodger Streitmatter, "Perverts on the Potomac: Homosexuals Enter the News Arena," paper presented at the Association for Education in Journalism and Mass Communication in San Antonio, Texas, August 2005. http://list.msu.edu/cgi-bin/wa?A3=ind0602a&L=AE-JMC&E=8bit&P=4270004&B=&T=text%252Fplain;%20 charset=iso-8859-1.

13. *Omaha World Herald*, 1938, quoted in Baxter, "'Homo-Hunting' in the Early Cold War: Senator Kenneth Wherry and the Homophobic Side of McCarthyism," *Nebraska History* 84 (2003): 119.

14. "Kenneth S. Wherry," Pawnee County History, http://www.pawnee countyhistory.com/yesteryear/wherry.html.

15. Unnamed members of the Senate Appropriations Committee to George Marshall, June 10, 1947. The letter was first printed in Joseph McCarthy, *McCarthyism: The Fight for America: Documented Answers to Questions Asked by Friend and*

Foe (New York: Devin-Adair, 1952), quoted here from Baxter, "'Homo-Hunting,'" 122.

16. Baxter, "'Homo-Hunting,'" 119–32.

17. Max Lerne, *The Unfinished Country: A Book of American Symbols* (New York: Simon & Schuster, 1959), 313–16.

18. Rao S. Sreenivas, "Why *Coronet* Failed," *Journalism Quarterly* 42, no. 2 (Spring 1965): 271.

19. Ralph Major Jr., "The New Moral Menace to Our Youth," *Coronet*, September 1950, 100–108.

20. Major, 100–108.

21. Rep. Arthur Miller, *Congressional Record*, vol. 96, part 4, 81st Congress, 2nd session (March 29–April 24, 1950), H4527–28, http://www.writing.upenn.edu/~afilreis/50s/gays-in-govt.html.

22. "Perverts Called Government Peril," *New York Times*, April 19, 1950.

23. *Employment of Homosexuals and Other Sex Perverts in Government*, interim report, December 15, 1950, Clyde Hoey, chair of investigations subcommittee, 81st Congress, 2nd session, document no. 241, p. 4, https://ecf.cand.uscourts.gov/cand/09cv2292/evidence/PX2337.pdf.

24. Stephen J. Whitfield, *The Culture of the Cold War* (Baltimore: Johns Hopkins University Press, 1991), 44.

25. Major, "New Moral Menace."

26. Exec. Order No. 10450, sec. 8(a)(1)(iii), https://www.archives.gov/federal-register/codification/executive-order/10450.html.

27. Baxter, "'Homo-Hunting,'" 128.

28. Bonnie Stark, "McCarthyism in Florida: Charley Johns and the Florida Investigation Committee, 1956–68," quoted in Karen Graves, *And They Were Wonderful Teachers: Florida's Purge of Gay and Lesbian Teachers* (Urbana: University of Illinois Press, 2009), 7.

29. Graves, *And They Were Wonderful Teachers*, 29–32.

30. For a more comprehensive look at morality clauses in American education see Marka B. Fleming, Amanda Harmon-Cooley, and Gwendolyn Mcfadden-Wade, "Morals Clauses for Educators in Secondary and Postsecondary Schools: Legal Applications and Constitutional Concerns," *Brigham Young University Education and Law Journal* 2009, no. 1 (2009): 67–102.

31. Alan Eisenberg, "Bullying and Being Gay in the 1950s (a Personal Story)," in Bullying Stories: Dealing with Bullying from an Adult Perspective, December 8, 2010, https://bullyinglte.wordpress.com/2010/12/08/1301/.

32. Rita Reed, *Growing Up Gay: The Sorrows and Joys of Gay and Lesbian Adolescence* (New York: Norton, 1997), 10.

33. "'We Just Stood Up for Our Own Self': James Justen Recalls Growing Up Gay in the 1950s" (interview by Miriam Frank, June 28, 1996), History Matters, http://historymatters.gmu.edu/d/6941/.

34. U.S. Navy, *Report of the Board Appointed to Prepare and Submit Recommendations to the Secretary of the Navy for the Revision of Policies, Procedures, and Directives Dealing with Homosexuality*, quoted in *Gay Rights, Military Wrongs*, ed. Craig Rimmerman (New York: Routledge, 1996), 272.

35. U.S. Navy, *Report of the Board*, quoted in Shauna Miller, "50 Years of Pentagon Studies Support Gay Soldiers," *Atlantic*, October 20, 2009.

CHAPTER 4. ORANGES, BANANA CREAM, AND BEAUTY QUEENS: THE FIGHT OVER GAY TEACHERS COMES OUT OF THE CLOSET

1. "A Resolution Commemorating the 40th Anniversary of East Lansing's First-in-the-Nation Ban on Discrimination Based on Sexual Orientation," SCRIBD, https://www.scribd.com/doc/84136141/A-Resolution-Commemorating-the-40th-Anniversary-1. Michigan State had a very active chapter of the gay liberation movement.

2. John Gish, telephone interview with the author, December 12, 2016.

3. Douglas McGill, "Beleaguered Teacher May Get Job Back," *New York Times*, June 28, 1981, http://www.nytimes.com/1981/06/28/nyregion/beleaguered-teacher-may-get-job-back.html.

4. Gish interview.

5. So labeled by *Time* magazine in "Americana: The Gay Goons," August 29, 1977, http://content.time.com/time/subscriber/article/0,33009,915339,00.html.

6. Joseph Kennedy, *Summer of '77: Last Hurrah of the Gay Activists Alliance* (New York: PPC Books, 1994), http://www.gaynewsandviews.com/.

7. Gish interview.

8. McGill, "Beleaguered Teacher."

9. Although this may be technically true, he appeared to assert his sexual orientation in several interviews, telling syndicated columnist Nicholas von Hoffman that "we're sexual niggers" and stating to the *Advocate* that "I'm tired of using women to accompany me to proms so the proper image is preserved."

10. Gish interview.

11. "Anita Bryant Biography," Anita Bryant Ministries International, http://www.anitabmi.org/3.html.

12. "Wanted in the County of Dade," *Rolling Stone*, April 5, 1969, https://www.rollingstone.com/music/news/jim-morrison-s-indecency-arrest-rolling-stone-s-original-coverage-20101210.

13. United Press International, "Teenagers Hold Decency Rally," http://cdnc.ucr.edu/cgi-bin/cdnc?a=d&d=DS19690324.2.14.

14. Anita Bryant, *The Anita Bryant Story: The Survival of Our Nation's Families and the Threat of Militant Homosexuality* (Grand Rapids, MI: Revell, 1977), 23.

15. Bryant, *Anita Bryant Story*, 114.

16. Jackie Blount, *Fit to Teach: Same-Sex Desire, Gender, and School Work in the Twentieth Century* (Albany: SUNY Press, 2005), 131.

17. "Anita Bryant, Save Our Children," SuchIsLife Videos, https://www.youtube.com/watch?v=IB5H—b3Xho&t=314s.

18. Bryant, *Anita Bryant Story*, 27.

19. "Anita Bryant, Save Our Children."

20. Bryant, *Anita Bryant Story*, 53.

21. Bryant, *Anita Bryant Story*, 43.

22. Randy Shilts, "How John and Randy Became Friends," *Healdsburg (CA) Tribune*, November 2, 1978, C1.

23. Gerald Uelmen, "California Death Penalty Laws and the California Supreme Court: A Ten Year Perspective," 1986, Santa Clara Law Digital Commons, http://digitalcommons.law.scu.edu/facpubs.

24. Fred Fejes, *Gay Rights and Moral Panic: The Origin of America's Debate on Homosexuality* (New York: Palgrave Macmillan, 2008), 183.

25. Karl Olson, "Berner Files Suit vs. Briggs, Lee," *Healdsburg (CA) Tribune*, August 9, 1979, A4.

26. "John Briggs—Proposition 6," interview with Tony Russamano, 1978, https://archive.org/details/01JohnBriggsSeries.

27. Shilts, "How John and Randy Became Friends."

28. Shilts, "How John and Randy Became Friends."

29. Associated Press, "Measure a Threat to Gays," *Palm Springs Desert Sun*, March 27, 1978, A3.

30. Blount, *Fit to Teach*, 146.

31. "John Briggs—Proposition 6."

32. Karl Olson, "Unconventional Priest's Adieu," *Healdsburg (CA) Tribune*, June 28, 1979, A1.

33. Ronald Reagan, "Two Ill-Advised California Trends," *Los Angeles Herald-Examiner*, November 1, 1978, reprinted by Gerard Magliocca at concurringopinions.com, http://concurringopinions.com/archives/2010/10/ronald-reagan-and-gay-rights.html.

34. Barbara Stewart, "From Star to Pariah, Now She's in Between," *Orlando Sentinel*, May 1, 1988.

35. Dudley Clendinen and Adam Nagourney, *Out for Good: The Struggle to Build a Gay Rights Movement in America* (New York: Touchstone, 1999), 329.

36. Quoted in Tom Shales, "The First Archie Bunker Award," *Washington Post*, July 31, 1977.

37. Shales, "First Archie Bunker Award."

38. Tom Shales, "Fate, Hope, Hilarity," *Washington Post*, July 10, 1980.

39. "TV Show Drops Anita Bryant," *Los Angeles Times*, May 12, 1985, 11.

40. YouTube, "Anita Bryant's Pie to the Face," NBC News footage, https://www.youtube.com/watch?v=5tHGmSh7f-0.

41. "Anita Bryant, Save Our Children."

42. Shales, "Fate, Hope, Hilarity."

43. Steve Rothaus, "Bob Green: Anita's Ex Paid Dearly in the Fight," *Miami Herald*, June 9, 2007, http://miamiherald.typepad.com/gaysouthflorida/2007/06/bob_green_anita.html.

44. Robert Medley, "Anita Bryant: Sunny Side of Life," *NewsOK*, http://ndepth.newsok.com/anita-bryant.

45. William Safire, "Miami Gay Activists Asked for Too Much," *Eugene (OR) Register-Guard*, June 9, 1977.

CHAPTER 5. HOMOSEXUALITY ENTERS THE CLASSROOM: SHINING A LIGHT ON THE PROBLEM

1. Anonymous interview with the author, October 2013. The epithet spawned what was one of the most notorious, if short-lived, faculty softball teams in school history, the "Social Studies Fags."

2. Anonymous interview with the author, October 2013. The teacher involved believed that since the students came out to him in confidence, it was best that he honor that by remaining anonymous.

3. Thomas Roesler and Robert W. Deisher, "Youthful Male Homosexuality, Homosexual Experience and the Process of Developing Homosexual Identity in Males Aged 16 to 22 Years," *Journal of the American Medical Association* 219, no. 8 (February 21, 1972).

4. Gary Remafedi, "Male Homosexuality: The Adolescent's Perspective," *Pediatrics* 79, no. 8 (March 1987).

5. John D'Emilio chronicles the same issue in San Francisco: a young minister working with street youth discovered that the Mattachine Society would provide no help to anyone under twenty-one, "fearful of charges of corrupting youth." John D'Emilio, *Sexual Politics, Sexual Communities: The Making of a*

Homosexual Minority in the United States (Chicago: University of Chicago Press, 1998), L 3723, Kindle. Gay teachers in Boston, among them Ferreira, also noted the fear of being labeled a pedophile if one were to work with LGBT youth. Arthur Lipkin noted in his interview that gay activist David LaFontaine, who eventually was instrumental in the formation of the Governor's Commission, was "very vocal about needing to do school and youth stuff . . . but he was just dismissed" by the leaders of gay and lesbian activist groups at the time. Arthur Lipkin, interview with the author, Cambridge, MA, October 28, 2013.

6. Al Ferreira expressed particular sensitivity to this issue from the teachers' perspective, although other interviewees, such as Arthur Lipkin, also discussed this dynamic.

7. Peter Atlas, interview with the author, Concord, MA, November 4, 2013.

8. Letter from Kevin Harding to Peter Atlas, 1992, Concord-Carlisle High School Spectrum archive.

9. Polly Bixby and Karen Grzesik, interview with the author, Orange, MA, November 3, 2013.

10. Bixby and Grzesik interview.

11. Virginia Uribe and Karen Harbeck, "Addressing the Needs of Lesbian, Gay, and Bisexual Youth: The Origins of Project 10 and School-Based Intervention," in *Coming Out of the Classroom Closet: Gay and Lesbian Students, Teachers, and Curricula*, ed. Karen Harbeck (New York: Harrington Park, 1992), 10.

12. In fact, without exception, all the pioneers of these efforts in Massachusetts expressed surprise at the degree of acceptance and support they received from their communities. Homophobia, it appears, was not as universal or deeply rooted (at least in some communities) as suspected.

13. Brian Marquardt, obituary for Eric Rofes, *Boston Globe*, July 2, 2006, http://archive.boston.com/news/globe/obituaries/articles/2006/07/02/eric_rofes_51_longtime_gay_rights_activist/.

14. Eric E. Rofes, *Socrates, Plato, and Guys Like Me: Confessions of a Gay School-teacher* (New York: Alyson Books, 1985), 24.

15. Rofes, *Socrates, Plato, and Guys Like Me*, 52.

16. Warren Blumenfeld, interview with the author, South Hadley, MA, November 11, 2013.

17. Blumenfeld interview.

18. In 1980 the Boston Area Gay and Lesbian Youth (BAGLY) also established a Youth Speakers' Bureau.

19. Blount, *Fit to Teach*, 121.

20. Andrei Joseph, interview with the author, Concord, MA, October 30, 2013.

21. Joseph interview. He did note that he felt he had a claim to "academic

freedom"—that what went on in his classroom was beyond the purview of the school administration.

22. Boston Gay and Lesbian Speakers Bureau, "Do We Make a Difference?," n.d. [1987?], CCHS Spectrum archive.

23. Blumenfeld interview.

24. Joseph interview.

25. Bixby and Grzesik interview.

26. Janice Doppler, "A Description of Gay/Straight Alliances in the Public Schools of Massachusetts," unpublished dissertation, 2000, 83.

27. Bixby and Grzesik interview.

28. Joseph interview.

29. Lipkin interview.

30. Kevin Jennings, *Mama's Boy, Preacher's Son: A Memoir of Growing Up, Coming Out, and Changing America's Schools* (Boston: Beacon, 2007), 155.

CHAPTER 6. REFORMS GO PUBLIC

1. Quoted from an article by Alice Cathcart in the *Andover Phillipian*, April 12, 1991.

2. "W. Hollywood to Recognize Non-married Partnerships," *Los Angeles Times*, February 23, 1965, http://articles.latimes.com/1985-02-23/local/me-1069_1_west-hollywood-city-council.

3. Michael Quintanilla, "Haven for Gay Teens," *Los Angeles Times*, December 7, 1989, http://articles.latimes.com/1989–12–07/news/vw-404_1_gay-teens.

4. Jerry Gilliam and Patricia Ward Biederman, "School Funds, Gay Counselor Linked," *Los Angeles Times*, March 11, 1988.

5. Patricia Ward Biederman, "Views Clash on Homosexual Students Program," *Los Angeles Times*, June 24, 1988, http://articles.latimes.com/1988-06-24/local/me-6027_1_students-program.

6. Gilliam and Biederman, "School Funds, Gay Counselor Linked."

7. Al Ferreira, interview with the author, Leominster, MA, October 26, 2013.

8. Al Ferreira, telephone interview with the author, November 8, 2013.

9. Karen Harbeck, interview with the author, Arlington, MA, November 6, 2013; Al Ferreira, interview with the author, Leominster, MA, October 26, 2013; Mary Hurley "Straight Talk for Gay Teenagers," interview with Al Ferreira in the *Boston Herald*, Sunday People section, September 20, 1992, 10.

10. Dan Levy, "Ever the Warrior," *San Francisco Chronicle*, June 23, 2000.

11. Michael Bronski, "The Real Harry Hay," *Boston Phoenix*, October 31–November 7, 2002.

CHAPTER 7. PULPITS, PINK TRIANGLES, AND BASEMENT MEETINGS:
PRIVATE SCHOOLS JOIN THE MOVEMENT

1. National Association of State Budget Officers (NASBO), *State Budget Report, 2014–16*, 8–11.

2. M. Danish Shakeel and Corety A. DeAngelis, "Who Is More Free?," University of Arkansas College of Education and Health Professions, EDRE Working Paper 2016-09.

3. Patrick Bassett and Mark Mitchell, *Financing Sustainable Schools: Six Steps to Re-engineering Your School's Financial Future*, NAIS, 2006.

4. Bassett and Mitchell, *Financing Sustainable Schools*.

5. Kevin Jennings, *Mama's Boy, Preacher's Son: A Memoir of Growing Up, Coming Out, and Changing America's Schools* (Boston: Beacon, 2007).

6. The first march was actually held on October 14, 1979.

7. Quoted in Jennings, *Mama's Boy, Preacher's Son*, 172–73.

8. Jennings, 166.

9. Jennings, 176.

10. Gail Ralston, "Andover Stories: Thomas Cochran and Phillips Academy's 'Golden Decade,'" *Andover Townsman*, November 3, 2011.

11. Notes in Phillips Andover GSA archive, box 1, believed to be from Nancy Boutilier.

12. Sharon Tentarelli, interview with the author, Concord, MA, August 1, 2017.

13. Quote from essay by Nancy Boutilier on the history of the GSA at Andover, Phillips Andover archives.

14. Essay on the history of the GSA by Sharon Brown, Phillips Andover archives.

15. *Phillipian*, May 1991.

16. Sharon Tentarelli, "The Birth of a Gay/Straight Alliance," *Speaking Out*, November 1993, 10.

CHAPTER 8. TEACHING, LEARNING, AND MOVING UP THE HIERARCHY:
SCHOOL LEADERSHIP JOINS THE MOVEMENT

1. Kevin Jennings, telephone interview with the author, November 25, 2013. In theory, Jennings could have talked to Al Ferreira at Cambridge, but the public and private school universes had yet to overlap.

2. Jennings interview.

3. For the rest of the book, I will refer to the group as GLSEN—even though the group became GLSTN (Gay, Lesbian, Straight Teachers Network) in 1994, and finally GLSEN in 1997. In 2009, the group chose to keep its name but refer to itself only as GLSEN (as opposed to Gay Lesbian Straight Education Network)—this in an effort to be more inclusive to transgender and other identities.

4. Jennings interview.

5. Arthur Lipkin, interview with the author, Cambridge, MA, October 28, 2013.

6. Al Ferreira, interview with the author, Leominster, MA, October 26, 2013.

7. CRLS student newspaper, October 1992.

8. Bob Parlin, interview with the author, Cambridge, MA, November 4, 2013.

9. Parlin interview.

10. Parlin interview.

11. Parlin interview, and "Newton South High School Anti-Homophobia Program," timeline in the Concord-Carlisle High School (hereafter CCHS) Spectrum archive, provenance unknown.

12. Ferreira interview, Leominster, MA, October 26, 2013.

13. Internal correspondence from Andrei Joseph to "Attendees of the GLSTN Conference and Friends," March 2, 1993, CCHS Spectrum archive.

14. Program, "Third Annual GLSTN Conference: 'Celebration and Challenge,'" March 1, 1993, CCHS Spectrum archive.

15. CCHS Spectrum archive.

16. CCHS Spectrum archive.

17. Parlin interview.

18. Internal correspondence from Andrei Joseph to "Attendees of the GLSTN Conference and Friends," March 2, 1993, CCHS Spectrum archive.

19. CCHS Spectrum archive.

20. Al Ferreira archive, Coll. 28, History Project, Boston.

21. Karen Harbeck, "Gay and Lesbian Educators: Past History / Future Prospects," in *Coming Out of the Classroom Closet*, ed. Harbeck (New York: Routledge, 1992), 121–40.

22. Bixby and Grzesik interview.

23. Pat Griffin, "From Hiding Out to Coming Out: Empowering Gay and Lesbian Educators," in Harbeck, *Coming Out of the Classroom Closet*, 167–96.

24. Warren Blumenfeld, ed., *Homophobia: How We All Pay the Price* (Boston: Beacon, 1992).

25. Karen Harbeck, "Legal Leverage Tip," *Newsletter of the National Institute for GLBT Concerns in Education* 1, no. 2 (1994). In Al Ferreira archives, Coll. 28, History Project, Boston.

26. "East High Gay Straight Alliance v. Board of Education of Salt Lake City School District," Lambda Legal, http://www.lambdalegal.org/in-court/cases/east-high-gsa-v-board-of-ed-salt-lake.

27. Richard Barbieri, telephone interview with the author, June 25, 2017.

28. Don McNemar, interview with the author, Waltham, MA, July 25, 2017.

29. McNemar interview.

30. Alexandre Wolf, "Ten Percent of Phillips Academy's Untold History: A Case Study of the Gay, Lesbian, and Bisexual Community," unpublished research paper, May 19, 2006.

31. Thomas Wilcox, "Doing What Is Right," *Speaking Out* 2, no. 2 (November 1993).

32. Jennings interview.

33. Tom Wilcox, telephone interview with the author, June 27, 2017.

34. CCHS Spectrum archives; Joseph interview and Atlas interview.

35. CCHS Spectrum archives.

36. McNemar interview.

37. McNemar interview.

38. Parlin interview.

39. Wilcox interview.

40. Quoted in Eric Marcus, *Making Gay History: The Half-Century Fight for Lesbian and Gay Equal Rights* (New York: HarperCollins, 1992), 50, e-book.

CHAPTER 9. PROMISES, PROMISES: THE MOVEMENT GOES POLITICAL

1. Michael Isikoff, "Parents Sue School Principal," *Washington Post*, August 13, 1983.

2. Leah Y. Latimer, "Dungeons and Dragons Banned by Arlington School Board," *Washington Post*, August 19, 1983.

3. "The Great 1980s Dungeons and Dragons Panic," BBC News, Magazine, April 11, 2014, http://www.bbc.com/news/magazine-26328105.14.

4. "Masterpiece Ultra Magnus," *Mahou Blog*, January 13, 2015, https://mahou.wordpress.com/2006/12/01/judas-priest-suicide-trial-article/.

5. Quoted in Scott Poland, *Suicide Prevention in the Schools* (New York: Guilford, 1989), 114.

6. Alcohol, Drug Abuse, and Mental Health Administration, *Report of the Secretary's Task Force on Youth Suicide* (Washington, D.C.: U.S. Department of Health and Human Services, 1989), 3–112.

7. *Report of the Secretary's Task Force on Youth Suicide*, 3–110.

8. *Report of the Secretary's Task Force on Youth Suicide*, 3–135.

9. *Report of the Secretary's Task Force on Youth Suicide.*

10. Susan Okie, "Sullivan Cold Shoulders Suicide Report," *Washington Post,* January 13, 1990.

11. Okie, "Sullivan Cold Shoulders Suicide Report."

12. Atlas interview.

13. See Janice M. Irvine, "One Generation Post-Stonewall: Political Contests over Gay and Lesbian School Reform," in *Queer Representations: Reading Lives, Reading Cultures,* ed. Martin Duberman, 572–88 (New York: CUNY Center for Lesbian and Gay Studies, 1997). She calls it the "deathstyle" argument.

14. Quoted in Irvine, "One Generation Post-Stonewall," 581.

15. From a recap of the March 5, 1995, speech at the Human Rights Campaign Fund Leadership Conference, posted, ironically enough, by the conservative group MassResistance, "Pro-family Activism That Makes a Difference!," http://www.massresistance.org/docs/issues/gay_strategies/framing_the_issue.html, accessed 11/20/13.

16. Peter Atlas, interview with the author, Concord, MA, October 2013.

17. Documentation from MTA Conference, "Affording Equal Educational Opportunity to Gay and Lesbian and Bisexual Students"—"What to Do," 1992.

18. David B. Wilson, "He Means What He Says, and Says What He Means," *Boston Globe,* October 2, 1978, 17.

19. Dominic Sandbrook, *Mad as Hell: The Crisis of the 1970s and the Rise of the Populist Right* (New York: Anchor Books, 2011), 109.

20. Brian Mooney, "Bellotti, Silber Hit Rough Spots in Final TV Debate," *Boston Globe,* September 12, 1990.

21. Mark Starr, "Archie Bunker with a Ph.D," *Newsweek,* June 17, 1990, http://www.newsweek.com/archie-bunker-phd-206430.

22. Curtis Wilkie, "A Stark Campaign, a Grim Vision," *Boston Globe,* May 26, 1990, 1.

23. Scott Lehigh, "Some Mothers' Career Pursuit Means 'Child Neglect' Silber Says," *Boston Globe,* October 26, 1990, 26.

24. Meeting minutes, GBLGPA, October 4. From "Lesbian, Gay, Bisexual and Transgender Political Alliance of Massachusetts records," box 4, folder 20, Northeastern University archives.

25. Frank Phillips, "Weld Courts Both Sides of the Bloc for Late Votes," *Boston Globe,* November 1, 1990, 1.

26. Quoted in Stephen Rodric, "Running Weld," *New York Magazine,* January 23, 2006, http://nymag.com/nymetro/news/politics/newyork/features/15551/index1.html.

27. Kay Longcope, "Gay Vote for Weld Was Heavy," *Boston Globe*, November 13, 1990, 13.

28. Peter Freiberg, "The Boston Bully," *Advocate*, November 26, 2002, 28.

29. Phillips, "Weld Courts Both Sides of the Bloc."

30. Curtis Willkie, "Dukakis Loyalists May Hold Key for Weld," *Boston Globe*, November 1, 1990, 1.

31. Matt Hertzog, *The Lavender Vote: Lesbians, Gay Men, and Bisexuals in American Electoral Politics* (New York: NYU Press), 127.

32. Hertzog, *Lavender Vote*, 108.

33. Martin Linsky, telephone interview with the author, July 12, 2017.

34. Quoted in Kevin Jennings, *Mama's Boy, Preacher's Son: A Memoir of Growing Up, Coming Out, and Changing America's Schools* (Boston: Beacon, 2007), 196.

35. Linsky interview.

36. Toni Locy, "Weld Creates Panel on Gay Youth Issues," *Boston Globe*, February 11, 1992, 18.

37. Quoted in the Governor's Commission on Gay and Lesbian Youth, *Making Schools Safe for Gay and Lesbian Youth: Breaking the Silence in Schools and Families* (Boston, February 25, 1993).

38. Linsky interview.

CHAPTER 10. AN ENORMOUS PRESSURE TO SUCCEED: FROM PROMISES, PROMISES TO A STATEWIDE POLICY

1. These were the terms used by Paul Gibson in the HHS report.

2. Letter from Kevin Jennings to GLSTN members, September 22, 1992, Phillips Andover archives, GSA carton 2.

3. Quotes in this section are taken from testimony before the Governor's Commission and are included in the commission's report, *Making Schools Safe for Gay and Lesbian Youth: Breaking the Silence in Schools and in Families* (Boston, February 25, 1993).

4. John Maltsberger, *Suicide Risk: The Formulation of Clinical Judgment* (New York: NYU Press, 1986), quoted in the Governor's Commission report, 20.

5. Sara Rimer, "Gay Rights Law for Schools Advances in Massachusetts," *New York Times*, December 8, 1993.

6. Rimer, "Gay Rights Law."

7. Quoted in Don Aucoin, "Weld Is Set to Sign Gay Student Rights Bill," *Boston Globe*, December 10, 1993, 39.

8. Letter in archive of Byron Rushing's office, dated May 20, 1993.

9. Kevin Jennings, *Mama's Boy, Preacher's Son: A Memoir of Growing Up, Coming Out, and Changing America's Schools* (Boston: Beacon, 2007), 201.

10. Christopher Muther, "Student Rally Draws 300," *Bay Windows*, October 21, 1993, 3.

11. Aucoin, "Weld Is Set to Sign Gay Student Rights Bill."

12. Kris Franklin, "Homophobia and the 'Matthew Shepard Effect' in *Lawrence v. Texas*," *New York Law School Law Review* 48, no. 4: 657.

13. Hilary Weaver, "Ellen DeGeneres' Groundbreaking Coming Out: 20 Years Later," *Vanity Fair*, April 28, 2017.

14. Ferreira interview.

15. Aucoin, "Weld Is Set to Sign Gay Student Rights Bill."

16. "Why William Weld Should Not Be Considered as Ambassador to Mexico," Republican National Coalition for Life, http://www.rnclife.org/faxnotes/1997/aug97/97-08-11.shtml.

17. Rimer, "Gay Rights Law."

CHAPTER 11. THE MASSACHUSETTS MODEL GOES NATIONWIDE

1. Governor's Commission on Gay and Lesbian Youth, *Making Schools Safe for Gay and Lesbian Youth: Breaking the Silence in Schools and Families* (Boston, February 25, 1993).

2. Eric Fehrnstrom, "Gov Diverts Tax $ to Aid Gay Students," *Boston Herald*, October 19, 1993.

3. David LaFontaine, telephone interview with the author, August 3, 2017.

4. "Controlling the Schools," *Salt Lake Tribune*, January 18, 1996, A6.

5. Dan Harrie, "Leavitt, Hatch Say Schools Have Right to Ban Gay Clubs," *Salt Lake Tribune*, February 10, 1996, A1.

6. Samuel Autman, "Club Ban Sparks Fear, Loathing," *Salt Lake Tribune*, February 22, 1996, A1.

7. Autman, "Club Ban Sparks Fear, Loathing."

8. Louis Sahagun, "Utah Board Bans All School Clubs in Anti-Gay Move," *Los Angeles Times*, February 22, 1996.

9. Sahagun, "Utah Board Bans All School Clubs."

10. Associated Press, "Ban on Student Clubs Aimed at Gays," *Southeast Missourian*, December 6, 1998.

11. Autman, "Club Ban Sparks Fear, Loathing."

12. Katherine Kapos, "Educators, Student Leaders Discuss Clubs with Board," *Salt Lake Tribune*, March 5, 1997, B1.

13. Samuel Autman, "S.L. School Officials to Pick Which Clubs to Allow," *Salt Lake Tribune*, March 30, 1996, D3.

14. Katherine Kapos, "State Will Dictate School Clubs," *Salt Lake Tribune*, November 2, 1996, C1.

15. Hilary Groutage, "Civil-Rights Groups Sue over School Clubs Ban," *Salt Lake Tribune*, March 20, 1998, A1.

16. Hilary Groutage "Gay-Straight Teacher Group Comes to Utah," *Salt Lake Tribune*, March 22, 1997, B1.

17. Samuel Autman, "Peterson Still Deals with Gay Club Fallout," *Salt Lake Tribune*, June 7, 1996, B1.

18. Heather May, "S.L. District Lifts Ban on High School Clubs," *Salt Lake Tribune*, September 6, 2000, B1.

19. Throughout the book, I have used the term LGBT, as it was the term most commonly used during the period I am writing about. In discussing more current events, it can be LGBTQ—the Q for queer / questioning. In many places, an *I* is added for intersex, an *A* for asexual, or a plus sign (+) to include and embrace all.

20. Joseph G. Kosciw, Emily A. Greytak, Noreen M. Giga, Christian Villenas, and David J. Danischewski, *The 2015 National School Climate Survey: The Experiences of Lesbian, Gay, Bisexual, Transgender, and Queer Youth in Our Nation's Schools* (New York: GLSEN, 2016), 62–65.

21. Kosciw et al., *2015 National School Climate Survey*, 113–20.

22. Kosciw et al., 102.

23. Russell B. Toomey, Caitlin Ryan, Rafael M. Diaz, and Stephen T. Russell, "High School Gay-Straight Alliances (GSAs) and Young Adult Well-Being: An Examination of GSA Presence, Participation, and Perceived Effectiveness," *Applied Developmental Science* 15, no 4 (2011): 175–85.

24. Elizabeth M. Saewyc, Chiaki Konishi, Hilary A. Rose, and Yuko Homma, "School-Based Strategies to Reduce Suicidal Ideation, Suicide Attempts, and Discrimination among Sexual Minority and Heterosexual Adolescents in Western Canada," *International Journal of Child, Youth, and Family Studies* 5, no. 1 (2014): 89–112, 99

CONCLUSION. NOW WHAT?

1. Mel Dahl, "The Battle Ahead," *Bay Windows*, November 19, 1992, 12.

2. Bernard Bailyn, *Education in the Forming of American Society* (Chapel Hill: University of North Carolina Press, 1960), 16.

3. Brown v. Board of Education of Topeka, 347 U.S. 483 (1954).

4. Thomas Pettigrew, "Intergroup Contact Theory," *Annual Review of Psychology* 49 (1998): 71.

5. Gordon Hodson, "Do Ideologically Intolerant People Benefit from Intergroup Contact?," *Current Directions in Psychological Science* 20, no. 3 (June 2011): 154–59.

6. Anonymous interview with author, November 1, 2017, Concord, MA.

7. Lawrence v. Texas, 539 U.S. 558 (2003).

8. Phyllis Scattergood, telephone interview with the author, August 4, 2017.

9. Martin Linsky, "Adaptive Leadership," Tedx St. Charles, April 13, 2011, https://www.youtube.com/watch?v=af-cSvnEExM. Linsky has collaborated extensively with Ronald Heifetz on this concept of adaptive leadership, developed further in books such as *Leadership on the Line* and *The Practice of Adaptive Leadership*.

10. Anonymous interview with author, November 15, 2017, Concord, MA.

11. S. Helper, M. Kleiner, and Y. Wang, "Analyzing Methods of Compensation in Manufacturing: Piece Rates, Time Rates, or Gain-Sharing?," NBER Working Paper 16540, 2010.

12. Ronald Heifetz, Alexander Grashow, and Marty Linsky, "Leadership in a (Permanent) Crisis," *Harvard Business Review*, July–August 2009.

Index